INDUSTRY AS A PLAYER IN THE POLITICAL AND SOCIAL ARENA

INDUSTRY AS A PLAYER IN THE POLITICAL AND SOCIAL ARENA

DEFINING THE COMPETITIVE ENVIRONMENT

John F. Mahon and Richard A. McGowan

Q

QUORUM BOOKS
WESTPORT, CONNECTICUT • LONDON

Library of Congress Cataloging-in-Publication Data

Mahon, John F. (John Francis).
    Industry as a player in the political and social arena : defining
the competitive environment / John F. Mahon, Richard A. McGowan.
      p.   cm.
    Includes bibliographical references and index.
    ISBN 0–89930–978–X (alk. paper)
    1. Industrial policy—United States. 2. Industries—Social
aspects—United States. 3. Competition—United States.
4. Competition, International. I. McGowan, Richard. II. Title.
HD3616.U47M288   1996
338.973—dc20   96–2213

British Library Cataloguing in Publication Data is available.

Library of Congress Catalog Card Number: 96–2213
ISBN: 0–89930–978–X

First published in 1996

Quorum Books, 88 Post Road West, Westport, CT 06881
An imprint of Greenwood Publishing Group, Inc.

Printed in the United States of America

The paper used in this book complies with the
Permanent Paper Standard issued by the National
Information Standards Organization (Z39.48–1984).

10 9 8 7 6 5 4 3 2 1

TO OUR FAMILIES AND OUR STUDENTS
WHO DAILY CHALLENGE AND INSPIRE US

[] [] []

CONTENTS

[] [] []

FIGURES AND TABLES

FIGURES

TABLES

[] [] []

PREFACE

This book evolved over many years, and its authors came to it through very different paths. John Mahon became interested in corporate political strategies in the late 1970s when he conducted work on his dissertation on the chemical industry. Richard McGowan became interested in political strategies during the work on his dissertation in 1988. Both authors have been collaborating on a variety of topics and presentations since 1988, and during this process became aware of their mutual interest in corporate involvement and response strategies to the political and social environment. As a result, this book has taken an exceptionally long time to develop while both authors pursued other topics and pondered this collaboration.

There has been a growing business school interest in the political activities of corporations, dating from the classic work of Edwin Epstein in 1969. Both of us were, are, and continue to be deeply influenced by this soft-spoken individual with a burning passion for knowledge and a communication of that knowledge to others. We hope that this work can measure up to the standards he set so long ago. In addition, as an undergraduate, John Mahon was taught political science by Roger Cobb. That early involvement and Roger Cobb's love for his subject matter ignited Mahon's interests in things political.

For a long time, Epstein was the only individual writing and researching on this topic in the business school arena; but near the end of the 1970s and into the 1980s (and beyond) a large group of business scholars began to look at the relationship of the corporation to the environment—in particular, to the political environment. Some of these colleagues who have continued on this stream of research, in addition to Epstein, include the following: Barbara Bigelow, Jean Boddewyn, Steven Brenner, Phil Cochran, Liam Fahey, Kathleen Getz, Amy

Hillman, Gerry Keim, William Martello, Barry Mitnick, Kathy Rehbein, Doug Schuler, Brian Shaffer, Sandra Waddock, Steve Wartick, and David Vogel. If we have forgotten anyone, the omission is clearly ours. These scholars pursued a rich research agenda, focusing on what we would term elements of political strategy (e.g., issues management, stakeholder management, etc.); but the topic of corporate political strategy still remains a vague term for most, especially for practitioners.

Concurrent with this growing academicians' interest in the political activities of business has been the expansion of practitioner interest. Managers have realized that political and social action can dramatically affect individual firm and industry-wide competitiveness. This impact is clearly seen in political and social actions that change the rules by which industries and firms play the competitive game. Policies that restrict trade in the international arena, regulatory interventions that impose additional costs, and public interest group activities that challenge the legitimacy of the firm and industry product and service offerings alter the rules of competitive engagement. Firms and industries that learn to be a player in the development of these rules can significantly improve their competitive positioning vis-à-vis other competitors and industries. What practitioners lack are models and approaches to the formulation and implementation of political strategies and tactics.

We believe, however, that the base of research in this area is sufficiently rich to allow the analytical focus to move on to a new level. Virtually nothing has been written on the topic of industry political strategy. There have been some works that look at trade association activities, but no single work that we are aware of deals with political strategy at the industry level. As competition moves increasingly to a more global playing field, the interactions among business, government, and society will only become more complex and more frequent. Industries and individual firms will need to deal with different national governments, regulatory agencies, and global organizations (e.g., World Court, U.N. Commissions, etc.) that will shape and alter the competitive landscape. An organization or industry that does not prepare for that future reality may find itself at a significant competitive disadvantage. Although the analysis here is based on the U.S. experience, we believe that the lessons developed in this text are applicable far beyond our national borders.

In addition to the "academic" content of this research, we have attempted to craft a work that has appeal to practitioners of management. Organizational leaders are not well served by business school curriculums that ignore the impact of political and social environments on the exercise of corporate discretion. We believe that this work has value for managers in organizations as they attempt to become more adept in developing and implementing political strategies.

This has been an extremely enjoyable collaboration for us, a natural follow-up to all the previous work that we have done. Many of our colleagues at Boston College, Boston University, and the University of Scranton have graciously listened to our never-ending commentary on corporate–political analysis and—when they could get a word in—offered valuable insights. To all of them, and to our colleagues around the country, we are deeply grateful. Any shortcomings and deficiencies in this work are, of course, the sole responsibility of the authors.

We hope this work will inspire a new generation of scholars to investigate the fascinating relationships between the corporation and its social and political environment. It is a research arena that offers no end of possibilities for the scholar and endless possibilities for practitioners to achieve success individually and for their organizations.

Chapter 1

INTRODUCTION

Case 1   American Telephone and Telegraph (AT&T) routinely made donations to the Planned Parenthood Foundation of America for more than twenty-five years. AT&T's funding was designated for relatively uncontroversial issues—family planning and sex education. However, in March 1990, in response to concerns that it would become embroiled in a public battle between anti-abortionists and women's rights activists, AT&T announced that it would no longer provide funding. The anti-abortionists had achieved success in their previous campaign to have other major corporations such as JC Penney and Union Pacific withdraw their financial support of Planned Parenthood. In announcing the withdrawal of support, an AT&T spokesperson noted that "advocates on either side of the issue began to equate AT&T's support of Planned Parenthood's family planning and sex education as really AT&T's political view of pro-choice. We had to keep explaining ourselves. We feel that [abortion] is not a corporate matter but a private matter." Did this mean that AT&T supports abortion rights? "No, it means that we don't have a stance, nor should we" (Keller, 1990).

Case 2   On January 24, 1996, Mattel, the world's largest toy maker, made a public offer to buy Hasbro, the second largest toy manufacturer, located in Providence, Rhode Island. The proposed combination would have sales of $5.9 billion, control as much as 40 percent of the $16 billion U.S. toy market and 61 percent of the doll business, and would have had first or second position in every toy category worldwide. It pitted "Barbie" (a popular Mattel toy) against "G.I. Joe" (a popular Hasbro toy). Mattel offered $5.2 billion to purchase Hasbro. This was a 73 percent premium over what Hasbro shares were worth on January 24, 1996. Hasbro management decided to fight this hostile takeover and took their battle to the political and legal arena. Hasbro convinced the attorneys general of Rhode Island and Connecticut to ask for corporate records, as they were both concerned that serious antitrust issues were raised by this union. The Rhode Island Congressional Delegation asked the Federal Trade Commission and the Justice Department to look into this proposal, and European antitrust regulators expressed their concern. The most telling weapon that Hasbro used was the Rhode Island state legislature and governor. In less than a week, the legislature repealed a key state law that allowed owners of 10 percent or more of a company's stock to call a special meeting of shareholders, and the governor signed it. The new law allows only a company's board of directors or people authorized by the company to call a special meeting. The day after the governor signed the legislation, Mattel withdrew its offer. An analyst at Smith Barney observed that "Hasbro was victorious in keeping its independence, and the company's political clout was clearly highlighted in the fight." The analyst also noted that "Even if the deal were to turn friendly, Hasbro would have a hard time returning the antitrust warheads it launched back to their silos" (Davis, 1996: 1a). The chairman of Mattel, in a letter to Hasbro made public, wrote, "You elected to take drastic steps, both politically and through the media to greatly increase the difficulty of achieving a merger in a timely manner. Unfortunately, your 'scorched earth' campaign has created an intolerable climate" (Reidy and Shao, 1996: 28).

Case 3 Daiwa Bank was embarrassed by the apparent actions of one individual in their U.S. operations in 1995. Later, it became apparent that these actions, in clear violation of U.S. law, were known to senior executives in the United States and in Japan. Owing to differences in culture, the Japanese officials decided to keep the information that they had quiet and not report it to U.S. officials. As a consequence of these violations, bank regulators in the United States stripped Daiwa Bank of its right to operate in the United States, and the Department of Justice actively pursued criminal indictments against several Daiwa officers. One observer, commenting on this situation, noted that "The punishment by the U.S. means the death penalty for Daiwa" (Otsuka, 1995: 3).

Since the dawn of industrialized society, practitioners in the business arena have been pursuing success. Success has been defined using marketplace criteria and the amassing of wealth in the form of what society used as an exchange device at any particular time in history. At one point, in some cultures, having stock of tobacco was a mark of wealth. In Western cultures, having gold, silver, or other precious minerals was once considered a mark of success and wealth. There is the very old story of King Midas, whose greed caused the gods to gift him with a magic touch—everything he touched turned to gold. In today's society, the amassing of wealth is measured by many through the use of currency.

In pursuit of wealth and success as defined by other marketplace measures (e.g., share of market, innovativeness, leadership on price and quality), organizations and individuals have attempted to develop plans and strategies to succeed in competition with other firms; but such plans and strategies did not address the types of situations described in the opening of this chapter. The use of political strategies can be critical to the success of an organization's product market or economic strategies, as will be discussed in this book.

The focus of these market-based strategies, as exemplified in the academic literature and in the practice of management, is on developing plans and implementing them to achieve a sustainable position of competitive advantage. A sustainable position of competitive advantage has been defined in a variety of ways, but the major focus has centered on developing specific capabilities that provide an "edge" to the firm and that cannot be easily duplicated by competitors. This "edge" is also meant to be sustainable; that is, it should yield an advantage to the firm in the marketplace that will last for a lengthy period of time. No advantage is sustainable forever, as innovations in both products and processes can make yesterday's advantage totally obsolete (or at least less formidable) today.

For example, Henry Ford introduced the concept of mass production in automobiles. This yielded his firm, Ford Motor Company, an impressive strategic advantage in the marketplace. He was able to produce cars quickly and at a sufficiently low enough price to capture the largest and most significant share of the market. General Motors (GM) and other car manufacturers copied these mass production techniques, but Ford Motor Company remained dominant. This dominance continued until GM developed the idea of different models to appeal to different segments of the marketplace. GM decided that it could out-maneuver Ford's competitive advantage. This erosion of Ford's advantage would take place by appealing to the ultimate customer in the form of variety in their selection of models and cars. GM moved to this strategy and quickly improved market share at Ford's (and everyone else's) expense. When Ford reluctantly shut down to retool in order to provide Fords beyond just black and the Model T, GM's dominance of the market was assured. Ford never regained its lead again in the U.S. automotive market.

History repeated itself in the 1960s in the U.S. automobile market again. This time, the challenge to GM's leadership arose from Japan. It should be clear that the Japanese faced an enormous handicap in entering the automotive market in the United States. The Japanese had no distribution network, they were not familiar with American consumers and their tastes, and they had no identifiable market image for their products. In addition, the U.S. manufacturers (Ford, GM, and Chrysler) had enormous economies of scale that dwarfed domestic production in Japan. So how did the Japanese car manufacturers enter the market? They entered the market at the low end, where price was one of the most important, if not the only, criteria for selecting an automobile. This yielded numerous benefits to the Japanese manufacturers. The large U.S. competitors ignored them, as this was a segment of the market where "there was not much money to be made." This ignorance of the major competitors allowed the Japanese car manufacturers to learn about the American market, build up a distribution system, and understand shifting consumer preferences and tastes. Gradually, over time, the Japanese car manufacturers did two things. The first action was to build an image of quality and move up into higher-priced and more feature-rich automobiles. The second, and more important, strategic action was to find a way to overcome the enormous economies of scale that American manufacturers enjoyed. The Japanese realized that they would not be able to beat Ford, GM, and Chrysler through imitation alone. As a result, one of the competitive advantages that the Japanese developed, among others, was the ability to shift from one model and style of car to another very quickly. This allowed them to be more sensitive to customer preferences and to reduce the size of finished goods inventory and the number of cars not sold in a given model year. This advantage in shifting model production continues to this day (Mahon and Vachani, 1992).

As knowledge of strategy and sustainable competitive advantage grew, more sophisticated studies were undertaken in order to understand competitive dynamics at the industry level of competition. Harvard's Michael Porter (1979, 1980, 1985) was one of several who led the way in this particular research. He argued that specific firm performance and positioning in an industry was a function of a variety of factors, including the nature and intensity of industry rivalry; the particular power relationships between and among the industry and its suppliers, customers, and likely new entrants; and the availability of substitute products or services for those offered by the industry under study. In addition, he highlighted the problems and opportunities with barriers to entry and exit within a particular industry setting. This approach is also referred to as the Five Forces Model.

Porter's work has proven to be immensely successful and relevant to the practice of management in large and small organizations alike. It is extremely difficult to find a leader of an organization, an academic, or a doctoral student who is not familiar with Porter's writing and thinking on this topic. The model and approach that he developed is easy to explain, relatively easy to apply and use, and has shown to be of significant strategic value to organizations.

The very success of Porter's work and others in the strategic management field has blinded both academicians and practitioners to situations raised in the opening of this chapter. It is abundantly clear that such events and actions have a strategic impact on both individual firms and on industry-competitive dynamics. What has been missing to date is a systematic approach to assessing these impacts and suggestions on how corporations and industries might deal with such strategic challenges. The focus of this book is on the assessment of social and political action on the strategic positioning of individual firms and the industries that they represent. Although some attention is paid to individual firm political strategy, the clear emphasis here is on industry political strategy. The teaching of political strategy is not as well developed as the more conventional business strategy; indeed, it is often downplayed or even totally omitted in most strategic management textbooks. In the political science field, scant attention is paid to the role of corporations and industries in political and social issues. Robert Dahl noted years ago to his colleagues in political science that "For all the talk and public curiosity about the relations between business and politics, there is a remarkable dearth of studies on the subject. What is written is more likely to come from the pen of a sociologist, a historian, a lawyer, or an economist than from a political scientist" (1959: 3).

This book is divided into three parts. In Part One, consisting of two chapters, the foundation of the approach utilized in this text is developed. Chapter 2 explores, in some detail, the research in three distinct fields—strategy, organizational behavior, and social issues in management—that contributes to our understanding of the impacts of political and social action and events on firm- and industry-competitive positioning. In order to develop a model for industry-competitive political dynamics, it is important to have a basic understanding of these diverse literature bases. Chapter 2 concludes with a model of political strategy that has utility for individual organizations. Chapter 3 analyzes in detail the flaws and lapses in the current approach to industry-competitive dynamics. A careful review of the current approach is undertaken, along with a clarifying example. Then, an example of the inapplicability of this model is shown to highlight its shortcomings. A complementary model of industry-competitive political dynamics is developed; and a detailed example is discussed, which is drawn from a recent, charged political situation involving the issue of television violence. This particular issue had potentially significant financial implications for a variety of actors, including, but not limited to, the television networks, advertisers, local stations, producers, writers, and actors in specific shows. Chapter 3 concludes Part One of this book.

In Part Two, we provide evidence and examples of industry-competitive political dynamics from four different industries chosen specifically to represent a broad spectrum of economic activity in four separate chapters. These industry examples develop and flesh out the details of the model of industry-competitive political strategy developed in Chapter 2, showing the impact of such issues on the competitive dynamics of the industry. The four industries chosen for more detailed analysis are the cigarette, beer, banking, and chemical industries. These industries were chosen for detailed analysis for a variety of reasons. First, they represent large and significant sectors of the economy, with powerful, individual firms in active competition with one another. Second, they represent industries that are heavily influenced by public opinion and action, and that have been subjected to long-term, at times intensive, government oversight and involvement. Third, they represent a range of industrial activity—cigarettes and beer are mass-marketed consumables; banking is a financial services activity and product; and chemicals are, for the most part, sold to industrial concerns. Fourth, each of these industries is currently (or will be) important in international competition. Finally, we believe that the political and social challenges that these industries have faced in the United States will be repeated in the international arena and that the lessons these industries have learned or failed to learn in dealing with political and social issues and events will be instructive to industries and firms both in the United States and in international competition.

Chapter 4 begins our industry analysis and focuses on a historical view of the cigarette industry and the waves of government and societal involvement that it has faced since its inception. In Chapter 4, one can see the evolution of issues and problems that the industry has faced and how government and societal involvements have dramatically altered the competitive landscape. The flow of Chapter 4 is carefully tied to the key concepts developed in Chapter 2. It allows the reader to see how issues and problems in the political and social arena develop and how they often accrue and build over time—that is, yesterday's issues are not completely resolved, and new issues are added on that the firm and industry has to resolve. In addition, the reader can view the industry's response to these issues over time and assess their success.

Chapter 5 deals with our second producer of consumer products—the beer industry. Again, a broad historical approach is taken; and the reader can clearly see the political strategies and tactics that the beer industry pursued in its attempts to separate itself from the general alcohol (wine and distilled spirits) industry. As in Chapter 4, the reader can view the development of issues and events, noting that an issue dealt with ten years ago may not go away and that the issue addressed today is a logical extension of that previous issue requiring an industry response to both the past and present issue. One of the interesting aspects of this analysis is how a segment of the overall alcohol industry (beer) followed a political strategy of differentiation for a lengthy period of time. The beer industry has argued that it is quite different from wine and distilled spirits. This strategy, as will be seen, yielded tangible financial results for the entire beer industry, perhaps at the expense of the wine and distilled spirits industries.

Chapter 6 shifts our focus to the financial services industry and, in particular, banking. Again, a historical overview is provided; but one key difference in this particular industry's competitive political situation is the presence of other powerful industries (insurance, investment houses, financial supermarkets, etc.) attempting to exert influence on the political process in which key issues will be resolved. The battles among these major industries took place at both the state and federal government arenas. The banking industry exerted its influence at the state level, where it was skilled and powerful. The insurance industry responded by exerting its influence at the federal level, where it was skilled and powerful. Each industry was trying to achieve success at the expense of the other industry.

Chapter 7 shifts both the focus of analysis and the style of presentation. In Chapter 7, the chemical industry is our unit of analysis. Chemicals, for the most part, are sold to other chemical firms and other industrial users. However, rather than pursuing a broad historical sweep of issues and events, the focus is on a single issue of salience to the industry—the cleanup of hazardous waste sites. The focus on this single issue is to allow the reader to move from the more macro presentations and broad historical events and issues in Chapters 4, 5, and 6 to a more micro view. The responses of the chemical industry (and key individual firms) to a pressing political and social issue is developed in detail in Chapter 7. The supporters of the issue were powerful political actors, and the impact of contextual factors and environmental conditions are evident in this issue and its unfolding. The political strategies and tactics pursued by the chemical industry to blunt those efforts and change the shape and nature of the debate are clearly presented. In addition, it is possible to assess the impact of this issue's resolution on the competitive dynamics of the industry in both the domestic and international markets. Finally, it seems that the chemical industry learned from its experiences with this issue and applied them to the subsequent extension of the law several years later.

Part Three of the book focuses on a review of these four industries and their experiences in dealing with political and social dynamics and their impact on overall industry competitive dynamics. We conclude with a set of key lessons that should be taken from this work and would encourage the reader to develop his or her own set of lessons that would be applicable to his or her own situation and specific circumstances.

The impact of social movements, interest groups, and government involvement in the business of business is not likely to recede in the foreseeable future. Firms and industries have two clear choices—ignorance or involvement. Firms and industries can choose to remain aloof from the political and social debates that swirl around them. Unfortunately, this aloofness can have severe impacts on the ability of the firm or industry to operate at a profitable manner, or even to exist at all. Aloofness ultimately means that the firm or industry surrenders its voice in shaping the debate and its ultimate resolution. We believe that such a course of action is short-sighted and a prostitution of both the individual firm's fiduciary responsibility to its owners and of the democratic process which encourages debate and discussion from all sides. Therefore, our position would be for an active, consistent, and constant involvement in the political and social debate that will set the rules for competitive conduct in the future. However, in order to engage in such a debate, the individual firm and industry must recognize that such an activity is desirous. Once this recognition comes to pass, then individual firms and industries must develop the tools and techniques to develop and implement political and social strategies. We believe that this work is but the first of many to follow that will address the need to improve an industry's capabilities in assessing competitive political dynamics and implementing political and social strategies to ensure success or, at the minimum, guarantee that the industry's voice in political and social debates is not silenced.

We would agree with the concluding comment in Edwin Epstein's (1969) classic work, *The Corporation in American Politics*. In this work, he addresses the legitimacy of corporate political activity and action. Although he is dealing with the individual firm, his comments are germane to industry political activity as well. He notes that out of the process of continuing adjustments to our environment "must come a modification of the traditional concepts of political participation, including a reappraisal of the political role of the corporation. Such a reappraisal should result in the explicit recognition that the corporation is a necessary and legitimate participant in the political process—a participant that, together with other social interests, contributes to the maintenance of pluralistic democracy in America rather than endangers it" (Epstein, 1969: 324).

PART ONE

THE THEORETICAL DEVELOPMENT OF COMPETITIVE-INDUSTRY POLITICAL DYNAMICS

Chapter 2

ORGANIZATIONAL ADAPTATION TO ITS ENVIRONMENT

> I owe the public nothing.
> —J. P. Morgan
>
> The public be damned.
> —W. H. Vanderbilt[1]

The sentiments expressed by Morgan and Vanderbilt were not unusual for their time. They reflect a view of the organization's relationship with its environment that, while recognized as unlikely today, nonetheless is at times desired by leaders of the organization. The problem is easily understood. Managers of any organization find the shaping, direction, and control of the enterprise from an *internal* perspective challenging and far from easy—but doable. Managers understand the beauty of accounting and finance and how to organize, staff, and direct a business. Managers have improved their skills in motivating and rewarding employees to achieve organizational goals and objectives. It is when managers are faced with the contingencies and challenges found in the world beyond the organization's boundaries—the external environment—that real difficulties set in. In this *external* world—beyond mere marketplace considerations of products and customers, where ideas and not money are the currency of exchange—managers have to deal with different agendas offered by different individuals and groups that are frequently themselves in conflict. The neat, clear, understood measures of performance and control (e.g., accounting and finance, budgets, returns on investment, profitability, etc.) are not applicable in this particular external environment. Groups clamor for the organization to be socially responsible, to care for the natural environment, to consider the safety of both the workplace and the community, and to, in general, be "good citizens." Yet the specific definitions of these terms and what constitutes acceptable behavior seem to be in constant flux over time. In some respects, Morgan's and Vanderbilt's comments can be seen as reflective of the frustration faced by managers in dealing with the public at large, interest groups, and government. It is not always the case, as those opponents of businesses argue, that business does not care, but rather that business leaders are perplexed in their dealings with this external environment. In many ways, the world of academe has not been helpful to generations of managers in preparing them for this disparate external environment. How have we reached such a position?

BUSINESS–GOVERNMENT–SOCIETY: AN EVOLVING RELATIONSHIP

The key organizational and strategic problems of Morgan's and Vanderbilt's era centered on the development of efficient manufacturing systems and tight control systems (Ansoff, 1979). The other major elements in the business environment—government and the public at large—were reluctant to press for business responsibility and accountability at this time. The concerns of business were to be left to business leaders, and the public's interest in business was largely confined to economic and employment issues. This rather benign relationship, with an external environment that was not intrusive into business affairs, was to undergo a gradual transformation—a transformation which continues to this day. Letwin captures this relationship quite well when he notes that "businessmen were already established in their high status when the United States emerged as a nation in 1789. Even as early as that, the United States could have been described as a nation of businessmen ruled by businessmen. That description would have violated certain of the more acceptable images of American life, but it would have fitted the larger facts" (1973: 18).

This comfortable and predictable relationship between business, government, and society continued for some time. Business seemed able to impose its will on society and government with little opposition. As Garraty states, "Flush times in the postwar era (Civil War) produced a new kind of business titan. Freebooters such as David Drew, Jay Gould, and Jim Fisk swindled each other as well as the public and boasted of the legislatures they bought; not even the Crédit Mobilier nor the worst political corruptionists were more brazen in their pillaging" (1966: 556). Documenting these attitudes and actions even further, Garraty notes that the battle to control the Erie Railroad in 1868, pitting Drew, Gould and Fisk against the elder Vanderbilt, was archetype of financial piracy; judges and legislatures in two states corrupted, 50,000 shares of stock illegally printed and sold, a railroad looted of millions. Victorious, Gould and Fisk next embarked on a scheme notable for its audacity—a corner on the nation's gold supply. Possessing enough cash to control the open market, they sought to neutralize the Treasury's stock of gold through the influence of President Grant's brother-in-law. The price of gold shot up at their bidding until September 24, 1869 ("Black Friday"), when Grant belatedly released the government reserves. Gould and Fisk slipped out from under their collapsing scheme, but hundreds of investors were ruined. "Nothing is lost save honor," said the carefree Fisk. "Let everyone carry out his own corpse." (1966: 556)

Lest the reader think that such actions are confined to the dust bin of history, we have only to look at the last twenty years for similar examples. We have seen manipulations in the savings and loan industry, where thousands were ruined; in the junk bond business, Boskey and Milken made millions with insider information; in the Hunt brothers' attempts to corner the silver market; in the recent collapse of a venerable British bank due to the derivatives trading of a single broker; and in the recent scandal over bond trading in the Japanese Daiwa Bank (Syrre, 1995).

The giants of business were able to pursue these actions in the past (and in the present) because of the secrecy with which they surrounded themselves. Tedlow notes that Vanderbilt concealed his business methods from his own son by keeping all accounts in his head, and J. P. Morgan was described by many as "broodingly silent" (1976: 1–2).

The relationships among business, government, and society can be viewed as shown in Figure 2.1. Business was clearly influential in government and societal processes, with little interference from these other parties in business affairs and operations.

Figure 2.1
Early Business–Government–Society Relationships

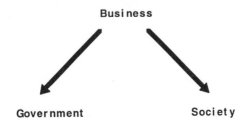

Business

Government   Society

The Relationship Begins to Change

This relationship, with business dominant, existed for quite some time and did not require the development of skills to deal with the external environment by managers and business leaders. Morison offers several reasons for this tolerance, noting that "these exactions and abuses were long tolerated by Americans, so imbued were they with laissez-faire doctrine, so proud of progress, improvement, and development, and so averse from increasing the power of government" (1965: 764). Even when the scandalous actions of businessmen were exposed for public scrutiny, little was done. "Such depredations, although denounced from the pulpit and cursed in the press, met with only halfhearted government censure" (Garraty, 1966: 556). These times were, from the business person's perspective, the golden age:

Until the late nineteenth century, legislation was designed, on the whole, to encourage business and commerce. After the War of 1812 it was clear that the new nation could not rely on the Old World as a source of manufactured goods, and protective tariffs were enacted to promote the growth of American industry. Government also subsidized business directly, especially the transportation industry. . . . Some 130 million acres were given away by the federal government—establishing a railroad empire twice the size of New York, New Jersey, and Pennsylvania combined. This action perhaps set a record (in one sense or another) for government support and encouragement of business in the United States. (Holton, 1973: 58)

However, public tolerance of the behavior of business and its actions waned over time, and government finally stepped in to control some of the worst situations. Chandler (1980) argues that the growth of government involvement in business and the switch to an adversarial relationship was a direct result of business taking advantage of the situation during nonregulated times. In 1887, the federal government made its first move to regulate railroads and break up the large trusts. The first Interstate Commerce Act was passed, declaring pooling, unreasonable rates, and other unfair practices to be illegal; and enforcement was vested in the Interstate Commerce Commission (Morison, 1965: 764). Government success in this area was initially limited, and business was quick to move the debate away from the legislative arena and into another one:

Administrative regulations were so foreign to the American conception of government that the federal courts insisted on their rights to review orders of the Commission and by denying its power to fix rates, emasculated the Act. So the railroads continued to charge "all the traffic would bear." Equally futile was the Sherman Anti-Trust Act of 1890, which declared illegal any monopoly or combination in restraint of interstate trade. When the Supreme Court in 1895 held that purchase by the sugar trust of a controlling interest in 98 percent of the sugar refining business of the country was not a violation of the law because it was not an act of interstate commerce, the Sherman Act became temporarily a dead letter. (Morison, 1965: 764)

Although these initial steps were not particularly successful, they marked the beginning of government regulation and involvement in business affairs that would eventually result in both industry-specific (banking, insurance, air transportation) and issue-specific (health, safety, environment, equal employment) regulation. This involvement is not limited to just regulation and has brought government as the representative of the public interest into almost every aspect of corporate action (Baron, 1993; Hoberg, 1990; Marcus, Kaufman, and Beam, 1987; Mitnick, 1993a; Shaffer, 1992). This government activity has altered the relationship in Figure 2.1 to that shown in Figure 2.2.

As a consequence, government has assumed a greater role in the affairs of business at both the state and federal level. Government has argued, among many other reasons, that their representation of the public interest is paramount in the oversight of business activities. This meant that business leaders and managers now had to consider the interests of a new factor—government—in their decision making and strategic planning. Although this addition of a new factor into business decision making complicated the decision process and analytical approach, it was still a manageable process as the pace of government action was slow and somewhat predictable.

If this level of involvement in business activities had stopped here, the process of organizational accommodation to societal interests as represented by government could have been managed. Unfortunately, the level of involvement of societal interests continued to

Figure 2.2
Evolving Business–Government–Society Relationships

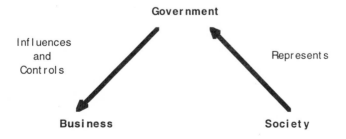

expand far beyond mere government oversight and regulation. The rise of such public interest groups as Common Cause, the Interfaith Council on Corporate Responsibility (ICCR), Friends of the Earth (FOE), the American Civil Liberties Union (ACLU), the National Organization for Women (NOW), and other groups too numerous to mention here has greatly expanded both the substantive debate on corporations and their responsibility to society and the process by which such disagreements would be resolved (Berry, 1984; Cobb and Elder, 1972; Freeman, 1984; Hilgartner and Bosk, 1988; Kingdon, 1984; Olson, 1965; Russo, 1993; Walker, 1991). Surprisingly, business in the past has, to a large extent, invited and actively welcomed this involvement (Dill, 1976). This involvement of a large and growing group of actors with different agendas, different criteria for measuring success and improvement, and a willingness to use different methods (boycotts, mass demonstrations, media events and the media itself, legal actions in various jurisdictions, lobbying and direct political action, legislative and regulatory involvements, etc.) has complicated the business manager's decision making enormously. As a consequence, the relationship has evolved as shown in Figure 2.3, becoming far more difficult to manage.

The early history of business–government–society relationships was one of accommodation of society and government to business. What business wanted, government and society were quick to grant. This pattern of accommodation changed, as we have noted, starting in the late 1870s. Louis Galambos (1975) investigated how public perception of big business in America changed from the 1880s to 1940. His work documents the shifts in public attitudes and perceptions of big business that occurred during this time. Galambos notes that this shift in attitudes and perceptions impacted on the business–government–society relationship and that this shift involved "a long-run process of accommodation between the corporation and middle class America" (p. 19). How, then, is business to

Figure 2.3
Current Business–Government–Society Relationships

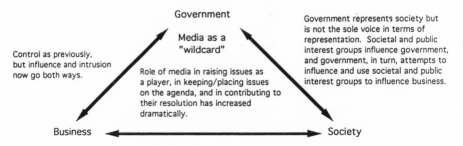

accommodate itself to these changing attitudes and perceptions and become a legitimate and recognized player in the political and social arena? It is assumed that dealing with such issues and problems is one of strategic importance to the organization.

The traditional economic orientation of the firm, its role, and its position in a free-market economy have become subjected to continuous, intense debate. Organizational critics have questioned the narrowly conceived economic mission of the firm, arguing that the performance of the business as an institution needs to be addressed within a political and societal framework. Certainly, a significant portion of these challenges to business have arisen from the growing interdependency of environmental elements (e.g., structures of authority and power resources, information) and the accelerating rate of changes within the environment itself. Another factor is the massive growth in the complexity and size of business organizations themselves (as seen in recent bank mergers and media mergers) and the counteractivity of downsizing to become more competitive and maneuverable (as in the recent breakup of AT&T into three separate businesses). In any event, the interaction of larger, more complex managerial units with a more dynamic environment has led to increased corporate exposure on a variety of issues involving both specific (product safety, equal employment) and general (firm governance) issues of legitimacy.

The first and short-term response to these pressures has been the development of a highly visible or "public" chief executive officer. The likes of Irving Shapiro of Du Pont and Jack Welch of General Electric (GE) to name but a few have dramatically altered the role of the corporate leader. By their example, they have shown that an articulate business executive can have a positive influence on the firm's relationship with its many publics.

This new role for the chief executive is a recognition by organizations that society is demanding more from its corporations and its corporate leaders. Unfortunately, this type of response is a function of the particular individual and his or her capabilities, talents, and interests. As such, it is transitory in nature. What is needed, then, is some way to institutionalize this sensitivity to dealing with diverse publics and issues within the corporation's structure and processes. One such method appears to be the establishment and growth of public affairs and corporate community relations departments within the firm (Fleisher, 1993; Marcus and Irion, 1987; Post, Murray, Dickie, and Mahon, 1982). These institutional changes help to perpetuate an awareness of societal and political interests within the decision-making structure of the organization. Notwithstanding these changes, it has been our experience in both teaching and consulting over the last twenty years that the influence of such offices and their continued existence is still largely a function of the chief executive officer's support and interest.

Why, then, is it so difficult for organizations to engage in sustained analysis, anticipation, communication, and response to political and societal issues? Perhaps a review of the relevant literature will provide insights for twenty-first century managers on the importance of such capabilities for all organizations.

ORGANIZATIONAL ADAPTATION TO THE ENVIRONMENT IN THE LITERATURE

There are several areas in which one can begin to investigate the treatment of the organization's adaptation to its external environment and the key issues that are raised by that environment for corporate decisions and actions. These approaches are, in some ways, dependent on the operating assumptions that one makes. For example, if an organization and its managers see external forces (legal compulsion, legislative action, boycotts, other pressures from interest groups) as the key factor in corporate responses and that managerial action and commitment occur incrementally, then no long-term planning or anticipation is possible or needed. The organization careens from one event to another, responding to pressures and problems as they arise. Since all of these events and pressures are seen as discrete situations, there is no possibility of organizational learning and no value in anticipatory actions or strategies. Such an assumption, in our view, guarantees poor corporate performance in dealing with diverse issues and publics.

If, on the other hand, the operating assumption is that political and social issues are environmental factors to be considered in shaping an organization's strategy, and that they are part of an overall pattern of situations that can be managed or influenced, then organizational strategies for anticipating, shaping, and responding to such issues and problems make sense. It is further assumed that the organization can learn from these events and improve on its performance in the future with related issues and problems. This particular view emphasizes managerial initiative and the values of the top management team as motivators of organizational behavior. The most realistic set of operating assumptions is to combine both views and recognize that there are crisis situations that cannot always be anticipated and, therefore, are unique and discrete and that there are streams of issues, events, and problems that occur that can be anticipated and acted upon by the farsighted and organized firm. If there is some advantage to organizational structures and processes for dealing with social and political issues and events, what information and assistance does the academic literature provide to the practitioner? There are three relevant literature bases that apply to this problem: (1) organizational behavior field (especially in boundary spanning and in environmental scanning), (2) the strategic management literature, and (3) the social issues in management literature (especially the subfield that deals with corporate political strategy). It is the intersection of these three literatures that is important to our understanding of the corporate–government–society relationship and how organizations can anticipate and respond to changes in that relationship over time (Figure 2.4). The goal in reviewing these literature bases is to familiarize the reader with their content and focus in order to lay a conceptual foundation for the remainder of this book and not to review these fields in significant depth.

Figure 2.4
The Intersection of Three Literature Streams

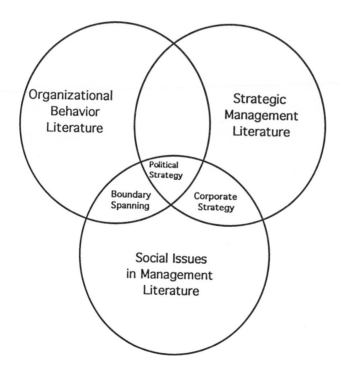

The Organizational Behavior Literature

The organizational behavior literature, like all literature areas, encompasses a large and diverse set of interests. Our major focus is on the boundary spanning and information processing area. Boundary-spanning activities can be defined as all those activities and relationships (market and nonmarket) that occur between organizational members and members of the environment (i.e., not members of the organization). More specifically, boundary spanning involves some parts of the organization that are interdependent with organizations not subordinated to the focal organization and, therefore, not subjected to the authority of the organization. The critical aspect of boundary-spanning activities, then, is not control or coordination but adjustment to constraints and contingencies not controlled by the organization. Examples of such activities include, but are not limited to, legal actions, public-affairs activities, lobbying, speeches, community relations, selling activities, and so on. These elements of an organization not only represent the firm to the external environment but also interpret and analyze that environment for the organization.

Assume for a moment that your entire view of a portion of the world relied on another individual. His or her interpretations and ability to communicate would be crucial factors in your understanding of that portion of the world and in shaping your responses to and anticipation of issues, events, and problems in that world. This individual, in effect, controls your understanding of this portion of the world through the information he or she provides (or does not provide).

March and Simon (1958) and Simon (1976) argued that information is a source of power and influence within an organization. Simon further stipulates that organizations ensure "satisficing" behavior (and not optimizing behavior) by controlling decision-making premises through the control of information provided to the decision maker. Galbraith (1973), expanding on this information theme, notes that organizations have two general approaches in dealing with information. The firm can elect to deal with information in a faster, more efficient manner, thereby improving the organization's ability to process and understand information and, therefore, act more quickly. This is clearly the preferred choice. On the other hand, the organization can elect to slow down the information flow in the organization through the establishment of what he calls "slack resources." An example of a slack resource is the addition of more hierarchies in management, which slows down the information flow and allows the organization more information processing time. A slowing of information processing time would doom the organization to a reactionary cycle of response; that is, if information is slowed through the organization, then key decision makers do not have the time to analyze information and prepare carefully crafted actions in anticipation of problems and issues. Galbraith argues that if the organization does not consciously choose a strategy, then it, in effect, selects the slowing down of information option. Therefore, boundary spanners have an important impact on the decision and decision-making process of the organization.

Weick (1969) takes this informational and boundary-spanning perspective one step further. He argues that organizations can "enact," that is, create their own environments. Pfeffer and Salancik (1978) also argue that organizations can create their own environments, and they offer several specific methods by which this environmental creation can be carried out. In both cases, the creation or enactment of environments involve the use of boundary-spanning elements of the organization. It should be clear that lobbying and advocacy advertising are examples of an organization and, in some cases, an industry attempting to create a certain environment.

Therefore, the lesson for managers is quite simple: Where and with what speed do you get your information, and how effectively do you use your boundary-spanning elements to represent the organization to the external world, to obtain information from that world, and to shape and create an environment? If a manager concentrates effort on marketplace and financial data, then he or she will likely miss informational cues about coming changes in regulation, legislation, or public attitudes. The speed with which information is gathered and delivered to the correct decision maker is often crucial to successful anticipatory and response strategies. In the Cuban Missile Crisis, Allison (1971) recounts the difficulty that intelligence officers in Florida had in getting critical information to the executive branch of government. When Union Carbide's chemical plant blew up in Bhopal, India, responses were confounded by the fact that there was only one telephone line in and out of the city. Information was delayed and frequently confused and chaotic.

The Strategic Management Literature

This literature has been concerned with, among other things, the relationship of strategy, structure, and economic performance in light of the corporation's environment. One would think that the environment would include political and social issues and concerns and the impact of government and societal action. This was not to be the case. Alfred Chandler was one of the first writers to explore historically the relationships among these variables. For him, strategy was "the determination of the basic long term goals and objectives of an enterprise, and the adoption of courses of action and the allocation of resources necessary for carrying out these goals" (Chandler, 1962: 13).

From the earliest time, the strategy literature excluded the nonmarket environment from consideration. Ansoff narrowed Chandler's definition, noting that strategy is

primarily concerned with external, rather than internal, problems of the firm and specifically with the selection of the product-mix which the firm will produce and the markets to which it will sell. To use an engineering term, the strategic problem is concerned with establishing an "impedance match" between the firm and its environment or, in more usual terms, it is the problem of deciding what business the firm is in and what kinds of business it will seek to enter. (Ansoff, 1965: 5–6)

Ansoff went on to emphasize that profitability (as defined by return on investment) is the key criterion for investment. For Ansoff, the elements of a successful strategy are an emphasis on product and market scope considerations and growth as well as the development of competitive advantages and synergy. Milton Friedman (1970) echoed this basic sentiment in the popular press in his article, "The Social Responsibility of Business Is to Increase Its Profits."

Andrews seems to agree with the position on strategy staked out by Ansoff and, combining it with elements of Chandler's earlier version, concluded that "corporate strategy is the pattern of major objectives, purposes, or goals and essential policies and plans for achieving those goals, stated in such a way as to define what business the company is in or is to be in and the kind of company it is or is to be" (Andrews, 1971: 28).

A clear theme in these definitions of strategy is the match that the organization achieves with its environment: The firm must align its goals and objectives with its capabilities (or distinctive competencies) in light of environmental considerations. This alignment process has been confined almost exclusively to the development of adequate product–market relationships; that is, the focus of the strategy literature and the definition of strategy is devoted to the maximization of the organization's economic performance. What remains consistent in virtually all models of strategy is the treatment of environmental analysis as just another block in the model to be filled in by economic and technical information only. As early as 1979, Utterback summed up this problem:

A large amount of work has been done in the development and use of forecasts of specific economic and market variables. A growing body of work has emerged in attempts to forecast technological change. Much less research has appeared in the literature reviewed related to forecasting social, political, and institutional changes which affect the firm. Often attempts to anticipate change in these areas are based on generalizations of methods tried in the economic market or technological contexts. (Utterback, 1979: 134)

Klein is also concerned with this narrowness of focus, but with a slightly different emphasis:

When reviewing the textual literature on formal planning systems, what must strike the student of formal planning processes immediately is the almost total elaboration of the environmental analysis step in the process. In short, otherwise exemplary treatments of strategy formulation and planning processes consider the assessment step more in terms of the results it yields, than in the process whereby such results are obtained. (Klein, 1979: 145)

In sum, while strategy attempts to deal with the matching of organizational strengths and weaknesses to threats and opportunities in the environment, it generally fails to adequately address the assessment of nonmarket factors. Even one of the acknowledged experts in the field, Michael Porter (1980), barely addresses this issue in his seminal work, *Competitive Strategy*. Although Porter recognizes that government can have an impact, it is confined to entry barriers, a brief commentary on regulations, and government impediments to international competition. There is no commentary or analysis of the role of interest groups and changing social mores on the competitive positioning of firms and of industries. Fried and Oviatt (1989) offer a more stinging criticism, noting that Porter (1980, 1985) ignores the challenges to corporate strategy posed by U.S. antitrust laws. The authors note that there is "little evidence that academicians and executives who use his [Porter's] work pay much attention to these risks" (Fried and Oviatt, 1989: 49). They conclude that Porter's work is missing a crucial key chapter on antitrust. We would conclude that Porter is missing several chapters on political and social strategies and tactics to deal with political and social events.[2]

Nonetheless, it is important to understand how the organization as a whole interacts with other entities in an environment characterized by dynamic social and political—as well as economic, competitive, and technological—forces. If appropriate attentiveness and successful adaptation to social and political issues are not forthcoming from the firm, a cost is incurred. If society incurs the cost in the short time, redistribution of the costs may be sought through the judicial, legislative, regulatory, or public action processes. Thus, the failures of corporate performance to meet public expectations may give rise to a social or political issue; and through the political and social process, the cost to society is reimposed on the firm—specifically, its industry, or the business community, in general—in the form of damages, penalties, prohibitions, regulations, or other constraints and limitations on the exercise of corporate and industry discretion.

A key factor in these relationships is the responsiveness of the political process. In some countries, including the United States in the early development stages, the political process fails to intermediate between business and society with the result that business can impose costs on society with impunity and, to a degree, vice versa, with an active set of interest groups that represent society. If government ceases to at least pose a credible threat of being able to constrain business activity, or to pass back to it certain costs, then at least some corporations in the system tend to lose any incentive to curtail and discipline any antisocial practices. This is frequently what occurs in third world or lesser developed countries when large, international firms enter and begin to conduct business.

Social Issues in Management Literature

The social issues in management literature concern the impact of the firm on the environment and the impact of the environment on the firm. This literature includes analyses that deal with the structure and process of corporate social responsiveness and corporate social performance (Wartick and Cochran, 1985; Wood, 1991a, 1991b; Mitnick, 1993b). Those that look at the structural aspects also deal with process (some classics here are Ackerman, 1975; Bauer, 1978) and look at issues and problems from the perspective of the corporation. Others analyze the relationship of the corporation with the environment from a societal or public policy perspective and focus on process (some examples include Lindblom, 1968; Post, 1978).

The research stream started with Ackerman and Bauer argues for the establishment of staff specialists to institutionalize the firm's response to societal issues (related to the boundary-spanning notions discussed earlier). This research stream also views corporate responsiveness as internally developed from subjective decision making. In addition to the institutionalization of organizational response in this area is the necessity for managerial awareness of various political strategies available to the firm. While it is obvious that there is a rational model of decision making in organizations, firms within the same industry often follow very different political strategies in dealing with a political or social issue. Therefore, if we are to understand industry political dynamics, we must first have a grasp of what it is that constitutes political strategy.

CORPORATE POLITICAL STRATEGY IN THE LITERATURE

In order to adequately address the firm's external resource dependencies (and, at the same time, achieve a workable accommodation between economic and other social goals on a basis broader than a single issue at a time), Ackerman advocates the formulation of a corporate strategy for corporate responsiveness, recognizing that there needs to be some accommodation between the strategy and social issues in management literature.[3]

As with corporate strategy, political strategy is concerned with the whole organization and its relationship with the environment. The primary focus in corporate political strategy is on the allocation of values, resources, and influence; not on economic outcomes. This does not mean, however, that the results of political strategy are not intended to generate economic consequences. They can and frequently do generate benefits that yield economic value to the firm and industries involved.

If we are to integrate these two literature bases, then four basic premises underlie much of the literature on political and the more traditional strategy. The first is that strategy is concerned with the link between the organization and the environment (Chandler, 1962). How this relationship is conceptualized differs among researchers (Chafee, 1985), yet whether the strategy is to be understood as initiating upon or adapting to the environment, the organization and its environment are seen as integrally connected.

The second premise is that strategy represents a stream of decisions made by the organization or individuals within the organization. Differences exist, however, on the rationality of the decision process as noted earlier. Andrews (1987), in a revision to his earlier 1971 work, argues that the process is rational, while Narayanan and Fahey (1982) and Smircich and Stubbart (1982) argue that the process is based on behavioral and political factors. Yet all agree that strategy concerns decisions about the future and the organization's fit or match with the environment.

The third premise is that the execution of strategy involves the use of resources to carry out organizational goals and objectives (Chandler, 1962). These resources include technological, human, and financial resources as well as supply and distribution contracts and channels.

The final premise is that strategy yields or leads to a "sustainable competitive advantage" (Ghemawat, 1986). This advantage can be based on economies of scale and scope, timing, control of access to customers and suppliers, and the use of advantageous public policy initiatives. Although the general focus of competitive advantage is on gaining an edge in the marketplace, we argue that the notion of competitive advantage is equally applicable to corporate political strategy and behavior.

A general definition may be developed that incorporates the notions of environment, decisions, resources, and advantage. Corporate strategy represents those streams of decisions concerning the use of the organization's resources to adapt, shape, and respond to the environment to gain an advantage over other competitors. The concept of "political" (to be discussed next) extends the notion of both resources and advantage.

The Meaning of Political

The term *political* has two distinct meanings in the political science literature (Bachrach, 1967). The first is the structurally oriented meaning in which *political* refers to government and legal systems and the organizations that comprise those systems. In this sense, one can speak of the political arena as that involving legislatures, judicial systems, and regulatory bodies. This is the meaning of the term in which most of the research in management literature has understood *political*.

The second meaning of *political* is the functional, or process-oriented, conception. *Political* in this context is understood as a process in which outcomes may be explained by the exercise of power (Allison, 1971). Power is broadly defined as the ability of a social actor to influence the behavior or overcome the resistance of another social actor (Dahl, 1957; Emerson, 1962). Murray and Isenman (1978) have argued that organizations shape their environments through a process of continued bargaining and negotiation with other actors in the environment. As a result, the exercise of political strategy and behavior can occur in a variety of circumstances and situations.

In addition to power, two other concepts are important to our understanding of the term *political*: resource allocation and conflict of interest. Political behavior may be expected when the existing allocation of resources is threatened or is changing (e.g., through legislation or regulation which changes the rules of the game, or through social and interest group action which change the attitude with which an organization's products or services are viewed by the consuming public) and conflict exists among and between the actors involved with these resources. Specifically, political behavior includes such activities as coalition formation and control of the agenda (Pettigrew, 1973; Kingdon, 1984). *Political* then, as used in this book, refers to a conflict where social actors decide to exercise power to influence or change the behavior of one another. When the premises of corporate strategy and this definition of political are joined, corporate political strategy is defined.

Corporate Political Strategy

Corporate political strategy typically defines *political* in its structural sense. As a result, it focuses on the relationship between organizations and government and the strategies organizations use to influence regulatory or legislative decisions (Epstein, 1980). The functional approach is also evident, however, in the specific strategies and tactics that are presented as examples of action in the political arena (Hillman, 1995; Getz, 1993; Schuler and Rehbein, 1995).

The definition offered in this analysis seeks to integrate the notion of corporate strategy with that of political as defined in the previous section. Therefore, for us, *corporate political strategy* is defined as those activities taken by organizations to acquire, develop, and use power to obtain an advantage (a particular allocation of resources or no change in the allocation) in a situation of conflict. Activities directed to the political arena (legislatures, regulatory agencies, judicial bodies) are only one forum in which corporate political strategy could be exercised. It is also capable of being exercised in mediation and arbitration situations, in dealing with public interest groups and the media, and in dealing with crisis situations. Resources can take on a variety of forms; for example, resources can be goodwill and image of the firm with the public at large, they can be contracts and relationships with key suppliers, they can be influence with a specific stakeholder or stakeholder set, and they can be specific sections of legislation or regulation that yield a competitive advantage in the marketplace.

Implicit in the definition in the preceding paragraph is that which instigates action and the general nature of the behaviors engaged in by the organization. An organization has the right to choose when and where to become engaged or to not become engaged at all. Political behaviors are found when the existing allocation of resources is changing because opportunities for increasing one's power relative to others increases (Hardy, 1987). Political behaviors may also occur, however, when the existing allocation of resources is threatened. As a consequence, social actors who benefit from the existing allocation of resources need to engage in political behaviors in order to maintain their power (Bachrach and Baratz, 1962). As in the exercise of strategy, what is sought is a position of advantage over one's competitors. In the political strategy framework, however, advantage can be either temporary (e.g., at the time of a given vote on a piece of legislation or the silencing of organizational critics through bargaining) or sustainable for a lengthy period of time (as in judicial decisions or specific contractual or bargained agreements). Finally, political behaviors can either yield tangible benefits to the firm in terms of profits, market share, and other financial measures or prevent the erosion of such existing benefits. It is often difficult, however, to measure these benefits and translate them directly into balance sheet or income statement items. For example, how do you "show" on a financial statement the impact of changing a line in a piece of legislation that yields significant future savings or preserves an existing market or an agreement with a public interest group that preserves the image and reputation of the corporation?

These political behaviors fall into three general categories to be discussed in greater detail later. The first category deals with behaviors directed at specific issues. These include such actions as control of the agenda (Bachrach and Baratz, 1962; Cobb and Elder, 1972), and the timing of issues arising on the agenda for action. The second category includes behaviors directed at the choice of the arena in which this allocation of resources will take place. It is this aspect in particular that distinguishes the approach in this analysis from all other views of corporate political strategy because it does not assume that the only arena for political action and strategy is in the judicial, regulatory, legislative, and governmental arena. In addition, it assumes that the organization (or the public interest group or industry), if it moves quickly, can select the arena in which the given issue will be resolved. The third category of political behavior is those behaviors directed at other actors or stakeholders (Freeman, 1984) and includes the formation of coalitions and co-optation (Selznick, 1949), as well as attempts to limit access to a particular arena.

A model of individual (as opposed to industry) corporate political strategy is shown in Figure 2.5. Changes or potential changes in the environment to an existing allocation of resources instigate action if perceived as a threat or an opportunity by the organization. The choice to act is reflective of contextual factors which include, but are not limited to, such things as organizational resources, the industry in which the organization operates, scanning and

Figure 2.5
A Model of Corporate Political Strategy

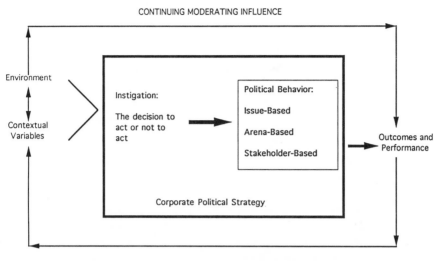

boundary-spanning mechanisms to read and shape the environment, and the overall resources of the organization. In addition, some assessment is made as to whether others will act in the corporation's behalf (the free rider effect). Finally, an organization will make an assessment about the likely impact and success of involvement in a particular issue or problem. The behaviors, already presented briefly, are issue, arena, and stakeholder based, as well as the perceived salience and threat of the changes in the resource allocation.

The performance of the organization on a given issue or problem will influence its choice to become involved and its selection of behaviors in future issues and problems (a feedback and learning loop). In addition, the actual outcome of the organization's behaviors (as distinct from how well the organization executed its behaviors) will also influence future involvement decisions.

In this model, corporate political strategy is conceived of as *both* the decision to act (instigation) and the specific strategies and tactics (political behavior) employed. These components are elaborated on further in the remainder of the chapter.

Instigation   Instigation is a necessary organizational choice whether to commit organizational resources in the face of a changing distribution of resources in the environment. This, out of necessity, involves choices concerning the costs and risks of political behavior on the issue or problem, as compared to other choices of action, including inaction. An organization may choose not to act because its interests are sufficiently protected by values inherent in the environment or because the costs of action exceed the likely benefits to be achieved.

Several factors influence the decision to act. The values of top management and their interest and understanding of the impact of political and social issues on the exercise of organizational discretion shape organizational action and political behavior. These can provide incentives for corporate political behaviors and involvement if top management values such actions. An organization may choose to act in the face of legal pressure or the threat of legal action. An organization may choose to act because it holds or enjoys a certain role in society (e.g., the community leader or renowned for product safety). Note that the past history of the organization in dealing with social and political issues and other variables that mold, shape, and alter the way in which the organization attends to and understands its environment (those contextual factors—see next section) will shape not only the actual behavior and strategy of the organization, but also the specific decision to act in a given situation.

As mentioned earlier, resources often drive the choice to become actively engaged in a political or social issue. In political issues, many actors in a given industry will let the larger organizations fight the battle. For example, in the automotive industry, many battles are fought by GM and Ford. Chrysler and American Motors (when it existed as a separate independent entity), while having a stake in the outcome of many of these battles, were simply not resource rich enough to enter the contest on the same scale of involvement and, therefore, were quite willing to let Ford and GM act as their agents on this issue. In some ways, this paucity of resources and lack of managerial attention to political and social issues explains the growth of trade associations and other multi-organizational political actors.

Another factor in the choice to act or not to act reflects the stake of the organization in the potential outcome(s). If an organization's stake in the issue or problem is low or high—but past, visible indiscretions exist—the organization may choose not to get involved or to be involved in a very limited way. The infant formula industry's response to Infant Formula Action Committee (INFACT) pressure is illustrative here. Those firms with major market share in third worlds fought long and hard against any restrictions on marketing and product sales in those countries; those with lower stakes and marketing and sales presence, and sensing an opportunity to develop a relative advantage in both third world and first world markets, quickly agreed with INFACT and supported their attempts to bring the other firms to heel (Post, 1978). The problems that some firms had with breast implant products did not allow them to take a leadership position when that issue emerged for discussion.

In brief, the instigation decision is not a trivial one. It is also important to note that organizational decisions are not a foregone conclusion because the issue is one of great importance. The organization needs to decide, within its own processes, to act and how it will act. Often, organizations lose their potential leadership on a given issue or problem, not because they failed to anticipate the issue but because they were unable to reach a consensus on what public position to take and how to implement that position in a timely manner. Once the decision to act is made, however, the focus of behaviors as noted earlier comes into play.

CORPORATE POLITICAL BEHAVIOR

The specific behaviors available to an organization are selected, we believe, in a specific hierarchical pattern. This should not be interpreted as limiting an organzation's action to only one set of behaviors at any given time. It is possible, and often the case, that organizations will pursue several of these behaviors simultaneously with one issue or problem or across multiple issues and problems. The distinctions made here are not static and should be understood in the framework of a constantly changing political context. The generic political behaviors organizations follow are (1) issue based, (2) choice of arena, and (3) influencing and engaging stakeholders. These behaviors are discussed in more detail in the following paragraphs. It is important to recall, however, that the choices of specific behavior are reflective of a variety of contextual factors. Some of these key contextual factors include the stake of the organization in the issue or problem at hand, the resources available, and the ultimate choice and preference of the organization's top management.

The first set of political behaviors available to the organization lie in attempts to control the definition of the issue or problem. This is so because the focus of action in the political and social arena is on ideas, and issues are the practical expressions of those ideas in the political marketplace. Until an idea is defined as an issue for attention, the issue will not be actively pursued in any arena, and no stakeholder positioning around the issue will occur (Mahon and Waddock, 1992; Wartick and Mahon, 1994). More specifically, an issue is a conflict between two or more identifiable individuals, groups, or organizations over preferred outcomes (Cobb and Elder, 1972). These conflicts can be based on value choices (Should we allow bio-genetic research?), facts (Does cigarette smoking cause cancer?), or on policy concerns (How shall we clean up the environment?) (Waddock and Mahon, 1991). Most of these issues deal with the distribution and allocation of scarce resources. This scarcity is not in an absolute sense however, but in light of the *expectations of the members of society* (Cobb and Elder, 1972).

Issue Definition

In managing an issue, an organization has two major tools: issue definition and the timing of an issue's emergence in the public arena for discussion and debate. The most powerful weapon that an organization has is in the definition of an issue and the symbols and symbolism associated with a specific definition (Edelman, 1964). In the continuing abortion debate in this country, for example, pro-life and pro-choice are not idly chosen terms as rallying cries for each side of the issue. Pro-choice conveys a specific message to large segments of society of constitutional guarantees of freedom and the rights of women to choose how their bodies will be used. Pro-life, on the other hand, conveys a specific message to large segments of the society that abortion is murder, a long-standing societal taboo. Note carefully how both sides have defined the issue in such a manner as to be almost mutually exclusive of one another's position. Pro-choice advocates never have to deal with the notion of murder because the issue is one of individual choice, and pro-life advocates never have to address the issue of choice because the issue is one of murder. It is no wonder that society is so divided on this particular issue. Three other examples of issue definition and re-definition should make the power of this behavior manifest.

When Ceasar Chavez decided to lead yet another grape boycott, he made a critical decision not to frame the issue or problem as another labor–management conflict, with its associated symbols and the generally recognized private nature of the actions (involving only the two parties directly involved). Instead, Chavez pressed the issue as one of the rights of the oppressed minorities. This definition served as a rallying symbol to a much larger segment of society than a simple strike and expanded the number of stakeholders and options for support and media coverage dramatically. It artfully drew in three powerful actors in the environment to articulate and support Chavez's position—the Roman Catholic Church, the National Association for the Advancement of Colored People (NAACP), and the American Federation of Labor and Congress of Industrial Organizations (AFL-CIO). As Cobb and Elder observed:

"I am here," announced an early arrival in clerical garb, "because this is a movement by the poor people to improve their position, and where the poor are, Christ should be and is." Other supporters . . . said much the same thing in their own way: this was part of their battle against society's power structure. (1972: 68)

The Church provided support for this injustice from the pulpit, the NAACP provided access to the media and Washington decision makers, and the AFL-CIO provided organizing assistance. All of these actors supported the union for their own specific reasons, independent of Chavez's goals and desires. The Church supported the movement for moral and ethical reasons, the NAACP for discrimination and minority rights concerns, and the AFL-CIO for a presence in the unionization of farm workers. None of these actors had been involved in previous Chavez-led strikes and would likely have not been involved in this one if it had been defined as another labor–management issue.

Not too long ago, the Commonwealth of Massachusetts was involved in a battle over containment of health care costs (Allen and Mahon, 1987). The issue of containing health care costs was, and is today, a very hot topic and subject to intense interest and stakeholder maneuvering. The Senate Majority leader was strongly in favor of the legislation; and it was also supported by the State Insurance Commissioner, the Massachusetts Business Roundtable, and the Life Insurance Association of Massachusetts (LIAM). The interests threatened by this reallocation of resources were the Massachusetts Medical Society (MMS), the Massachusetts Hospital Association (MHA), and Blue Cross–Blue Shield (the Blues).

After extensive consultation with lobbyists and other interested parties, it seemed that the MMS, MHA, and the Blues would be unable to stop the adoption of this legislation, as the support for it among large and powerful stakeholders was too strong to overcome. Then it was determined that the legislation would adversely affect a segment of the population at large—the elderly. The elderly in Massachusetts, as in other states, are a potent political force. The Blues contacted all of the elderly in the state, telling them that if the legislation passed, one of the following outcomes was likely to occur: (1) costs for elderly coverage would rise for the same level of service; (2) costs would rise and services would decline; or (3) costs could remain the same, but services would decrease. As a consequence, the elderly contacted not only their legislators but also their own children. They told their children that if their benefits changed, the children would be responsible for assisting them. The legislation was defeated because the Blues redefined the issue from one of health care cost containment with its own constellation of stakeholders and actors to the issue of erosion of benefits for the elderly with a different set of stakeholders and actors. In this manner, the Blues were able to use the elderly as their agents—not to preserve the Blues position in health care—but to preserve their own benefits level.

Finally, the experience of Procter and Gamble (P&G) in dealing with a crisis: that toxic shock syndrome is helpful in advancing our understanding the power of issue definition. As may be recalled, the media and government authorities leapt on P&G's Rely tampon as the cause of toxic shock in women that resulted in sickness and, in some cases, death. The issue quickly became defined as "Rely causes toxic shock" or, more emotionally, "Rely kills women" and, therefore, P&G must do something about this. P&G, the marketing powerhouse that it is, was unable to shake the association of toxic shock with its product. Women's groups from around the country supported the decision of the Centers for Disease Control and the Food and Drug Administration to force P&G to withdraw the product. P&G argued (as would be proved subsequently) that Rely was not the problem but that the entire super-absorbant tampon market and every product in it was the problem. P&G argued for a warning label to be placed on the product and moved to establish funded research in toxic shock. The product was removed from the market, and the incident of toxic shock in other competitor's super-absorbant tampons shot up by as much as 400 percent because women who had been using Rely switched to another super-absorbant tampon product. If you purchase such a product today, it contains a warning about toxic shock as P&G had proposed. Rely as a product died, and more innocent women were hurt because of the definition of the issue that prevailed—Rely causes toxic shock—and not the actual issue—super-absorbant tampons are likely to cause toxic shock.

In addition, timing of an issue's emergence is the other tool for managing an issue. Firms have to decide if they wish to push the issue on to an agenda for resolution or wait for others to do it. The risk in moving ahead on an issue that has not come into clear focus in the political or social arena is that a firm or industry may be so far ahead that the issue is quickly dismissed as not requiring resolution at this time, or that stakeholders will be able to delay the issue's discussion until they firm up their positions and garner support from others. On the other hand, delay in pursuing an issue may yield benefits to one's competitors and adversaries (see the discussion on arena choice in the next section).

This brief discussion of issue-based action is not meant to be all-inclusive of the actions available to the organization (including public and societal interest groups and elements of government). It is meant to be suggestive of the range of activities available and to emphasize that the fundamental step in political behavior is the definition of the issue and whether it deserves organizational support and commitment of resources. It is entirely possible, and often the case, that early definitions of an issue would result in a specific firm or actor deciding not to act in the issue at that time. As the definition of the issue or problem undergoes discussion and change, then organizations must reconsider their decision to become engaged in the issue or, alternatively, leave the political contest as a redefinition as reduced the salience of the issue to the firm.

Choice of Arena

The organization can choose to place an issue in play in a specific arena for resolution and thereby push the socialization and expansion of an issue, or it can choose to keep an issue from going to a specific arena for resolution. In short, organizations will select arenas for the resolution of issues and problems and the exercise of political and social strategy that afford the greatest flexibility for organizational action, limit the absolute number of disputants involved, control costs, preclude or limit the involvement of the media, and offer the highest probability of success. One arena for action, as noted earlier, is the structural one, which includes those generally recognized societal institutions and mechanisms for resolving disputes. Examples of these arenas would include judicial action, regulatory action, legislation at all levels, and compulsory arbitration. Yet, the opportunity for political strategy through the choice of arena occurs in other situations as well. Bargaining with the local community over right of way or waste site location are examples of political behavior outside of the formal structural arenas previously noted. The National Coal Policy Project (Hay and Gray, 1985) is an excellent example of an industry and its major critics attempting to resolve disputes and problems outside of the formal structural system. It is also a subtle attempt to create more allies for the coal industry on a variety of issues. In general, an organization has more control over the potential resolution of an issue if the number of disputants is held to an absolute minimum and if the involvement of the media is contained. The minimum number of disputants serves to limit the number of alternate definitions of the problem or issue to be resolved; and the limitation on the media can prevent the issue from expanding and thereby involve more disputants, different issue definitions, and the possible move of the issue to another agenda.

This would suggest that an organization would serve its own interests quite well if it could keep the issue or problem off the formal structural agendas and in the arenas of informal discussion, negotiations, and private agreements. The Nestlé boycott is an example of how the choice of arena may be utilized by a public interest group to compel corporate action and response. The boycotters, INFACT, have focused on Nestlé in an attempt to arouse public disapproval (and associated financial consequences) and compel Nestlé to change its practices with regard to sale of infant formula in third world countries. The arena chosen, then, is public opinion in the United States. The boycott is an attempt to enhance the power (and resource base) of INFACT in order to press their demands on Nestlé. Curiously, these third world countries do not seem disposed to take action and have not been subjected to the same kind of pressure from INFACT. It is clear that it is easier to target one organization that is prominent in a country that shares common values about children than it is to target several nations, their legislatures, and their peoples that may not share the same set of common values.

In the legal arena, numerous court cases are settled out of court with the stipulation that the parties involved will not release the terms and conditions of the settlement. This is a clear attempt to contain the issue or problem and limit the flow of information to other interested actors with a stake in the resolution of the issue. Yet, corporate admission of culpability can have favorable impacts. Several years ago, Boeing admitted to some culpability in the crash of a Japanese Airlines (JAL) plane that killed all aboard, except for a small child. This admission reduced media interest in the issue and allowed the key actors (Boeing, JAL, those harmed directly, and the Japanese government) to achieve a settlement to the issue.

If an organization acts quickly, it can determine the arena in which the issue will be addressed for resolution. A. H. Robins's and Johns Manville's filings for bankruptcy are clear examples of firms not only choosing the arena for resolution but also impacting on the definition of the issue itself. The filing for bankruptcy by these two firms meant that product liability claims against the firm would be treated within the framework of bankruptcy law and not solely within the rules of product liability. Those persons injured by the product, under bankruptcy law, become another creditor of the organization. It can be argued that this was not only a smart strategic political move for the firms involved but also a beneficial move for those injured, as it assured that all injured parties would receive some compensation for their injuries. What value to the individual is there in an enormous financial judgment against a firm that had no further ability to pay because it has gone bankrupt paying previous enormous claims?

The key question for any organization entering into a politically based contest is this: What specific arena should serve as the battleground for the resolution of this problem? The answer will obviously depend on the nature of the problem or issue, but it will also reflect the exercise of organizational will. *Organizational will* is meant as the recognition that, ceteris paribus, an organization will choose as an arena whatever venue provides the best prospects for winning the contest. To be effective in this choice requires that the organization act quickly to define the issue or problem and move it to an arena of its choosing. In many cases, as noted earlier, organizations fail to recognize that an issue even exists, fail to define it, lose control of the definition early on, or allow others to select the arena. In that case, the organization has to regroup its efforts around both issue redefinition and stakeholder influence and action.

Influencing and Engaging Stakeholders

Following Freeman (1984), stakeholders are those individuals, groups, and organizations that can influence or are influenced by the decisions of the focal actor (be it individual, group, or organization), the implementation of those decisions, or both. Political behavior is often defined solely in terms of influencing the behavior of others. Consequently, political action reduces to stakeholder management. The tactics employed in stakeholder management have received considerable attention and include such actions as coalition building, constituency building, and co-optation. According to Schattschneider (1960), the root of all political action lies in the development of group action. It follows from the definition of political strategy that organizations must direct their actions to the development of coalitions of support for their positions and the prevention of such coalitions being formed by those opposing the organization. These coalitions form in an attempt to influence actions and decisions in political contests, but active participation is not guaranteed. That is, in many political contests, what is desired is that some stakeholders (or a set of stakeholders) do not become involved in the issue or problem in any way (i.e., the "sit out the issue on the sidelines" and observe what occurs). Depending on the issue, this "sitting" can be the desired behavior at times for those who support and for those who oppose the organization's position.

There are several ways in which an organization can foster the development of coalitions among stakeholders. The first and most obvious way is through the definition and redefinition of the issue or problem as this serves as the primary organizing tool for like-minded stakeholders—simply put, those with common interests tend to travel the same paths. In many political contests, for example, a naturally occurring relationship is based on industry or interest group affiliation.

Another method of stakeholder influence is through co-optation. This often involves efforts to change the positions of powerful stakeholders through inducements they value (e.g., affording them a role in the decisions of, or participation in, the organization in some manner). The form of inducement is usually a positive one, where they can be offered tangible benefits. Mothers against Drunk Driving (MADD) came out against proposed restrictions on the advertisement of alcohol in return for the brewing industry's agreement to run more public service announcements featuring the MADD logo prominently. The MADD group joined with the brewing industry to oppose action based on benefits to be received by MADD. However, the inducement can also be of a negative nature in the form of threatening actors with undesirable consequences if they do not change their position. Trade associations use this tactic to keep member organizations in line on crucial legislative issues, and so do political leaders. The threat is that the individual firm will be ostracized for its non-team-supporting position. When Chrysler was lobbying the federal government for loans, the Business Roundtable in New York came out publicly against this bailout. Chrysler immediately resigned its position on the Roundtable. Although it did not work in this specific instance, the threat of a large and powerful actor to withdraw from a coalition or joint effort can influence other actors to accede to the organization's position.

In many ways, the influencing and engaging of stakeholders is a function of the issue definition and the arena in which the issue will be resolved. It is also a function of traditional public relations and public affairs techniques to influence actors to see the correctness of the organization's position on the issue and to energize and lend support to the effort. It can involve direct organizing action or the use of agents to represent the organization's interests. The use of agents can allow the organization the luxury of not entering the specific issue or problem debate but have their position represented and possibly not draw in those stakeholders who routinely opposed the organization. In addition, the use of agents may allow for the development of coalitions that would not occur if the organization were directly involved. Finally, the organization, if it used agents, can always disavow the agent's actions and enter the debate at a later time when positions and issues are more clearly focused.

STRATEGY AND THE POLICY PROCESS

If we envision the issue-development process as proceeding through simple and identifiable stages, then the use of political strategy can come into even sharper focus. Although many have noted that issues go through life cycles or stages, very few have attempted to articulate managerial strategies and tactics through those stages (Eyestone, 1978; Mahon, 1989; Mahon and Waddock, 1992). Table 2.1 shows possible relationships between issue and problem life cycles and the appropriate political tactics at each stage that can be pursued by the organization.

Containment/Advocacy Tactics

The purpose of containment tactics in dealing with emerging and growth-stage issues and problems is to limit their growth and damage. This limitation can take two principal forms. First, contain the issue and prevent it from achieving broad-based recognition and attention. The second form is to limit entry and access to the discussion of the issue itself. Numerous examples of these tactics have been offered thus far, the clearest being the National Coal Policy Project. This project was an attempt by the mining industry and environmentalists to resolve the divisive issues that separated them. The process used was to gather invited participants in a secluded setting devoid of media attention and work on the issues and problems. Obviously, those invited were given access and entry to the process, and many thereafter supported the mining industry's interests. The very establishment of this process also served to stifle open debate and thus limited the scope of the debate, media attention, and the general society-at-large's knowledge of the issues.

Table 2.1
Political Tactics and Issue Life Cycles

Life Cycle Stage	Appropriate Political Tactics
Introduction	Containment/Advocacy
Growth	Containment/Advocacy
Entry into a Specific Arena	Arena Manipulation
Resolution	Policy Adaptation

The other alternative tactic to contain issues or limit their growth is through advocacy, where the organization takes the lead in the development of the issue, its specific definition, the constellation of stakeholders in support of the organization's position, and the overall strategy and tactics to press for resolution in a given arena. The strategy driving this choice of tactics is the recognition, in many cases, that legislation, regulation, judicial action, or public interest action is imminent and that the organization wishes to shape the issue definition and have a say in how it will be resolved. Therefore, the thrust of the action is not solely on containment per se but on focused expansion of the issue to a specifically chosen arena for resolution.

Agenda Manipulation

The majority of attempts to contain an issue or limit entry and access on a specific issue will not be successful. Therefore, organizations must have a backup set of tactics to follow, and this is where manipulating the agenda is to be considered. There are, as stated previously, two primary tactics that the organization can pursue. The first (from a chronological view) is to select the specific arena in which a given issue will be resolved. The earlier examples of Johns Manville and Robins apply here.

The second method is to manipulate the manner in which the issue is to be considered within the chosen arena. The Massachusetts health care cost-containment issue is a case in point here. An additional example is the manner in which Union Carbide manipulated the arena in the Bhopal disaster. It was clear that Union Carbide was going to be sued by a variety of stakeholders on this particular issue. The real question was, which jurisdiction? The United States has a more liberal record in dealing with such cases and, in general, a much higher payout in terms of financial rewards. Union Carbide argued forcefully and successfully that the litigation should occur in India, the site of the accident. It also just happened to be a legal system that favored large, rich, and powerful litigants. One should not assume in this and all the examples we have offered that we either applaud or condemn the organization's actions. The examples are meant to illustrate the strategies and tactics that are available to the organization. Indeed, the judgment of such actions is an example of another issue requiring organizational and stakeholder attention, debate, and resolution.

Policy Adaptation

It is folly to assume that any organization will win on each and every issue and problem. Therefore, the resolution of an issue will demand policy adaptation by the organization; that is, the organization will be expected to do something unless it can find a way to limit the impact of the resolution. One method of limiting the impact of a given resolution is to appeal it to a different arena, for example, appeal legislation or regulatory action to the judicial arena, or appeal a judicial decision to the legislature. A more subtle, less visible manner in which to appeal the resolution is through involvement in the actual implementation and development of oversight procedures associated with the resolution. A clear example of this is presented in Chapter 7.

CONCLUSION

This chapter has tried to define key terms that will be useful in digesting the remainder of this book. We have attempted to advance a specific view of corporate political strategy that is useful both analytically and theoretically (for academics and researchers) and of practical import for managers and leaders of organizations.

In Chapter 3, we will take these concepts and develop them into a model of industry political dynamics and show how this model complements and advances the earlier work on industry competitive dynamics of Michael Porter.

NOTES

1. Quoted in Matthew Josephson, *The Robber Barons* (New York: Harcourt, Brace, and Co., 1962), pp. 187, 276, 441.

2. We shall return to this issue in Chapter 3. Porter's very success, we argue, has inhibited investigations into political and societal strategy as an important element within strategy.

3. This section draws heavily on John F. Mahon, "Shaping Issues/Manufacturing Agents: Corporate Political Sculpting," in *Corporate Political Agency: The Construction of Competition in Public Affairs*, edited by B. M. Mitnick (Newbury Park, Calif.: Sage, 1993), pp. 187–212.

Chapter 3

INDUSTRY POLITICAL DYNAMICS:
A FRAMEWORK FOR
ANALYSIS AND ACTION

Chapter 2 laid the foundation for our concern over the lack of serious and continued research attention to corporate- and industry-based political strategies. The research into corporate and industry political strategy is likely to originate in two different academic areas—business policy (strategy) or political science. The political science field, for the most part, has been disinterested in the strategies and tactics of businesses and industries in the political arena; and where such research exists, it is not informed by a well-grounded knowledge of business and organizational practices. The most likely place for such research to take place is in the field of business policy and, more specifically, strategy. Strategy is, after all, concerned with the long-term survival and success of the organization in a competitive environment. Unfortunately, strategy researchers, for the most part, have conceived of strategy being confined to the product–market–technology arenas. The strategy field has neglected the impact of government and political and social groups on the strategy of the firm and the industry. The notable exception has been in the field of regulation, where the impacts are clearly evident and somewhat easy to measure, model, and theorize about.

The social issues in the management field, a branch of the management policy field, is where the most relevant, interesting, and practitioner-oriented political strategy research is being conducted. This research is firmly grounded in business and organizational practices and arises out of a multidisciplinary perspective. It is here that the importance of organizational skills in political strategy and tactics is recognized as important (Baron, 1995; Getz, 1993; Hillman, 1995; Mahon, 1989, 1993; Mahon, Fahey, and Bigelow, 1994), especially as the nature of competition becomes more global and intense (Boddewyn, 1993; Lenn and Mahon, 1993). As noted earlier, it is crucial that organizations understand both political and social issues and the absolute need for organizations to anticipate, shape, and respond to them.

The purpose of this chapter is threefold: (1) to introduce and develop a model for understanding and managing political and social issues that has both theoretical and practical implications; (2) to provide a brief example of the applicability of the model; and (3) to transition to Part Two of this book, which provides more detailed evidence from four different industries (in manufacturing, in services, and in consumer and industrial goods).

MICHAEL PORTER'S LEGACY

Michael Porter is a legend in the strategy field, and his work has contributed enormously to the development of industry competitive analysis (see Porter, 1979, 1980). Porter's work has deep roots in the industrial organizational economics field and was heavily influenced by the work of Bain (1968) and Caves (1967). One of his major accomplishments has been the development of structural analysis of industries, more commonly known as Porter's Five Forces Model (see Figure 3.1). This framework is well known, and every undergraduate and graduate student in business schools is exposed to it at some point in his or her education. It has broad applicability and has won the respect of managers around the world. The model has been successful, in our opinion, because of its simplicity, which manages to capture the powerful forces of industry dynamics in an easy-to-understand-and-apply format. In the academic field, the Porter Model has led to the development of an enormous number of case studies that lend themselves to the use of the model and to numerous strands of research that continue to develop and support the basic utility of the model itself.[1]

The model consists of five major components that impact on the competitive dynamics of a specific industry: suppliers, industry rivalry, substitute products, new entrants, and customers. In addition, Porter's model recognizes the importance of barriers to entry and barriers to exit for a given industry. The fundamental approach rests on the notion of power in the relationships—where power lies at a given point in time, and that that power can and does shift over time. The shifts in power mirror the strengths of the players in the industry and the forces that are buffeting it at any given

Figure 3.1
Porter's Model of Industry-Competitive Dynamics

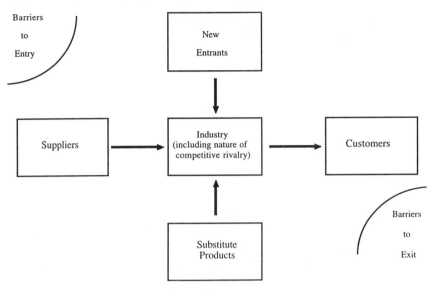

point in time. That is, doing industry analysis is a continuous activity because the competitive dynamics change over time, as power shifts between and among the five forces, and effect relationships. As a consequence, a successful industry with few substitutes, a low likelihood of new entrants, and great power over either customers or suppliers can be transformed in a very short period of time.

For example, if one were to look at the computer time-sharing industry in the mid-1960s, we would see an industry that had tremendous power over its customers but very little power with regard to suppliers. The nature of the industry was such that a competitor (or player) in the industry would buy one mainframe computer (hence, the limited power over the supplier) and provide time-sharing services to small- and medium-sized businesses. Since there were few alternatives (no personal computers, local area networks, or mid-sized computers) to doing processes by hand, and there were enormous numbers of potential customers, the time-sharing business did quite well, as it had a power advantage relative to its customer base. It should also be evident that at this time there were few substitute products and the possibility of new entrants was slim. The nature of the business was to provide tailored computing services to individual clients, and that is where competitors would differentiate themselves and attempt to achieve a sustainable competitive advantage. Barriers to entry into this industry were not particularly high—the major costs lay in the purchase of a mainframe computer and knowledgeable workers to apply and develop software for use by major customers. Barriers to exit were also relatively low, as competitors could come and go nearly at will. As a consequence, being a competitor in the time-sharing business held the promise of reasonable financial success because of segmentation in the market. There were numerous ways to specialize (e.g., geographically or by type of business [manufacturing vs. service] or by type of computing needs [accounting, personnel, statistical, quality control, logistics, etc.]), which further limited the possibility of ruinous competition and maintained the power of the industry over the buyer or customer.

Unfortunately, this rather successful business was turned upside-down with the advent of mid-sized and personal computers. Suddenly, there was an affordable and efficient substitute to time sharing that dramatically reduced the power the industry had exercised over customers. The industry went through a period of large-scale consolidation and shrinkage because the buyer had a reasonably priced alternative to relying solely on a time-sharing firm. Notice how the power relationships changed over time—initially, the industry (time-sharing firms) had significant power over the potential customer market. Although the time-sharing business lacked clout with its suppliers, there was little fear of forward integration because the time-sharing business was mainly a service industry and the mainframe computer business was mainly a manufacturing and hardware service business. As technological advances were made in computing, allowing the development of powerful, small, reasonably priced computers, time-sharing customers had, for the first time, an alternative product/service package. There are still time-sharing firms in existence today, and their competitive edge is on the specific services that they provide to the customers in terms of software development and support that is not provided by the seller of a personal computer.

Therefore, the use of Porter's model requires not only a recognition of competitive dynamics over time and how they change and what is the source of that change but also the ability to identify and recognize the strengths and weaknesses of the industry and the individual firms within the industry. It is in the recognition of strengths and weaknesses that individual firms must plan for the future to adapt, survive, and prosper.

Porter's analysis takes place completely within the confines of the product–market–technology arena. That is, Porter's model is concerned with industry competitive rivalry in the marketplace, where success is measured in terms of share of the market, profitability, return on equity, and, indeed, survival over time. Unfortunately, Porter's model does not pay much attention to nonmarket sources of change on competitive rivalry and industry relationships. In our view, this is one of the greatest shortcomings of the Porter Model as it may mislead organizations into believing that they are prepared for the future when they are only prepared for the future in a narrow product–market–technology sense.

For example, the utilization of the Porter Model in the analysis of competitive dynamics in the semiconductor industry would have been of little use to Intel and its 1995 problems with the Pentium chip. The problem with this chip was that it would produce erroneous mathematical results under some conditions. A "typical" Porter-based analysis would have suggested that once the decision had been made to produce the product, given the market and technological lead, Intel was correct in moving to large-scale production. After all, the problem with the chip, the argument went, was only in very sophisticated mathematical applications; and those customers dealing with such applications were only a small portion of the overall market. Besides, over time, Intel would solve the problem and replace the chips for those customers who use the product for sophisticated problems. Unfortunately, Intel did not foresee the firestorm of controversy that this problem would raise from all users. Once the controversy surfaced, Porter's model was irrelevant and of no help to Intel's managers in deciding how to deal with this issue; for the resolution process required technological, media, public relations, political, and public interest group skills. The model afforded Intel no assistance in responding to a fast-moving public issue and image problem (Gonzales-Herrero and Pratt, 1995). Intel stumbled in their response—at first, stonewalling the problem, then arguing that it was not of sufficient merit to require any large-scale recall. Intel seriously underestimated the anger of a computer user in receiving a chip that, no matter what careful phraseology was used, was defective. Intel's response had a negative spillover effect on their customers that used the chip in their products—like Compaq. Intel's poor performance in handling this issue opened up a competitive window of opportunity that IBM was quick to act upon. IBM took the high road on this issue and refused to use the Pentium chip until such time as all defects were removed. IBM was forced, so they argued, out of concern for its customers, to use its own manufactured chips instead. Make no mistake about it, this problem with the Pentium chip had financial and competitive positioning impacts for Intel and for Intel's customers. It is precisely these types of impacts that can be planned for, and responded to, if an organization looks beyond just the marketplace and the technological arena.

The situation with Intel is meant to be seen not as a total indictment of the Porter Model but as a partial one. In fairness to Porter, the model was never meant to deal with issues in the public and social arena; and that is a key weakness, as many of the sources of surprise for an industry and an individual firm arise out of changing social mores and action in the social and political arena. Our purpose here is to offer an approach that complements the Porter Model in that it assists practicing managers in understanding and dealing with political and social issues. Do not be confused here. The Intel problem was originally a technological one—the chip would generate an error in some of the more sophisticated mathematical processes which it might be called upon to do. Intel's failure to deal effectively with the controversy over the chip, after it had been shipped and installed, converted the issue from a purely technical one to an issue imbued with public interest. The solution to this problem was not only a technical one but also a political–social solution that would both deal with sets of angry customers as noted earlier and restore Intel's image as a premier manufacturer of chips for computers.

The last legacy of Porter's model is its very success in both the business and academic world. Its success has made it extraordinarily difficult for alternate conceptions of industry competitive dynamics to be developed, modeled, and discussed in the academic and practitioner worlds. This is not, as some might argue, a strawman argument. Porter's model has driven out creative thinking and new approaches in the modeling and conceptualization of industry competitive dynamics. Rugman and Verbeke (1991) have argued that in addition to Porter's Five Forces, one must add government regulation and external pressure groups. For example, they note that ". . . skills in business–government relations may result in an increase of government imposed entry barriers against rivals" (1991: 13). Yet their call for a broadened analysis has fallen largely on deaf ears.

Even Porter's most recent work (1990) has been criticized for its missing the crucial role of government in *directly* influencing and creating competitive advantage. Bosch and de Man (1994) have argued persuasively that government should be an additional determinant in the development of competitive advantage, and that timing and level of government involvement is important to national (and individual firm) competitiveness.

In addition, the general success and ease of Porter's model has lulled managers into a feeling of security in their strategic and competitive analysis. If one uses Porter's approach, then there is reasonable security from unanticipated situations. If one really uses Porter's approach well, then even in a situation of surprise the planning skills that have been developed will ensure a quick recovery and response. This is not only incorrect but potentially dangerous for the industry and individual firm (Mahon and Cochran, 1991; Mahon, Fahey, and Bigelow, 1994).

A MODEL OF SOCIAL AND POLITICAL INDUSTRY ANALYSIS

As noted earlier, the major purpose of this text is to propose a model that will enable managers to capture the political and social dynamics surrounding an industry and an individual firm within that industry. In our consulting on this topic, many managers are concerned that they will have to learn a difficult new approach that will in itself inhibit their individual and organizational success. This is not the case, for we use the Porter Model as a foundation to develop our model shown in Figure 3.2. The major purpose of this model is to enable managers to recognize and address social and political action and to develop credible responses and strategies for shaping these concerns. Although we are not interested in the financial and economic impacts of political and social action per se, we recognize that these actions can and often do have profound economic and financial impacts on an industry and on individual firms (Shaffer, 1992).

Like the Porter Model, this model recognizes that the fundamental approach is to analyze where the power lies at a given point in time and how these dynamics change over time. In the Porter model,

Figure 3.2
A Model of Industry-Competitive Political Dynamics

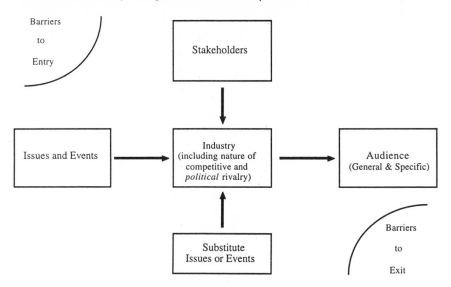

in addition to the five elements noted earlier, there are what we call three underlying, but critical, assumptions. These assumptions center around the raw materials and product, the theater of transaction, and the unit of currency (see Table 3.1).

In Porter's model, competitors obtain services and raw materials from the suppliers and transform them into products for sale to customers. In Porter's model, the product is either a good, a service, or a combination of goods and services that identify the industry and its competitors. For example, the automobile industry is clearly identified by its production of a good called an automobile and related services involved with that product. The financial services industry is identified by the range of both goods and services that it provides and produces to individuals, banks, and other financial institutions through a varied set of financial instruments. The theater of transaction is the marketplace, which can be conceived of on several levels. There is a local market, a state market, a regional market, a national market, and an international market. In addition, one can conceive of markets based on specific needs and desires that are addressed (commonly referred to as niche markets). Each of these levels has certain shared characteristics and concerns, as well as unique aspects.

Finally, the unit of currency in industry and business is money. Organizations keep "score" by using monetary-based measures (sales, profit, costs, returns on sales, equity, invested capital, etc.). The traditional definition of money is a medium of exchange, a store of value, or a unit of account. Therefore, how do we use money? We use it to get what we want (exchange), to bank it for later use (store of value), and to measure how much we have (as a unit of account).

In our model, the three driving assumptions are the same—that there exist a product, a theater of transaction, and a unit of currency. However, the specific meaning of each of these terms is different because of the focus on political and social dynamics and not on marketplace dynamics. The raw materials supplied in this approach are an issue or an event that demands (or has the potential to demand) industry- and firm-specific responses. This "raw material" is being supplied not only to the industry in question (although it is generally relevant to the industry and often very specific to the industry) but also to external actors (stakeholeder) that can impact directly and indirectly on the industry and its competitive dynamics (Bigelow, Fahey, and Mahon, 1991, 1993a, 1993b). The product in our model is not tangible in the form of a good or service but rather is the creation of a position or desired outcome that needs to be "sole" to a customer; in this case, the audience (discussed later in the chapter). The unit of currency is influence, and it is also discussed later.

Table 3.1
Critical Assumptions

	Porter's Model	Our Model
Raw Materials	Goods and/or services	Issues, ideas, or events
Product	Goods and/or services	A position or desired outcome
Theater of Transaction	The "marketplace"	A chosen arena of resolution
Unit of Currency or Exchange	Money	Influence

Issues

An issue can be defined as a disagreement between at least two individuals or groups over the facts, values, or means (either individually or in combination) for resolution to a given problem (Waddock and Mahon, 1991). Shell Oil was recently involved with the British government and Greenpeace (an international environmental public interest group) over Shell's proposed abandonment of an offshore oil rig. Shell decided not to sink the rig into the North Sea. Greenpeace opposed sinking the rig, and effectively argued that such a procedure would dump a great deal of oil into the ocean. Shell was precluded from carrying out this plan because of opposition from the British government largely because of Greenpeace's efforts and publicity on this issue. In September 1995, Greenpeace apologized to Shell because it had its facts wrong. Greenpeace had argued that a much greater volume of oil was contained in the rig and its piping than Shell's calculations showed. Indeed, Shell was right; but it, nonetheless, lost on this issue.

In the United States, the battle over the use of alachor on apples reflects disagreements over the "facts" of the situation. In both situations, the industries and firms involved lost the debate and were regulated in some manner, even though later research revealed the original factual concerns to be incorrect. It is clear, then, that being "right" on the facts is not a guarantee of success.

Issues may also arise from disagreements over the values around a situation. Values reflect people's beliefs and the rightness or wrongness of a given action. The field of genetic engineering reflects this type of conflict. It is recognized from a factual basis that we can alter genetic tissue. The arguments by opponents to this process are not based on facts but, rather, on values—we should not do this because it is not the right thing to do. Issue disagreements rooted in value conflicts are extremely difficult to deal with from an industry or individual firm perspective. The difficulty lies in the degree to which the values held are deeply ingrained in the opposition and their unwillingness to yield to fact-based arguments.

Finally, issue disagreements can be based on means conflict. Means conflict deals with the proposed solution and implementation of that solution to a given issue. The current debate in many countries around how to increase national competitiveness is illustrative. Every nation desires to increase the international competitiveness of its goods and services. The benefits can be easily demonstrated on a factual basis, and most value-based positions support it. The problem arises in the specific manner in which competitiveness is to be enhanced, and some questions that get raised are the following: Is it to be accomplished by private or public funds and oversight? Are specific firms and industries to be targeted, and, if so, by whom and based on what criteria? As a result, the dealing with a specific issue is far more challenging than might be initially imagined.

For example, an issue or idea that may arise with regard to any industry is regulation. The accounting profession, for example, is currently self-regulated; that is, the members of the accounting profession police themselves (also found in law and medicine). In recent years, there have been proposals for government regulation of the industry from individuals outside of the industry itself. This idea or issue becomes, in a sense, a "supplier" to the industry that requires a response from the industry (Mahon and Waddock, 1992; Waddock and Mahon, 1991; Wartick and Mahon, 1993). An interesting aspect of the response is whether the response will be an industry-wide one or differentiated by individual member firms.

An issue or an event serves as the trigger for action or reaction by the industry. Issues and events are what ignite an industry or firm to specific action. It is issues or events in the political or social arena that fuel the debate and require industry response. For example, when Union Carbide's plant in India blew up, it fueled intensive investigations and scrutiny into the issue of plant, worker, and community safety for the entire *industry*, not just Union Carbide. As such, issues and events as noted serve as the basis for industry action and reaction. They are the elements in the supply chain.

Arena

Just as a product is put up for sale in a given market (the theater of transaction), so too is an issue put up for discussion (and purchase through the development of support by various stakeholders) in a given forum. These forums also have different levels. An issue can be discussed at the local, state, regional, national, or international level as well as being addressed in different arenas. These arenas can be either informal or formal. Informal arenas include such things as public discussion in the electronic media and meetings between organizational representatives and members of the public or of elected bodies. Informal arenas do not necessarily lead to the resolution of an issue but can lead to an understanding of where each participant is in relation to the issue and can result in useful coalitions for action later on. Formal arenas include mediation, arbitration, legal action, regulatory action, and legislative action. Each of these levels and arenas has certain shared characteristics and concerns as well as unique aspects.

The choice of an arena is important, as it defines the target audience that needs to be addressed and satisfied if a resolution is to be achieved on the issue. Therefore, when a firm or a public interest group files a lawsuit, they are, in essence, defining the critical audience as the judiciary. Note that the specific tactics used in each arena will be different because of the arena selected and the specific target audience contained therein.

Influence

In the product market situation, the unit of currency is money. In the political and social arena, the unit of currency is influence. Influence, like money, can be used as a medium of exchange, held for later use, and measured over time to see how much an organization has and how it has used it. In the book, *Bonfire of the Vanities* (Wolfe, 1987), there is a wonderful discussion of the "favor bank." The favor bank, as described by one of the characters, is something that everyone knows exists and that people routinely make deposits into so that in the future a "withdrawal" can be made. According to the character in the book, the idea is to bank favors for the future and never make a withdrawal that will bounce (i.e., there have not been enough favors done or the favors are not of sufficient value to merit a response in kind). This is what influence is about—the trading of favors over time. Such favors can take a variety of forms: information provided, services rendered or not rendered, and the like. A firm will support a given position now in the expectation that a favor may be requested in the future. In the political and social arena, this is the major unit of exchange. Let us now turn our attention to the five elements in our model. One we have already discussed earlier is issues, so we will begin our discussion with substitute issues.

Substitute Issues

Just as a manufacturer has to be concerned with the possible entry of substitute products, in the political and social arena, we must be concerned with substitute issues. Over time and with discussion of an issue, its focus may be changed. The changed focus may be narrower or broader than the initial issue, and this may or may not have implications for the industry and individual firms within the industry. As the issue changes, the pattern of stakeholder involvement changes; and the arena of resolution may shift as well. If an issue, for example, initially begins as a civil rights–based disagreement, then it is reasonable to conclude that civil rights organizations (e.g., the NAACP) and civil liberties groups (e.g., the ACLU) will become involved. Over time, if the issue is redefined to mean something else, these two groups are likely to withdraw from the contest. More important, as briefly noted earlier, the specific nature of the issue and its definition can have very different implications for individual members of an industry.

As an example, one proposal for the regulation of the accounting profession several years ago included the notion of severing accounting and consulting services. That is, an accounting firm such as Arthur Anderson could not provide accounting and consulting services to the same client. Price Waterhouse opposed such a proposal, even though it is one of the smaller accounting firms, because of its significant position in consulting (Berton, 1995). Other accounting firms supported the proposal because their businesses, consisting largely of accounting services, would not be affected. Price Waterhouse sees the future of accounting firms as including such services in greater numbers. Therefore, the financial implications of such restrictions on the accounting profession would have far greater impacts on a large accounting firm such as Price Waterhouse than it would on a smaller accounting firm. It should be evident that even though the focus of the model is on political and social analysis, these events can have a differentiated impact on the financial performance of the firm, competitive dynamics, and its long-term success.

Stakeholders

Closely allied with the entry of substitute issues is the entry of stakeholders (Freeman, 1984) into the debate and ultimate resolution. Similar to new entrants in the product market sense, the entry of stakeholders into the debate can dramatically alter the competitive issue framework in terms of both definitions and the balance of power and influence with the target audience. Stakeholders can be defined in a variety of ways; but in this particular framework, we would suggest that stakeholders are those individuals, groups, and firms that can alter the definition of an issue, impact on the power relationships among players involved in the issue at hand, and influence the target audience and the resolution of the issue and the implementation of the resolution. As an example, the entry of someone like Ralph Nader into the discussion of automotive safety dramatically alters the issue dynamics, the number of additional stakeholders likely to be involved, and the costs of dealing with the issue or problem.

Industry Rivalry

Just as in the Porter Model, the degree of intensity of industry rivalry and differentiated market position impact on the dynamics of the situation. Issues have impacts on the industry as they arise but not necessarily in an equal and uniform impact. Recall the accounting example discussed earlier with the different views of Price Waterhouse and Arthur Anderson. Accounting firms are differentially impacted by the precise wording and approach of regulation supporters. Curiously, when one uses an analysis of industry that breaks the competitors into strategic groups, those groupings can often be insightful on how the industry might shake out on a political or social issue.

For example, an analysis of the soft drink industry reveals several strategic groups. Some of these groups are (1) Coke and Pepsi, the behemoths of the industry; (2) the second-tier players, such as Dr. Pepper; and (3) regional players like Shasta and Franks. When Congress proposed eliminating saccharin as an approved artificial sweetener, the impact on the industry was very uneven. The greatest impact was on Shasta, who received approximately 70 percent of their income from diet drinks. As such, they had the most to lose by this proposal and fought it, whereas the rest of the industry either did not care or supported it. Similar patterns can be observed in the banking industry with regard to deregulation of banking. The national and international banks are for it, while the state and local banks are opposed to it. The state and local banks are opposed to deregulation because they see it as having profound economic and financial impacts on them.

Audience

In Porter's model, the final element is the customer. The customer is the one who purchases the good or service and who can exercise power over the industry and individual players if dissatisfied. The concept in Porter's model is that customers serve as a feedback mechanism to the industry regarding how they are performing in addressing, meeting, and satisfying their needs. If their needs are not being met, customers react by not buying the industry's or individual firm's products and services; that is, they withhold financial support in the form of purchasing. The industry or individual firm then has to either change what it is doing or seek a different customer base that will be satisfied with the given product or service.

The audience in the political and social arena is the equivalent of Porter's customer. Schattschneider (1960) knew of the importance of the audience in political and social contests: "Every fight consists of two parts: (1) a few individuals who are actively engaged at the center, and (2) the audience that is irresistibly attracted to the scene. The latter are an integral part of the overall situation" (p. 1). Schattschneider goes on to argue at length that it is not the strength of the individuals who are directly involved in the dispute that necessarily determines the winner but, rather, the side that the audience chooses to join and support. We can see, then, that in the political and social arena, the audience serves two purposes. The audience is both a stakeholder, as defined earlier (and can be in the observer role in Schattschneider's view), and the judge that can provide resolution to the issue or problem if they (the audience) are convinced by the participant's arguments and presentations on the issue or event. That is, there is a "general audience" and a "specific audience." A specific audience is the one with the power and legitimacy to resolve the issue or problem. Political strategies *must* appeal to both audiences. The manner in which the firm and industry approaches an issue must then appeal to the audience in some way. Much like the customer in Porter's model, the audience must have its needs addressed and satisfied in some manner. The audience in this model can be defined as that set of individuals (or groups) that exercise recognized control over the solution to the issue and problem. Therefore, an audience can be society at large, the media, the judiciary, the legislature, the regulatory agency, and so on. The argument is straightforward—if the given audience is satisfied with the arguments by the firm or industry over an issue, the audience will rule (as in an act of law, a regulatory or judicial finding, or in the support of society at large that notes it is no longer interested in the problem) and the given issue is resolved at that time. If a given audience is satisfied (e.g., a regulatory agency), then the issue *may* go away permanently. It is important to note that these audiences have limited attention spans and time to deal with an enormous set of issues. As a consequence, some important issues may never get the attention of a target audience because their agenda is too crowded to deal with this issue or because an issue of higher priority and importance demands immediate action, and thereby throws an issue off the agenda until a later time.

Unfortunately, issues and problems are often resolved that deal with a very narrow subset of the main issue due to the overall context of the situation, or one of the stakeholders involved in the issue appeals the resolution of the issue to a different arena. For example, when the judiciary was deciding on the exact breakup of AT&T, AT&T was frustrated in seeking its goals. At one point in time, AT&T unleashed its lobbyists in Congress, seeking to force Congressional interest in the issue and possibly engineer a legislative vice in a judicial solution. Although AT&T was not successful in this attempt, the judiciary got the message and moved faster on the breakup and resolved some points in AT&T's favor. Therefore, the threat of moving an issue to another arena may be sufficient to compel favorable action in the current arena where the issue is being resolved. We often see such attempts when firms are seeking tax breaks at the state or county level. If the tax breaks are not granted, a firm will threaten to move to another jurisdiction where they will obtain more favorable treatment. This threat, with its obvious impact on local employment, is an attempt to bring the general audience (employees, customers, suppliers, etc.) into play and have them influence the specific audience (in this case, the taxing authority) to provide a favorable response. This is precisely the tactic that Hasbro utilized in fighting off Mattel's hostile takeover attempt.

Nonetheless, an issue considered resolved may arise again at some future date. An example of an issue being repeatedly dealt with, among others, is plant and worker safety. When situations change or new technological knowledge is developed, it can lead to new demands for workplace safety, and the regulations and legislation are revisited. In addition, a given audience may be satisfied; but the losing party can raise the issue in a different arena with a different audience as noted earlier. In this example, a firm may lose in the regulatory arena because the agency rules against them. However, the firm (or individuals or representatives of public interest groups) may appeal the decision to either the judicial or legislative arena with a different audience and a different set of rules and mix of stakeholders. Fixes to the social security funding situation occur at fairly frequent intervals. A logical question is, Why isn't the problem fixed permanently? It might be that this particular problem is so difficult and imbued with strong and active stakeholder interests that a permanent solution is just not achievable, so temporary "patches" are placed on the system with the understanding that this problem will be addressed again at a later date.

Audience satisfaction can also include nonresolution. That is, nothing happens at a given point in time because adherents and

opponents are so evenly balanced that no change in the status quo occurs, or another more pressing issue arises that demands attention; so the original issue is dropped from consideration. The issue of abortion is one that seems to be evenly balanced and, at this time, incapable of any final resolution.

Barriers to Entry and to Exit

In addition to the forces noted earlier, there are barriers to entry and barriers to exit in the political and social field. Barriers to entry in the political and social field center around access and legitimacy, and they are closely related. Access to the system is the ability to meet with and influence key actors and stakeholders in the process. In the Porter Model, money allows an organization to purchase rivals or to engage in intense price cutting to weaken rivals in the marketplace. Access allows for the exercise of influence; without access, influence does not exist in the political and social arena. Stakeholders in an issue that do not have access to the system can, and often do, engage in violent or illegal action to gain attention to their cause and thereby gain access to the arena where the issue will be resolved (Cobb and Elder, 1972). Legitimacy is the recognition by others that you have a reason to be involved—that it is legal or that the issue affects you or your organization in some clearly defined manner and that your involvement is not damaging. For example, People for the Ethical Treatment of Animals (PETA) is recognized as a militant supporter of the rights of animals. PETA's militancy, however, has denied it access and legitimacy because its approach to defending animals includes destruction of laboratories and years of research. Few stakeholders and public officials wish to meet with PETA because of these actions. As a result, PETA has encountered a barrier to entry into the political and social process.

In addition, barriers to entry can be raised by an organization's own past performance. Many years ago, GE was involved in a price-fixing scandal. Prior to that, GE had an excellent reputation. When Congressional hearings were held on the issue, GE was not a credible witness to address the issue of price fixing and what should be done about it, as they were tainted by past behavior—again, a barrier to entry. A key difference here is that the barrier to entry is not raised by the industry's actions (as in the Porter Model) but by the combination of the specific issue, the arena in which it is to be resolved, and the stakeholder or firm's prior performance.

Barriers to exit are similar. An industry or firm may be precluded from exiting the political or social issue because of the nature of

the industry and the nature of the issue itself. As noted earlier, if the issue is centered on a discussion of government regulation of the accounting profession, the accounting profession cannot exit the discussion of the issue without profound consequences. During the discussion of plant safety in wake of the Bhopal accident, Union Carbide might have preferred to stay out of the discussion. Indeed, the chemical industry as a whole might have preferred Union Carbide to remain silent on this issue, but the target audience (Congress) would not let them exit the discussion of the issue.

An industry that exits a discussion of issues that impact on its performance and survival loses all rights to complain about the resolution of the issue and has no role in the shaping of the issue or the enforcement of the outcome. This is one of the key reasons for raising industry and individual firm understanding of the political and social process and their need for intimate and ongoing involvement in it.

TELEVISION VIOLENCE: AN ILLUSTRATIVE EXAMPLE

In 1994 and 1995, the issue of violence and its source assumed major importance in the United States. There were individuals and groups that looked into violence in music and television shows, with the emphasis on the exposure to violence that children received daily from television. Several groups started tracking the number of violent episodes per show, per network, per hour, and per day to demonstrate the extent of the problem (Elber, 1995). Congress held hearings on this issue and invited the major networks to these hearings. The target of the inquiry seemed to be closely focused on the major networks—American Broadcasting Corporation (ABC), Columbia Broadcasting System (CBS), National Broadcasting System (NBC), and Fox Broadcasting. Cable-based broadcasting, while subjected to some scrutiny, was relatively easily dismissed because not all homes had access to cable but did have access to network television. As a result, cable television was defined out of the issue by many of the key stakeholders. The industry-competitive political dynamics are shown in Figure 3.3.

It is difficult to trace the beginning of any issue, particularly one such as violence. All interested parties seem to agree that violence in American society was on the increase and that something had to be done about it. That is about the extent of the agreement. After that, there has been marked and heated disagreement about the source of violence, television's role in encouraging violence, and what should be done about it.

This issue of violence is very susceptible to redefinition and interpretation. The problem could be interpreted in a variety of ways

Figure 3.3
The Network Television Industry

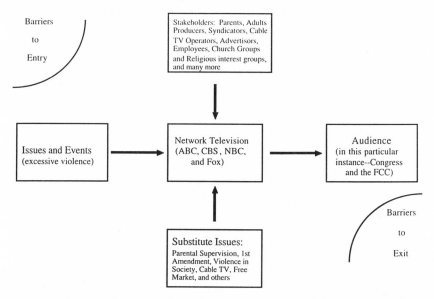

as shown in Figure 3.3. The problem is not with television but with the lack of parental supervision of children, or the issue is really one of network television trying to remain competitive with cable television and its level of graphic violence and sex (with the not-so-subtle argument that cable television should be investigated and regulated more tightly). Arguments were made that this is a First Amendment issue, that the networks have the right to televise it, and that individuals can make choices about what they wish to see by changing the channel on their televisions. Others argued that television is being made the scapegoat for all society's ills and that violence in society is the issue, not just violence on television. There are many other alternative definitions that might be offered; but it is important to understand that if the issue is redefined, it has an impact on stakeholder involvement and the potential arena and target audience.

The potential for varied and large-scale stakeholder involvement in this issue is quite high. Figure 3.3 provides a list of some of the potential individuals and groups that could become involved. Parents obviously have an interest in this issue, and so do adults who might desire to view adult subject matter on their televisions. The producers, syndicators, local television stations, advertisers, and their employees have a direct financial interest in this issue. Churches and other religious groups have an interest in this issue, as do educators. The balancing of stakeholder interests in this issue encompasses moral and financial grounds.

As has been consistently noted, the degree of financial impact is differentiated across stakeholders and the industry on this issue. The networks and the individual television stations make their money on ratings of television shows. The higher the ratings (meaning more people watching the show), the higher the advertising rates and the more profitable the show is for all concerned. As a result, the time of day, the specific day, and the ratings of the individual show all contribute to the financial outcome. Therefore, if a network made substantial sums of money from violent drama shows that aired in the late evening hours, that network might readily agree to substantial and substantive regulation of Saturday morning shows that appeal to young children. As in government, an industry's position on a given issue is not unified around a single proposal or plan of action. Indeed, part of the challenge for the target audience and for other stakeholders is to find these areas of industry differentiation and use them to achieve a compromise solution.

The solution achieved in this specific instance was that the networks would study their own performance in this area and move toward more stringent self-regulation. The issue was resolved, but only temporarily. Congress reserved the right to revisit this issue at a later date if the industry did not respond appropriately. Apparently, the appropriate response was to limit violence on network television. Although cable television operators escaped unscathed on this issue, movie producers have also been put on notice regarding violence and sex in their products. This is an issue that is likely to be addressed again in the future, for the current "resolution" does not seem likely to satisfy crucial stakeholders and the target audience.

GOING ALONE OR COOPERATING WITH OTHERS?

One of the challenges for an organization in dealing with issues such as those discussed thus far lies in the selection of the appropriate response. A key aspect of this decision is this: Does the firm "go it alone," or does it join with other organizations? We would suggest that this decision is a function of the type of impact that the issue has on the organization. For ease of analysis, issues have been broken down into three categories related to their impact on the organization: technical issues, administrative issues, and institutional issues.

Technical issues emerge with respect to some aspect of the organization's core technology, or what Porter and others in the strategy field might term distinctive competence (i.e., what the organization does exceptionally well; better than all of its competitors). Such issues will affect the fundamental resource transformation activity in which the entity engages. Transformation may be of physical resources, such as natural resources and energy production, or of human resources, as in service industries.

Administrative issues arise with respect to the way an organization acquires needed resources for its primary activities or sells and distributes the goods and services it manufactures or provides. The manner in which an organization acquires needed inputs, whether they be physical or human resources, can give rise to issues. The importation of labor, purchase of resources and agreements with foreign governments, or financing of core activities (e.g., universities entering agreements with pharmaceutical firms for support of genetic engineering research) can raise serious concerns among various stakeholders. Similar questions frequently arise with respect to the manner in which products are sold in the marketplace. These concerns may involve marketing techniques, advertising programs, distribution arrangements, or the very act of selling to certain types of clients (e.g., sale of computers to China). Virtually all businesses face the potential of such issues.

Institutional issues involve questions of the fundamental legitimacy of the firm or industry and the propriety of their continued existence and operation (see Chapter 4). Calls for changes in corporate governance to make the firm more accountable to the public and others is an example of an institutional issue.

Although individual firms face different configurations of technical, administrative, and institutional issues, it is clear that many industries tend to be dominated by issues of a particular type for long periods of time. In thinking about the strategic management of such issues, then, it is important to examine the relationships that are of primary concern in environments dominated by one of the three aforementioned issue types.

In environments dominated by technical issues, a key relationship is usually between the organization or industry and government agencies. Industries with natural monopoly characteristics, such as utilities, tend to have both a history of heavy government regulation and close scrutiny of capital investment in plant and equipment, rates, and technical improvements in the basic business of the industry. In such circumstances, regulatory agencies can buffer the organization and industry against direct challenge from other stakeholders in society. Regulatory hearings are frequently the formal, ritualized framework in which conflict is resolved. The regulatory agency decides both the outcome of the specific conflict (therefore serving as the target audience) and the "rules of engagement" by which the conflict will be addressed and resolved. The strategic management of such issues, then, begins with a clear focus on the interests and roles of the government agencies and their relationship to other interests and stakeholders in society at large.

In environments dominated by resource acquisition or product sale and distribution issues, the primary strategic relations are with nongovernment stakeholders in society. Heavy industries such as steel, automobiles, and natural resources (oil, mining) operate in such environments and have often found that government agencies are far less independent of stakeholders and societal forces than is true in an environment dominated by technical issues. Little technical expertise is necessary to recognize that one is without heating oil, that Japanese cars are cheaper and better than American cars, or that interest rates are prohibitively high for an individual seeking to purchase a home. In a similar vein, alcohol and tobacco firms constantly face issues around the sale and distribution of their products. The key strategic relations in such situations are between the firm and its suppliers, competitors, and customers. It is unlikely that a single firm in an industry will be successful in dealing with government agencies and stakeholders in society without recognizing the more fundamental driving forces to be found in the public at large.

In environments dominated by legitimacy issues, public mistrust of the industry or firm is itself the fundamental problem that needs to be addressed. In such circumstances, the firm or industry must develop a strategy for simultaneously dealing with the public, the media, stakeholders, and government; for government response may be internally initiated as well as stimulated by public pressure. The nuclear power industry is perhaps the most dramatic illustration of the legitimacy problem; but industries such as tobacco, banking, chemicals, and toxic waste disposal all suffer similar problems. Moreover, individual firms within such industries often develop reputations as particularly egregious violators of acceptable standards. The behavior of Hoffman–Laroche in dealing with the dioxin release in Seveso, Italy, or that of the Chisso Corporation in responding to the claims of Minamata disease victims, have become the basis for more intense public and government scrutiny. For the firms and industries involved, the task is nothing less than to persuade the public, stakeholders, and the government that they are, on balance, positive contributors to society and the welfare of the nation.

In such a milieu of issues, what are the response options available to the firm and industry? Technical issues, for example, because of their intimate tie to individual firm distinctive competence, may be dealt with best on an individual firm basis, unless a key aspect of this competency is distributed industry-wide. For example, changes in regulations dealing with effluent levels may have a markedly different impact on firms because their treatment processes differ. Therefore, firms might be better off to go it alone on this issue. However, a change that affects the distinctive competency of the entire industry as a whole would demand an industry-wide response. Administrative issues suggest that industry responses are more likely, with occasional cooperation among and between several industries. Finally, institutional issues can demand either individual or industry response dependent on the specific issue.

CONCLUSION

In this chapter, we have tried to weave together the themes of political and social analysis of industries with competitive analysis. The idea is that managers can use political and social industry analysis in concert with competitive analysis to improve overall organizational performance. In Part Two, we shall turn to an analysis of this model in four different industries: cigarette, beer, banking, and chemical. These industries represent a range of products and services and are large and important players in the U.S. and international economies, and all have had a sufficient and well-documented history of involvement in the political and social arena. In addition, these industries allow us to explore political and social strategies in consumer products, in financial services, and in industrial goods.

Chapters 4, 5, and 6 take a broad historical perspective, tracing the evolution of social, economic, and political issues that have permeated these industries and shaped their competitive dynamics. Chapter 7 focuses on a particular issue at a given point in time to allow the reader to explore in great depth the model developed in this chapter.

NOTE

1. Skil Corporation (HBS 9-389-005) and the CFM International, Inc. (HBS 9-793-091) cases available from the Harvard Business School are examples of a much larger set of cases that deal with and use Porter's industry analysis framework.

PART TWO

EVIDENCE OF COMPETITIVE-INDUSTRY POLITICAL DYNAMICS FROM FOUR INDUSTRIES

Chapter 4

THE CIGARETTE INDUSTRY

The cigarette industry is one whose very existence has always been the center of controversy and subjected to continuous scrutiny by public policymakers. The various government interventions have taken many forms: antitrust actions, price fixing charges, excise tax increases, warning labels on tobacco products, advertising bans, and public smoking bans. All levels (federal, state, and local) and branches (executive, legislative, and judiciary) of government have been involved in regulating this industry.

The history of government intervention of the cigarette industry can be divided into "three waves." (See Figures 4.1, 4.2, and 4.3 for a pictorial summary of all the various "stakeholders" during these three periods of regulatory activity of the cigarette industry.) In viewing each of these figures, one can immediately see that the cigarette industry has been confronted with a different issue during each of these "waves" of government regulation. These different issues have, in turn, caused the cigarette industry to operate in a variety of government arenas as well as attracting the interest of numerous other stakeholders that have an interest in either maintaining or destroying this quite profitable industry. The political and economic environment that has accompanied each of these waves has, in turn, determined how the cigarette industry developed its response to the challenges of its legitimacy as well as the desirability to enter or exit this industry.

Thus, the cigarette industry provides the reader with three opportunities or cases to evaluate the utility of the model that was developed in Chapter 3. Each case will be divided into five parts. First, the issue concerning the cigarette industry that has been the focus of public attention will be delineated. Second, the various stakeholders will be defined along with their stances toward the various policy instruments proposed to deal with the problems encountered by the cigarette industry during a particular wave. Third, the substitute issues proposed by the cigarette industry will be discussed along with the tactics used by the other stakeholders in trying to present their cases to the public policy forum. Fourth, the barriers to entry and exit will be examined to ascertain how a particular wave of regulation affected the actual structure of the cigarette industry itself. Finally, there will be a discussion of the actual effects that various public policy measures had both on cigarette sales as well as the overall business strategies of the cigarette firms. An evaluation of the strengths and weaknesses of the various stakeholders will conclude these discussions of outcomes.

FIRST WAVE: THE STRUCTURE OF THE CIGARETTE INDUSTRY (1911–1964)

Issue: A Competitive Market for the Cigarette Industry

Competition enjoyed a short and very turbulent existence in the American tobacco industry. The person who brought order to the chaotic competition of the 1880s was James B. Duke. Duke's objective was to garner all the various tobacco products under one trust or combine, known as the American Tobacco Company. He succeeded in his objective so well that his trust became one of the first targets of the Sherman Antitrust Act. In 1911, the Justice Department won a landmark decision breaking up the trust. Yet, even after the breakup of the trust, in no sense could one say that competition existed in the cigarette industry. There are a number of reasons for the failure to establish competition, but the chief reason lies with the nature of the trust and the industry that Duke created. The methods which Duke used to establish his tobacco empire are, in some ways, still being employed by the cigarette firms today. Therefore, it does behoove us once again to review the rise of the Duke tobacco combine. Figure 4.1 offers a summary of the various stakeholders that had an interest in the cigarette industry.

James Duke, along with his brothers, had been in the smoking tobacco field for seven years when it was apparent that their brand of smoking tobacco, Bull Durham, would not be the number-one smoking tobacco in the United States. Duke did not want to play second to anyone; and so he looked to the small, but highly disorganized, cigarette field where he could become number one in the industry. In the early 1880s, the annual expenditure on cigarettes

Figure 4.1
First Wave: The Structure of the Cigarette Industry (1911–1964)

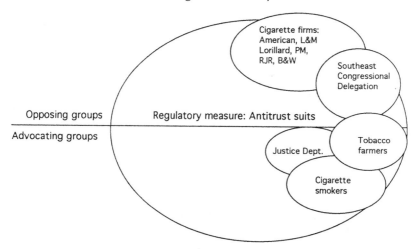

was estimated to be, at most, $1.5 million per year, or less than 3 percent of total tobacco sales (Jacobstein, 1908: 46). This was one reason why there were so few producers in the emerging cigarette industry. Another reason for this lack of competitors in the evolving cigarette industry was that it required a fairly substantial investment in patented machinery. However, the advantage that cigarette makers had over other branches of the tobacco business was that their labor costs were one tenth of those for other tobacco products. Hence, the early industry consisted of four firms that controlled 90 percent of the small, but profitable, cigarette market.

In 1884, Duke entered the cigarette market with a rather modest sum of $100,000, which hardly impressed the existing cigarette firms. But in 1887, after borrowing $800,000, Duke deliberately initiated a costly advertising campaign and employed cutthroat pricing tactics that brought him to the forefront of the cigarette industry. By 1889, independence seemed to be a very costly luxury for his rivals so that by 1890, all the firms had merged, and Duke had control of more than 90 percent of the market (Jacobstein, 1908: 107). New Jersey was chosen for incorporation, and Duke's American Tobacco Company was born. Duke's new tobacco trust was enormously successful. In 1890, the profit margin on cigarette sales was about 10 percent, and this was to increase to about 25 percent by 1911. American Tobacco controlled more than 90 percent of the cigarette market throughout this period (1890–1911) and, at the time of the breakup of the trust, had 96 percent of the market. By 1895,

American Tobacco paid its preferred dividends, built a surplus of $8 million, and paid a common stock dividend of between 8 and 12 percent (Jacobstein, 1908: 109). Indeed, Duke was number one in cigarettes and was now ready for the challenge of becoming number one in the whole tobacco industry.

With the help of its cigarette profits, and through the use of the same tactics that built the cigarette monopoly (economies of scale, heavy advertising, and cutthroat pricing), the American Tobacco Company rapidly gained control of all other tobacco fields except cigars. Duke even went international by invading the British market using the same tactics he had used in the United States. Imperial Tobacco of Great Britain sued for peace and agreed to form the British–American Tobacco Company, whose task was to market cigarettes throughout the British empire. As part of the agreement, American Tobacco received two thirds of the profits of the new firm; and both home markets were left to their respective domestic companies. While Duke viewed his consolidation of the tobacco industry as a personal triumph, officials in the U.S. Justice Department viewed with alarm the monopoly he had formed and decided to take action to rectify the situation.

The Cigarette Industry (1911–1964)

In May 1911, the Supreme Court ruled that Duke's Tobacco Trust was a monopoly in violation of the Sherman Antitrust Act and ordered that it be dissolved into a number of separate companies. This decree divided the business of the trust into fourteen independent companies. Table 4.1 summarizes the status of the largest concerns after the trust was dissolved.

Although the trust was broken up into fourteen different entities, it is fairly obvious that the net result of the government's antitrust activity was the creation of an oligopoly that, in many respects, still forms the basic structure of the cigarette industry today. Duke's American Tobacco was given the most generous settlement, and R. J. Reynolds (RJR) became very much the struggling young cousin. However, all this was to change dramatically within two years of the dissolution of the trust. The reason for this change involved the rise in cigarette use. In 1911, cigarettes still accounted for less than 6 percent of all tobacco sales. With the breakup of the Duke Trust, three firms accounted for more than 80 percent of the cigarette market, with RJR not producing any cigarettes. But in 1913, using its chewing tobacco profits, RJR introduced Camel as a "Turkish and Domestic Blend." The success of Camel was phenomenal. By 1917, cigarette sales had increased by more than 500 per-

Table 4.1
Percentage of Market Share after the Breakup of the "Tobacco Trust"

Company	Cigarettes	Smoking Tobacco	Fine Cut	Cigars
The Trust (1910)	86.1	76.2	79.7	14.4
American	37.1	33.1	9.9	6.1
Liggett & Myers	27.8	20.1	- - - -	- - - -
Lorillard	15.3	22.8	27.8	5.7
Reynolds	- - - -	2.7	41.6	- - - -
Big Four	80.2	78.7	79.3	11.8

Source: W. Nichols, *Price Policies of the Cigarette Industry*, Nashville, TN: Vanderbilt University Press, 1951, p. 31.

cent, with Camel claiming 34.7 percent of this market. With Camel, RJR had found a formula for greatly expanding not only its own but the entire cigarette market: national distribution based upon large-scale national advertising of a single brand. RJR's strategy was to establish a nationwide reputation through advertising and to cut prices while introducing the brand. While American Tobacco might have originated with James Duke, it was Reynolds that used his formula for success after 1911.

The other firms in the industry eventually followed RJR's lead. American Tobacco introduced Lucky Strike in 1917, and Liggett & Myers (L&M) developed Chesterfield in 1918. All these brands used the Camel formula—concentrate advertising on just the one brand, and avoid price competition. RJR was acknowledged as the price leader, and the other firms set their prices accordingly. By 1925, these three brands alone accounted for 82 percent of the national cigarette consumption. Lorillard was the backward cousin that did not develop a domestic blend cigarette (Old Gold) until 1926, by which time its market share had fallen to less than 2 percent. Table 4.2 provides a summary of the market shares of the various firms during the first wave.

Table 4.2
Percentage of Cigarette Market Share (1913–1965)

Year	RJR	PM	B&W	American	Lorillard	L&M
1913	0.2	- - -	- - -	35.3	22.1	34.1
1925	41.6	0.5	- - -	21.3	1.9	26.6
1930	28.6	0.4	0.2	37.6	6.9	25.0
1939	23.7	7.1	10.6	23.5	5.8	21.6
1949	26.3	9.2	5.9	31.3	5.0	20.2
1955	25.8	8.5	10.5	32.9	6.1	15.6
1960	32.1	9.4	10.4	26.1	10.6	11.3
1965	32.6	10.5	13.3	25.7	9.2	8.7

Sources: R. Tennant, *The American Cigarette Industry*, New Haven: Yale University
Press, 1950 (1913–1949); *Business Week*, Annual Survey of the American Cigarette
Industry (1955–1965).

The other obvious change that took place during this period was
the appearance of two other cigarette manufacturers—Philip Morris
(PM) and Brown & Williamson (B&W). By 1964, the sales of both
these two firms accounted for nearly 24 percent of the market. These
sales came at the expense of the two backward cousins, Lorillard
and L&M. Still, the overall structure of the industry had not changed
since 1913, with RJR and American being the dominant players
and price setters. The question of how competitive the cigarette
market remained and still remains is a controversial one.

Stakeholders

Besides the cigarette firms themselves, the major stakeholders
that had an interest in a competitive cigarette market were the
Southeast Congressional Delegation, tobacco farmers, cigarette

smokers, and the Justice Department. The role that each of these stakeholders played in determining appropriate public policy to ensure that
there was a competitive cigarette market differed markedly.

The role of the Southeast Congressional Delegation was mostly
defensive. Representatives and senators from Virginia, Maryland,
Tennessee, Kentucky, North Carolina, and South Carolina made
sure that excise taxes on cigarette taxes were kept low and supported agricultural subsidies for the tobacco farmers. However, since
they had little control over the executive branch and the Justice
Department, there was little they could do to stop the antitrust
action taken against the industry. In fact, they supported these
antitrust actions because of the intervention of two other stakeholders—tobacco farmers and cigarette smokers.

The economic power that accompanied the oligopolistic structure
of the cigarette industry became a source of great consternation to
both tobacco farmers and cigarette smokers. Tobacco farmers were
faced with what economists label a "monoponsy," that is, many sell-
ers but few buyers. Although there were many thousands of small
tobacco farmers (where the size of a farm averaged between ten
and twenty acres), they could only sell their product to the six cigarette firms, which easily dictated the price that farmers received.
Meanwhile, cigarette consumers could only choose among the products provided by the six cigarette firms. Thus, the cigarette industry had control over both their suppliers and customers. Clearly,
government had to decrease this power and placate the consuming
public and the farm interests.

Finally, it is significant that it was the federal government that
confronted the issue of the structure of the cigarette industry. The
two branches of the federal government that became involved in
this question were the executive and the judiciary. This limited
government interest in this issue worked to the advantage of the
cigarette industry. The industry could focus all its efforts at the
executive branch, realizing that Congress and state governments
viewed the cigarette industry as providing a needed source of revenue through the imposition of cigarette excise taxes.

Substitute Issues

The cigarette industry's response to criticism that its market was
not competitive was twofold. First, the industry maintained that
its structure was a "natural" oligopoly, so that it was futile for government to try and foster competition in the cigarette industry.
William Tennant was a prominent economist of this period who
agreed with this contention of the cigarette industry. He maintained

that the oligopolistic structure of the cigarette industry was "natural" because of economies of scale needed to manufacture cigarettes and because of the high cost to conduct the national advertising to sell cigarettes. His overall conclusion was as follows:

Although there is an usually good opportunity to reform the structure of the industry and although there is ample precedent in this industry for legal measures to secure greater decentralization, we do not find that it would be economically desirable or, according to political criteria, very urgent. (Tennant, 1950: 385)

The second issue that the cigarette industry used to substitute for the structure issue also involved economics, namely, the overall economic contribution that the cigarette industry made to the whole economy. First, there were the tobacco farmers, as well as cigarette factory workers, who were directly helped by the selling of cigarettes. Second, there were firms and businesses that indirectly benefited from the selling of cigarettes. These include retail operations such as food stores, drug stores, tobacco shops, and media operations such as newspapers and magazines that received advertising income from the cigarette industry.

Thus, the cigarette industry used economic arguments that it was efficient and natural to counteract the charge that its prices for both its suppliers and customers were predatory. While these arguments did not satisfy the critics of the cigarette industry, they were useful in preventing the industry from suffering more and prolonged attacks about the structure of the industry.

Barriers to Entry and Exit

Even though the structure of the cigarette industry was periodically under attack during this period (other antitrust suits were filed by the Justice Department in 1941 and 1954, but none were successful) in both the legislative and judicial arenas, the overall legitimacy of the industry was never questioned. There was never any mention of nationalizing the industry, which had occurred in most other major industrial countries. Certainly, the cigarette firms maintained access to all levels and branches of government through extensive lobbying efforts, and its economic might was never seriously questioned by other powerful stakeholders. Nor did this antitrust activity make it any easier to achieve the economies of scales in distribution or advertising needed to operate a successful cigarette firm. So the entry barriers to the debate over this issue were not very high, but many did not choose to get involved.

As for exit barriers, none of the six major cigarettes gave the least indication that they would exit this profitable industry or leave the resolution of the issue to the politicians and the judiciary without industry input. The federal government's antitrust activity was hardly an impetus to exit the debate.

Audience

Although the 1911 antitrust activity did break up the former Duke Cigarette Trust into six firms, it did not make the industry any more price competitive; nor did it afford its suppliers (i.e., tobacco farmers) any more leverage in dealing with this industry. The cigarette industry had managed to keep the courts as the primary audience for this dispute with its stakeholders. Clearly, it had the power to overwhelm the stakeholders in this arena.

The cigarette industry grew dramatically throughout this wave of antitrust activity. Advertising was the sole means through which these firms competed; and ironically, this increase in cigarette advertising not only increased sales but made cigarette smoking much more socially acceptable, especially with women. The cigarette became a symbol of sophistication and modernity. Cigarette smoking became a rite of passage into adulthood. As this industry entered the 1960s, it was one that had amassed enormous economic and political power at all levels and branches of government; and the cigarette industry would need to utilize this power if it was going to survive the next two waves of regulation.

SECOND WAVE: THE HEALTH OF THE SMOKER (1964–1985)

Issue: Smoking and Health

If the driving force behind the first wave for both government action and the pricing policies of the cigarette firms was the structure of the cigarette industry, the impetus for the second wave was undoubtedly the smoking and health issue. In 1964, the Surgeon General published a report which concluded that "cigarette smoking is a health hazard of sufficient importance in the United States to warrant remedial action" (Department of Health and Human Services, 1964: 231). The nature of these "remedial" actions and how the cigarette industry reacted to them are the focus of this section (see Figure 4.2).

As the anti-smoking sentiment increased throughout the country, it was Congress (as opposed to the executive branch, which

Figure 4.2
Second Wave: The Health of the Smoker (1964–1985)

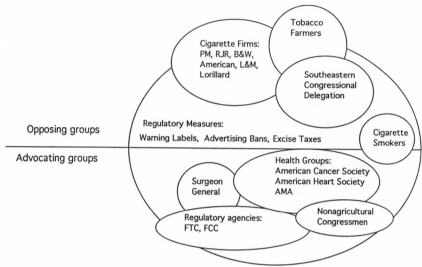

initiated action during the first wave) that responded to the demand for more regulation of the cigarette industry. No longer was the government concerned with the structure of the cigarette industry but with ways of reducing the number of smokers—and hence, cigarette sales. The executive branch of the federal government was divided throughout this period with the Surgeon General's office; Health, Education, and Welfare (HEW); and the Federal Trade Commission (FTC) wishing to take further actions against the industry and the Departments of Agriculture and Commerce, leading the opposition to any further restrictive measures. The executive branch was extremely sensitive throughout this period (1964–1985) about further alienating tobacco interests and never gave its full support to any of the anti-smoking measures proposed.

The chief measures enacted by Congress during this era were the Cigarette Warning Label Act of 1966; the TV and Radio Cigarette Advertising Ban of 1971; and finally, the doubling of the federal excise tax on cigarettes in 1983. The effects that these acts had on the sales and structure of the cigarette industry will be examined later, but now it is time to evaluate the various groups that had interests in the passage of these acts.

Stakeholders

The smoking and health issue has had and continues to have a tremendous impact on both the strategies of the cigarette firms and the structure of the cigarette industry. Unlike the first wave of government intervention, this issue changed not only the strategies of the cigarette firms but also the structure of the cigarette industry itself. Before 1964, cigarette sales had grown at least 3 percent per year. After 1964, this sales growth rate slowed. For the first time in its history, the cigarette industry faced declining sales for more than one year in the United States, when sales declined by an average of 1 percent from 1982 until 1993. While this decline in cigarette sales was radical enough, it was the way in which the smoking and health issue changed the business and corporate strategies of the individual cigarette firms and, subsequently, the structure of the cigarette industry.

As mentioned earlier, during the first wave (1911–1964), nonfiltered cigarettes were very popular and there was little need for product innovation. Because consumers tended to stick to one brand throughout their smoking careers, advertising and marketing strategies were aimed at attracting and keeping new smokers. This changed with the advent of the smoking and health issue, and only those firms that could adapt to the new environment would prosper.

Responding to the health concerns of their customers, the cigarette firms introduced various brands to satisfy the consumers' desire for a "healthy" cigarette. This change in consumers' desires forced cigarette firms to diversify their product offerings to satisfy the variety of consumer tastes. Filtered cigarettes, such as Marlboro, Winston, and Viceroy, which were presumed to be less hazardous to the smoker's health, surged in popularity; filtered menthol brands also began to flourish. After the rise of the filter cigarette, the "low-tar" brands of cigarettes were introduced. Then, in the early 1970s, new brands were targeted at such market segments as women (Virginia Slims) and the black population (Merit). The result of this effort to target the needs of smokers was an extremely segmented market with a dramatic increase in the number of brands. No longer the simple promoters of several well-known brands, the cigarette firms had to become masters of marketing and advertising. As can be seen in Figure 4.3, the two firms that became the experts at marketing and producing not only the less hazardous cigarette but a cigarette for every taste were RJR and PM.

Thus, the period from 1964 to 1985 was one of great change in the cigarette industry. The marketing strategies of the firms changed from promoting one basic brand to showering the public with various brands to satisfy a variety of tobacco needs and tastes. The structure of the industry also changed radically. The firms that learned to diversify their product lines most effectively were

Figure 4.3
Cigarette Market Share: 1965–1985

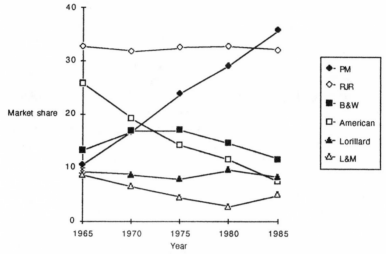

Source: Business Week, Annual Review of Cigarette Industry (1965–1985).

awarded market share. By far, the two firms that adapted themselves to this new environment were PM and RJR. Because of their success, PM and RJR had formed a duopoly which had cornered almost 73 percent of the cigarette market ("The Concentration of the Cigarette Industry," 1985: 90). Hence, these two firms had the greatest stake in opposing the various anti-smoking measures, while the other firms in the cigarette industry were, for the most part, mere spectators in the battle to preserve the cigarette industry.

The cigarette industry did have allies in its fight against these anti-smoking measures. The Southeastern Congressional Delegation and the tobacco farmers and workers formed a solid base of support that the cigarette industry could use to hold up anti-smoking legislation in committee, especially in the U.S. Senate.

Meanwhile, the groups advocating these anti-smoking measures were primarily health groups whose concerns were about the detrimental effects of cigarette smoking. These groups included the American Cancer Society, the American Heart Society, and the American Medical Association. Since these were traditional groups, the measures that they advocated were also quite traditional and were hardly radical in the sense that they were urging Congress to adopt measures that had been enforced in European countries for many years. Even the cigarette excise tax increase enacted (from $0.08 per pack to $0.16 per pack) was extremely modest, especially if one compares it to the cigarette excise tax rates imposed during this time period in Canada ($0.90 per pack) or a typical European rate of between $0.50 per pack and $1.25 per pack.

Substitute Issues

In dealing with this increase in regulatory measures, the cigarette industry mustered a variety of economic and social issues to counterattack and lessen the severity of any proposed regulatory measures of their industry.

The economic issues were familiar ones: the financial contributions of tobacco to suppliers (tobacco farmers, paper firms); customers (cigarette distributors, retail stores); and the amount spent on advertising. The fact that cigarette firms emphasized the most, however, was the amount of excise taxes paid on each pack of cigarettes. While cigarette excise taxes accounted for a little more than 1 percent of the federal budget, cigarette excise taxes were a major contributor to the financial well-being of state governments. State governments depended on this tax for nearly 5 percent of their revenue (Tobacco Tax Council, 1994: i). Hence, state officials were loath to raise cigarette excise tax to any level that would actually discourage cigarette smoking, since they would have to raise either sales taxes or income taxes to make up the shortfall in state revenues. It was often pointed out to state legislators that decreasing cigarette sales would, in turn, lead to lower state spending on health in the long run. This argument was of little comfort to state officials who would have to explain increase in taxes to constituents in the short run in order to balance a state's budget.

It was during this second wave of regulation that the cigarette industry also developed an ethical argument that used the concept of "rights" as its ethical counterattack against the anti-smoking forces. First, the cigarette industry used the concept of rights to oppose advertising bans. The industry maintained that any advertising ban was a denial of the industry's right to free speech. After all, if the product is legal and safe, do not cigarette firms have the right to inform the public of the availability of the product? A second ethical argument that the cigarette firms used against the imposition of any dramatic increase in cigarette excise taxes was the rights of the smokers. After all, why should cigarette smokers have to pay high taxes on a product they enjoy? If there is any harm in the product, they are only harming themselves. So why should their right to smoke be restricted through the imposition of higher taxes and hence prices? The cigarette industry had regularly referred to cigarette excise taxes as regressive and unfair; so while critics of the cigarette industry managed to get through their modest agenda to curb cigarette smoking, the cigarette industry was able to defend itself from any extreme proposals and was quite successful in delaying and modifying these proposals so that the industry could exist with them quite comfortably.

Barriers to Entry and Exit

Throughout the second wave of regulation, the cigarette industry sought to maintain legitimacy through a variety of tactics. First, the cigarette industry has never admitted that cigarette smoking directly causes cancer, heart disease, or any other ailment that health officials were attributing to cigarette smoking. While the cigarette industry might admit that cigarette smoking could contribute to smokers' chances of getting cancer or heart disease, it maintained that it sold a legal product that, used in moderation, would cause no harmful health side effects. It hired researchers who would dispute any direct causal connection between smoking and health.

Second, it was pointed out that the cigarette industry had developed into a duopoly during this second wave of regulation. The financial strength of these two leading cigarette firms was enormous. For example, in 1970, PM was the fourth-largest cigarette firm in the United States. By 1985, with its acquisition of Miller Beer, 7-Up, and General Foods, it had become the seventh-largest firm in the Fortune 500 ("The Tobacco Lobby," 1987). RJR Nabisco had also followed a similar strategy of diversification and was ranked tenth on the Fortune 500 list. Certainly, this diversification strategy gave both of these firms, as well as the other cigarette firms, legitimacy and easy access to the political and social arena.

Yet, for all their acquisitions, these firms were still highly dependent on cigarette sales and revenues for more than 70 percent of their profits. Hence, they could not afford to abandon the cigarette segment of their businesses if they hoped to continue this diversification strategy; thus, they could exit themselves from any public policy discussion that sought to further regulate their industry. Still, even though it was experiencing many more public policy initiatives, the cigarette industry never experienced during this second wave of regulation any entry or exit problems as it sought to enter the public agenda forum.

Audience

Throughout this second period of government regulation of the cigarette industry, the legislative branch of government took the place of the judiciary as the primary branch of government which was responsible for regulating the industry. The following measures summarize the activity of Congress in regulating the cigarette industry during this period.

Cigarette Warning Label Requirement

For anti-smoking forces, the requirement that cigarette makers include a warning on the packages of their product was the opening salvo in their campaign against cigarette smoking. The rationale behind this warning label was simply to remind cigarette smokers continuously that cigarette smoking was dangerous and, therefore, that the cigarette smoker should consider giving up the habit.

Even though the warning requirement was considered to be extremely mild, another benefit (at least from the standpoint of the anti-smoking groups) was that the government had finally committed itself to an official position on the dangers of smoking. The issue had been brought to the congressional agenda, and a victory had been won. For the first time, the tobacco lobby had been defeated. The long-term effect of this victory was to legitimize the smoking and health issue as an object for vigorous public policy experimentation and public debate.

Yet the passage of this measure has often been portrayed as a Pyrrhic victory for the anti-smoking forces. Although the warning label requirement was opposed vigorously by the industry, it did have one curious, major, unintended benefit for the industry. Over the years, many suits have been filed against cigarette firms claiming that the product is a dangerous one and, therefore, these firms should be liable as a result of selling this dangerous product. In the past, the courts have ruled that smokers did know of the dangers of cigarette smoking, in particular, because of the warning label requirement. However, in the famous Cipollone case, a New Jersey judge ruled against the cigarette firms. But even though the court held the cigarette firms liable, it still rewarded the plaintiff only $400,000 (Belluck, 1988). So it remains to be seen how successful this "warning label" defense will be in the future for the cigarette firms and how the anti-smoking forces propose to attack it (Van Gelder, 1988).

The Ban on Television and Radio Advertising

On January 1, 1971, cigarette advertising on the television and radio was banned as a result of the Public Health Cigarette Smoking Act of 1969. The ban was hailed as a major victory by the anti-smoking forces. The rationale behind this legislation was that cigarette advertising stimulated sales and, therefore, if advertising was banned, cigarette sales would fall.

There have been previous studies trying to measure the effect of this ban on cigarette sales. Both Bass (1969) and Hamilton (1972), using somewhat similar econometric models and national data, disputed the claim of the anti-smoking forces. Hamilton maintained that cigarette consumption was actually increased because of this action, since the broadcasters could no longer be required to broadcast anti-smoking spots. The influence of the smoking and health controversy was dampened, and the cigarette firms had ironically won once again. Hamilton's conclusion offers a sober assessment about the effectiveness of the advertising ban:

Actions that intensified the health scare would have been a more effective policy than banning advertising. Policy makers must evaluate policy models carefully. Action based on wishful thinking seldom is as effective as that based on carefully specified models accurately depicting the forces influencing the policy objectives and connections between forces and proposed policy actions. (1972: 409)

Another unforeseen effect of this advertising ban was that it became extremely difficult to enter the cigarette market. This barrier to entry in the competitive sense was erected by legislation and not the normal workings of the marketplace. No brand of cigarettes that has been introduced since the inception of this ban has managed to garner any more than a 5-percent market share. The firm that appears to have been the chief beneficiary of this advertising ban has been PM. PM's Marlboro brand has managed to achieve a 20- to 25-percent share by itself. One reason for Marlboro's popularity is that the majority of new smokers start their smoking careers with Marlboros. RJR has also benefited form the advertising in that two of its brands, Winston and Camel, also enjoy high brand recognition, but not nearly that of Marlboro. Hence, the ability of other cigarette firms to gain market share has been greatly reduced, leaving PM and RJR to divide this lucrative cigarette market.

Doubling the Federal Cigarette Excise Tax (1983)

The excise tax is the most frequently employed weapon in the anti-smoking movement's arsenal. There is a twofold rationale behind this policy measure: First, since the excise tax raises the price of cigarettes, it is thought to prevent people (particularly teenagers) from starting to smoke; and second, the cigarette excise tax generates tremendous revenues for federal, state, and local governments. For example, in 1993, almost $26 billion was collected by government at all levels through cigarette excise taxes (Tobacco Tax Council, 1994: iii). Hence, the cigarette excise tax is considered a "sin" tax—one where the government "does well, while doing good."

It is generally agreed that the demand for cigarettes is inelastic, and that Tennant's (1950) estimate for elasticity of between –0.4 and –0.5 is still accurate today. Therefore, one might expect that the same would be true of the excise tax—that only a large increase in the cigarette excise tax will produce a decrease in cigarette sales. Economists who have studied this issue have based their studies on European data which show a uniform excise tax rate that is not the case in the United States. For example, Chappell (1984) used econometric models to estimate the effect that excise taxes had on cigarette consumption in various countries (France, Belgium, and Great Britain, respectively). The general conclusion of these studies was that these increases in the excise tax rate were not great enough to have a significant impact on cigarette consumption.

However, the doubling of the federal cigarette excise tax was effective only in those cases where a state also raised its cigarette excise tax, thereby reinforcing the negative effect on cigarette sales. For example, in 1983, Michigan doubled its cigarette excise tax from $0.16 per pack to $0.32 per pack, while the federal cigarette excise tax was being increased from $0.08 per pack to $0.16 per pack. The result of this dual increase in cigarette excise tax was a dramatic and permanent decrease in Michigan cigarette sales (McGowan, 1989).

While the second wave of regulation was intense, the cigarette industry did survive virtually intact. The structure of the industry had become more concentrated, but all the firms in the industry remained very profitable. It was an industry that experienced a unique situation—decreasing sales but increasing profits. The smoking and health issue was addressed, but it was hardly resolved to the satisfication of the anti-smoking stakeholders. But the anti-smoking measures enacted during the second wave of regulation would merely be a preview of the fierce attacks that the cigarette industry would undergo during its third wave of regulation.

THIRD WAVE: THE RIGHTS OF THE NONSMOKER (1986–PRESENT)

Issue: The Effects of Secondary Smoke and the Nonsmoker

On December 20, 1985, Surgeon General C. Everett Koop announced the results of new research by his staff on the effects of smoking. One of the findings of this report indicated that there was a significant increase in the rate of lung cancer among nonsmokers in households where nonsmokers were living with cigarette smokers (Department of Health and Human Services, 1985: 1). This report sparked off a flurry of medical activity into the phenomenon called "passive smoking" or "secondary effects" of smoking (see Figure 4.4).

Figure 4.4
Third Wave: The Rights of the Nonsmoker (1986–Present)

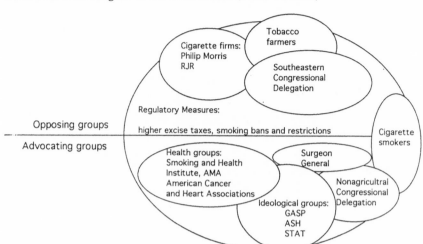

With the Surgeon General's report, the rights of the nonsmoker were raised anew by anti-smoking groups. No longer could it be claimed that smoking harms only the individual smoker; hence, it is the smoker's right to smoke or not to smoke. This issue gave anti-smoking forces an entirely new way of arguing their case against smoking. With the passive smoking issue, nonsmokers can claim that smoking affects their health even if they do not smoke.

Among the results of the controversy surrounding the passive smoking issue has been a dramatic increase in the number of legislative proposals regulating smoking in public places or proposing increases in cigarette excise taxes (see Figures 4.5 and 4.6). One of the factors that has made this third wave of regulation unique is the new interest shown by state and local governments in regulating the cigarette industry. Legislation that involves restrictions on smoking in various public places has been much more severe at the local and state level than at the federal level. This burst of legislative activity has not been confined to just the state and local levels of government. Figure 4.5 illustrates that Congressional interest in the smoking and health issue has increased fourfold since 1986.

It does not appear that the furor surrounding the smoking and health issue is subsiding. A survey of major news publications (*Time, Newsweek,* the *Wall Street Journal,* and the *New York Times,* as well as major newspapers throughout the United States) has revealed that the smoking and health issue—in particular, the passive smoking issue—has appeared at least 500 times since January

Figure 4.5
State and Local Legislative Activity

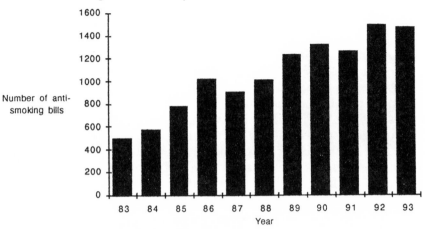

Source: Annual Survey of Tobacco Observer (1983–1993).

Figure 4.6
Congressional Activity

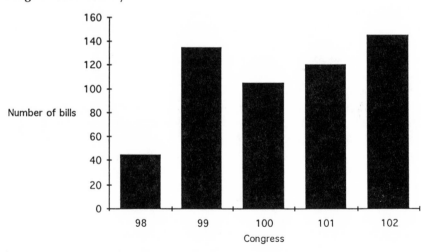

Source: Annual Survey of Tobacco Observer (1983–1993).

1988 ("Passive Smoking as an Issue," 1994). In fact, the topic of passive smoking has been a cover story for *Time* and *Newsweek* eight times since 1988. Thus, the controversy surrounding this issue seems to be intensifying instead of lessening with the passage of time.

Stakeholders

Traditionally, the anti-smoking movement was led by groups such as the American Cancer Society, American Lung Association, and American Medical Association, which in the past tended to be politically cautious and to be much more willing to strike political compromises. The federal agencies that handled the smoking and health issue include Health and Human Service (HHS), the Surgeon General, and the Office of Smoking and Health. Again, because of the political sensitivity of these issues, these bodies advocated, for the most part, noncontroversial solutions to the smoking and health problem (especially during election periods) and were ready to settle for less than an ideal solution.

But with the rise of the passive smoking issue comes the emergence of activist groups such as Association on Smoking and Health (ASH), Groups against Smoking Pollution (GASP), and Stop Teenage Abuse of Tobacco (STAT) that are dedicated solely to the anti-smoking movement. The rhetoric and tone of these groups is much more strident than that of more established multi-issue health organizations. These groups consider themselves as crusaders against an evil empire, namely, the cigarette industry. Inflammatory phrases such as "the six murderers" (used by STAT) are used to describe the cigarette firms, and mottoes such as "Sue the Bastards" decorate the office of John Banzhaf, the executive director of ASH (Troy and Markle, 1986: 66). As the rhetoric has grown more hostile, strong anti-smoking language has even crept into the federal establishment. The Surgeon General has said, "Smoking is the single most important preventable cause of death" (Department of Health and Human Services, 1986: 2) and declared that cigarette smoking is an "addiction" (Department of Health and Human Services, 1988: 1), stating a national goal of a smoke-free society by the year 2000.

It is interesting to note that the anti-smoking rhetoric has also become much more normative in tone. Smoking is wrong and should be wiped out. No longer is the cigarette industry confronted with an anti-smoking argument based solely on a cost–benefit analysis; it now faces what some have called an "ideology of anti-smoking" (Berger, 1986: 234). The goal upon which this ideology is built is the utopian dream of a smokeless society, and nothing less will do.

Academic Interest: Economists and Health Care Specialists

How has the academic world reacted to this renewed interest in the cigarette industry? Not surprisingly, economists have returned to familiar themes from the two previous waves of regulation. Economists are again studying the effects of excise tax increases and advertising bans on the consumption of cigarettes. An example of this would be a study conducted by the Congressional Budget Office suggesting that the elasticity of demand for cigarettes has remained constant at −0.4 and −0.5 (Congressional Budget Office, *The Tobacco Industry,* 1987). Other economists are exploring the topic that was the chief concern of economists during the first wave of regulation: the structure of the cigarette industry. Jeffrey Harris, a medical doctor and economist at MIT, has made the suggestion that a windfall profits tax be levied against the earnings of the cigarette firms because of the oligopolistic nature of the industry (Harris, 1986: 24). One example Harris gives that illustrates the oligopolistic nature of this industry is the manner in which cigarette firms deal with cigarette excise tax increases. Harris charges that the price increases for cigarettes far exceed the level justified by the tax increase. In other words, the excise tax increase is an excuse for milking the consumer. Another group that has a stake in this renewed interest in smoking and health is, of course, health care specialists. The chief spokesperson for this group of scholars is Dr. Kenneth Warner, who has been teaching at the University of Michigan's Public Health Institute since 1984 and has been secretary for the Council on Smoking Prevention since 1985. Warner has written extensively (at least fourteen articles on smoking and health since 1979) on almost every aspect of smoking prevention and has advocated all the various measures that are thought to decrease cigarette smoking, including advertising bans, smoking bans, and excise tax increases. In his articles, Warner's arguments combine an interesting blend of medical research about the effects of cigarette smoking on the health of individuals with empirical results about the effectiveness of policy measures designed to discourage cigarette smoking. Besides the "traditional" anti-smoking measures, Warner and his fellow health care scholars have also advocated some more radical solutions to the smoking and health problem. Examples of these radical proposals would be nationalization of the cigarette industry, total abolition of the price support system for tobacco (Warner, 1980: 348), and a 15-percent tax on cigarette profits to be used to finance anti-smoking advertisements (Tye, 1986: 23). Once again, it is apparent that passive smoking has given new life to an old issue—smoking and health—and enabled the anti-smoking forces to go on the offensive in order to achieve their goal of a smoke-free society.

The Cigarette Industry's Response to the Third Wave of Regulation

The reaction of the cigarette industry to the dramatic increase of government interference in the cigarette industry was to intensify the developments already taking place as a result of the second wave of regulation, but there were significant differences. The amount and type of diversification activity which has taken place since the inception of the third wave of regulation is quite different than that which occurred in the second wave. The trend toward "internationalization" becomes much more significant. Finally, a majority of the firms were simply faced with the question of when and how to exit the industry with the industry becoming even more concentrated than it had been during the second wave of regulation (see Figure 4.7).

Substitute Issues

With the advent of the passive smoking issue, the cigarette industry's argument concerning the rights of the smoker seemed to pale in comparison to the anti-smoking groups' assertion that the rights of the nonsmoker had superseded those of the cigarette smoker. No longer could a cigarette smoker or the cigarette industry claim that the only person being hurt by cigarette smoking was the cigarette smoker. While the cigarette industry pleads for tolerance of the smoker, this plea has fallen on deaf ears in regard to public policymakers. Figure 4.5 illustrated the dramatic increase

Figure 4.7
American Cigarette Industry: 1980–1993

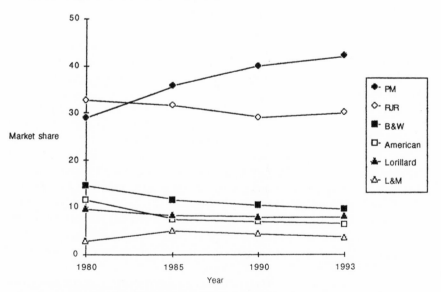

Source: Business Week, Annual Survey of the Cigarette Industry (1980–1993).

in the number of anti-smoking measures passed at the state level, and the vast majority of these measures were ones that place restrictions on where cigarette smoking was permitted. The cigarette industry had lost the "ethical" argument surrounding the cigarette controversy and now depends solely on the economic argument to justify its existence.

One of the economic arguments that the cigarette industry uses to defend itself from its critics still includes an emphasis on the income which the cigarette industry contributes to tobacco farmers, retail stores, and so on; but as the number of tobacco farmers declines and as cigarette sales decline, this argument has lost some of its impact. Another familiar economic argument that the cigarette industry continues to use is the regressivity of cigarette excise taxes along with the huge contribution that the cigarette excise taxes make to state treasuries.

However, the newest economic aspect of the cigarette industry's defense is the amount of cigarettes that are exported to other markets. Cigarettes are certainly one of the few American export successes in the 1980s, and American trade negotiators certainly made sure that markets for American cigarettes were opened throughout Europe and Asia. As a result of this export activity, cigarettes have made a significant contribution to the U.S. balance-of-payment problems. While critics dismiss this contribution as merely exporting death, State Department officials, as well as officials from the Department of Commerce, have paid close attention to the needs of cigarette firms in establishing their products in various foreign markets. But this minor success of exporting cigarettes has not mitigated the overall failure of the cigarette industries to deal with the passive smoking issue. The passive smoking issue has been the Achilles' heel of the cigarette industry and has certainly made the cigarette industry extremely defensive in dealing with public policy measures.

Barriers to Entry and Exit

Although the cigarette industry continues to deny the effects of passive smoking, the general public has become increasingly skeptical of any claims made by the industry. For the first time in its history, the legitimacy of the cigarette industry is being called into question. The cigarette firms have acquired the label "the merchants of death," which is one of the least disparaging descriptions that the industry has acquired (White, 1988).

As for the matter of access to the public policy process, the problem for the cigarette industry is not access but is the number of arenas that it has to enter. With the coming of the third wave of regulation, the cigarette industry could no longer confine to the federal level of government the major public policy measures that would affect it. The cigarette industry was forced to defend itself in nearly every state and locality, as if guerrilla warfare had been declared upon it. The vast majority of smoking prohibition laws were passed at the state and local level of government, where the cigarette industry could conjure very little sympathy for the plight of its consumers. Indeed, the individual legislator's association with cigarettes and with tobacco lobbyists was becoming increasingly strained.

The measure that the cigarette industry has found increasingly difficult to defend itself against is the large increase in cigarette excise taxes. While it has succeeded thus far in stopping the Clinton administration's call for a dollar-per-pack tax, the cigarette industry has not been able to stem the tide of large increases in state cigarette excise taxes. In 1985, state cigarette excise taxes ranged from $0.02 per pack to $0.30 per pack. By 1995, these state cigarette excise taxes had more than doubled, ranging from $0.05 per pack to $0.65 per pack (McGowan, 1995). Clearly, revenue-starved state legislators have found the cigarette industry to be a cash cow that has to be milked.

As for the ability to exit this political debate, this choice is one that is being faced by the four smaller cigarette firms that now divide slightly more than a 20-percent share of the cigarette market. Even with this small market share, the tobacco operations of these firms still remain profitable, although these profits might not be worth the risk of being involved in the many suits that have been filed against the cigarette industry claiming damage from the relatives of cigarette smokers who have died from complications due to cigarette smoking. American Brands, the original cigarette firm founded by Joseph Duke, has recently been sold to B&W. Obviously, executives at American have decided that the profits from their cigarette operations are not worth risking the rest of the firm's business portfolio should America become a target of a successful liability suit filed against the cigarette industry or if regulations become increasingly more restrictive and onerous.

Meanwhile, even though the two largest cigarette firms—PM and RJR—have diversified their portfolio of businesses, they still depend on their tobacco segments for at least 70 percent of their profits. Despite the overwhelming negative image and political pressure, they are in no position to exit the cigarette business. These two firms are as addicted to cigarettes as cigarette smokers are to the "golden weed." In their view, the cash flow resulting from cigarette operations outweighs any possible payments from losing a lawsuit.

Audience

During the third wave of regulation of the cigarette industry, the industry experienced a dramatic change in the primary audience for regulatory activity. In the two previous waves, the federal government had been the level of government where stakeholders went to do battle with the cigarette industry. As we have just seen, the state has now become the branch of government where the interactions between the cigarette industry and government take place.

Despite the passage of numerous smoking prohibition laws, as well as large cigarette excise tax increases at state level of government, the structure of the cigarette industry is the same at the end of the third wave of regulation as it was at the end of the second wave of regulation. Perhaps, the only change has been that the industry has become even more concentrated than it had been during the previous wave of regulation so that its structure now resembles the soft drink industry—two large competing firms trampling over the market share of the remaining smaller firms.

However, even with this flurry of public policy activity that has occurred throughout the third wave of regulation, the passive smoking issue has certainly not been solved to the satisfaction of the anti-smoking groups, since their goal of a smoke-free society does not seem to be achievable in the near future.

In fact, the cigarette industry, while still under relentless political pressure, is enjoying a resurgence on two fronts. First, in 1994, cigarette sales actually increased for the first time in twenty-two years, despite the increase of funds available for anti-smoking campaigns and school programs. Second, the 1994 Congressional elections produced a much more sympathetic Congress, especially in regard to any proposed hike in the federal cigarette excise tax. Thus, on both the economic and political grounds, the cigarette industry's future appears brighter.

However, the industry is once again faced with an increase in activity on the legal front. State governments are filing suits to collect damages from the firms as a result of health expenses that states incurred to treat cigarette smokers. There has also been a whole new round of liability suits filed on the behalf of cigarette smokers over the fact that the cigarette firms knew that they were selling an addictive product. It appears that what goes around comes around for the cigarette industry. As the legislative arena has become more favorable (or at least less hostile), opponents have stepped up their attacks in the judicial arena.

CONCLUSION

This chapter utilized the model of political and social analysis introduced in Chapter 3 as the vehicle to analyze the very complex but fascinating cigarette industry. Each element of the model (issue, stakeholders, substitute issues, barriers to entry and exit, and audience) made a contribution to an understanding of why a particular public measure was enacted and how the cigarette industry, its customers, and stakeholders reacted to these measures.

This analysis of the cigarette industry also illustrates three other features of the model that need to be taken into account in trying to understand the workings, the business, and public policy processes in other industries.

First, no issue has been completely resolved between the cigarette industry and its critics. The oligopolistic structure of the cigarette industry that fueled the first wave of regulation was still the target of critics of the industry in the next two waves of regulation. The issues (smoking and health and passive smoking) that started both the second and third waves of regulation have also never been resolved to the satisfaction of any of the stakeholders. In fact, the momentum of previous issues over time seems to add to the intensity of the various anti-smoking interest groups.

Second, the level of government (federal, state, and local) or audience also changed with each wave of regulation. During the first wave, the federal government—in particular, the Justice Department and the courts—provided the chief opposition to the cigarette industry. During the second wave, the federal government was still the battle for most of the public policy measures that were enacted; but the states were becoming more active, particularly in using the cigarette excise tax as a public policy instrument. Finally, during the third wave, the arena switches almost entirely to the state and local levels of government. Smoking prohibition laws were passed by state legislatures and local councils, and the cigarette excise tax was used by the states as a weapon to discourage cigarette sales and prices.

Third, there were changes in the branches of government that became involved in the cigarette controversy. The executive and judicial branches of the federal government were the most involved stakeholders for the first wave of regulation. Congress became the battlefield during the second wave of regulation, while state legislatures and courts have become the primary government voices during the third wave of regulation.

Thus, the cigarette industry has had to deal with every branch and level of government throughout its brief but turbulent history, yet issues that have confronted it have never been fully resolved to any of the stakeholders' satisfaction. Now it is time to examine an industry whose history has also had its share of government interventions and interactions, the beer industry.

Chapter 5

THE BEER INDUSTRY

The production and distribution of beer was one of the earliest commercial activities in America. Puritan leaders generally agreed that beer was a wholesome and nourishing beverage, especially in comparison to the consumption of distilled spirits such as whiskey or brandy (Baron, 1962). In Virginia, even though the wealth of the colony depended upon tobacco, John Smith's description of his new colony made special mention of the high-quality "barley from which excellent malt could be made" (Baron, 1962: 13).

Soon, however, colonial governments began viewing the commercial production of beer as an excellent source of revenue and began regulating the amounts of beer that could be brewed at home. It was this revenue issue that launched government's involvement in the beer and alcohol industries. This involvement has now gone well beyond just collecting revenue.

The involvement of government in the beer industry has had four periods. Table 5.1 provides a summary of these phases which have social, economic, and political aspects to them. As in Chapter 4, the model of political and social analysis that was developed in Chapter 3 will be utilized to describe the interactions between government and the beer industry throughout its history.

FIRST PERIOD: GOVERNMENT AND THE PRODUCTION OF BEER

Issue: The Availability of Beer

Although it sounds strange to our ears, one of the most serious problems confronting the early American colonists was what to drink. Even though New England possessed clean water (this was not the case in Virginia), the English colonists yearned for their

Table 5.1
The Four Periods of Government and Beer Industry Interactions

Time Period	Social Issues	Economic Issues	Political Issues
Colonial times to 1850	Availablity; "safe form of alcohol"	Home producers; English port or ale	Excise taxes as a source of revenue for government
1850 to 1933	Prohibition	Rise of brewing dynasties; German larger salons	Federal involvement
1933 to 1985	Tolerance	Concentration of industry; economies of scale	Age restrictions and "local" options
1985 to the present	The MADD Movement	The rise of the micro breweries	Passage of drunk driving laws by states

beer. During their journey to America, these colonists depended on beer to avoid scurvy and other vitamin-deficiency diseases. However, the crews of the ships that had taken the colonists were not willing to part with their beer for their voyage back to England, and so they left the colonists beerless.

This problem—the lack of beer—had to be solved, and the early colonial leaders (including the Puritan leaders of New England) permitted colonists to brew their own beer. The type of beer for which the colonists had developed a preference was English porter or ale. It was the traditional drink of the English working class. But the single-vat home breweries that produced the vast majority of beer up to the early 1700s were hardly efficient, nor did they produce the quality of porter or ale that the colonists had drunk in England. Eventually, commercial breweries developed. These breweries could brew beer in greater quantities and at less cost, since they could buy the malt and hops from England needed to make beer. This advantage would be maintained even after the colonists were able to grow the barley and hops needed for the production of beer. The primary centers of colonial brewing became Philadelphia and New York, and beer from these two brewing centers was shipped to nearby villages and towns. Philadelphia's beer became the standard of excellence in the area of the city and in the South (particularly in Virginia), while New York's beer had New England as its chief export market, although the Adams family of Boston did develop a reputation for producing quality beer.

However, as soon as the beer industry had been established, it was viewed by local and state governments as a source of revenue that could be tapped in order to provide desperately needed funds. The controversy was to run much deeper than merely the idea of taxing commercial beer. The brewers maintained that it was unfair to tax their product if home brewers did not have to pay taxes on their production also. Thus, the beer industry brought to the local and state levels of government the same question that was facing the early federal government: What should government's role be toward the developing industry? Should government help to develop the struggling beer industry, or should it use its taxing power which might lead to its demise? The question was not whether someone should be able to drink beer but, rather, how beer was to be provided and taxed.

Stakeholders

The issue of the availability of beer had two sets of stakeholders. The first was represented by Thomas Jefferson, a great advocate of home beer production, who was famous for the beer he brewed. His dream was of a nation of "free" self-sufficient farmers who could provide for all of their needs and would no longer be dependent on European influences. Jefferson had no doubt that every farmer, or at least every region, could develop a unique tasting beer.

Meanwhile, Alexander Hamilton was the leader of those forces that demanded that American industries had to be developed so they would no longer depend on European imports. It is interesting to note that both men wanted to rid the new nation of dependence on European goods, but the means that they wished to achieve this independence by pitted an ideal agrarian community of self-sufficient farmers against a developing native American industry that could compete with British or European imports. The beer industry was merely one of many potential industries that was caught in the crossfire of two different scenarios for the future of the newly independent United States.

Substitute Issues

Besides developing native industries, advocates for the fledgling beer industry used another argument against the imposition of an excise tax upon their product. In 1789, future-President Madison persuaded the House of Representatives to limit the tax on beer to 8 cents per barrel because "this low rate will be such an encouragement as to induce the manufacture and use of beer in every State of the Union" (Jackson, 1986: 208). Monroe believed that beer was a "healthy" form of alcohol, and he wanted to show this support through the imposition of low taxation. We have already seen that the earliest settlers viewed beer as a source of food and vitamins. Beer advocates also portrayed their product as the preferable form of alcohol because its alcoholic content was much less than either distilled spirits or even wine. Throughout early American history, leaders such as Jefferson and Monroe bemoaned the amount of drunkenness that resulted from the consumption of whiskey. Since wine was strictly the alcoholic drink of the well-to-do, its consumption was never questioned. However, our leaders thought that beer consumption certainly ought to be encouraged, since it was viewed as a form of alcohol that could entertain without leading to addiction or loss of time working. The newly formed commercial brewers maintained that they were providing a public service by making beer available to all and, hence, should not be taxed unfairly. While these new brewers did not avoid taxation, they did set the precedent (which still remains today) of taxing beer at much lower rates than other alcohol products.

Barriers to Entry and Exit

As we have seen, the ability of the fledgling beer industry to enter into the public policy process depended upon the case it could make that its product was a "necessity." It made its case using two arguments that have been repeated many times throughout American history. First, the industry should be developed in order to free the country from foreign dominance. This argument is often used to justify tariffs on foreign goods. The second argument was "public good"—the consumption of beer was deemed a better alternative than the consumption of distilled spirits especially whiskey. A product should be offered because it is deemed the better of two evils. Once again, this is an argument that has been used repeatedly in American history. For example, anti-gun control groups maintain that it should be the choice of every citizen to be free to buy a gun in order to defend himself or herself from criminals who obtain guns illegally.

Audience

The controversy that surrounded the beer industry during this period was its right to exist and what level of government would regulate it. The beer industry was successful in establishing its right to exist. It should be noted that during this first phase of government interactions, the beer industry faced no religious opposition. The opposition it did face was based on ideological purity, and these opponents did not favor any sort of prohibition. While the beer industry did have to accept an excise tax on its product, it could count on its own consumers to make sure that the tax remain small. It was an industry that produced traditional English porter and ale and, in general, had the support of the public, since it was able to separate itself from the other segments of the alcohol industry—in particular, distilled spirits. All of this was about to change, however, as the beer industry entered its second phase of government regulation.

SECOND PERIOD: PROHIBITION

Issue: The Legality of Drinking Beer or Any Alcoholic Beverage

This second phase of interactions between government and the beer industry was characterized by a number of changes, both in the beer industry and the level of government that regulated it. These changes were to lead to one of the most disastrous social experiments in the history of the United States.

The primary reason that there were drastic changes in the U.S. beer industry from 1850 to 1933 was immigration; in particular, German immigrants. While there were many other immigrant groups such as the Irish, Italians, Poles, and so on during this period, it was the Germans who took a keen interest in the beer industry. These German immigrants brought with them a well-developed taste for lager beer. Lager beer differed from the English beer and ale in two respects. First, lager beer used hops that gave the beer an amber color as opposed to the dark colors of English beer and ale. Second, the German techniques resulted in a lighter, sweeter beer than traditional English beer and ales. It was this German beer that became very popular with the other immigrant groups and eventually became the favorite type of beer of the majority of beer drinkers.

This rise in popularity of German beer caused a profound change in the brewing industry. No longer would the big city breweries merely supplement the homebrews of farmers and rural locations. With the rise of lager beer, German breweries in the big cities dominated the production and distribution of beer. German brewers such as Schlitz (Milwaukee), Anheuser–Busch (St. Louis), Hamm (Minneapolis), Schmidt (Philadelphia), Ballantine (Newark), and the

Schmidts of Olympia (Washington State) sold the bulk of their beer within a wagon ride of their breweries, but they were not content with merely selling beer; they also operated their own saloons in urban areas dominated by immigrant populations. These German brewing firms were fully vertically integrated ventures. They grew their own grain, hops, and barley; transported their beer; and sold it in their own saloons. The net result, even with a limited geographic market, was the formation of brewing dynasties (Krebs and Orthwein, 1953: 62).

The prosperity of the brewers was quite evident and, at times, a cause of public scandal. For example, in celebrating their golden wedding anniversary, Adolphus Busch crowned his wife, Lilly Anheuser with a $200,000 diamond diadem, and they ate on plates worth $1,000 each. Such ostentatious shows of wealth provoked a great negative reaction from the Puritan American society, especially when the source of wealth was such a common product. The beer industry had developed into a lucrative business that was dominated by immigrant Germans who supplied lager beer to their fellow immigrants, and it was looked upon with increasing alarm by the established American society (Krebs and Orthwein, 1953: 78).

Stakeholders

Throughout the late 1800s and into the early twentieth century, urban unrest had become a major concern of the public and its representatives. This unrest was centered in urban areas populated by the newly arrived immigrants, and the vast majority of this unrest had its start in the saloon. These immigrants were resented by the native population for two reasons: (1) the economic competition that caused wages to be held down; and (2) the religious differences, in particular, the dramatic rise in the number of Roman Catholics. Thus, the Prohibition movement (which sought to eliminate the drinking of all forms of alcohol) was fueled by a number of factors. First, there was genuine concern over the amount of alcohol being consumed and the violence associated with drinking that occurred both in the streets and in the homes of the immigrants. Second, the "Know Nothing" movement (which decried the rise of Rum and Romanism associated with immigrants) also latched on to the Prohibition movement as a vehicle to further its own anti-immigrant aims.

There were also economic interests that helped support the Prohibition movement. For example, both Henry Ford and John Rockefeller gave substantial amounts of money to support the movement, though they themselves did not drink alcohol and viewed the drinking of their employees as inefficient and dangerous to the goal of their businesses.

Thus, the Prohibition movement was supported by a curious mixture of religious, social, and economic elements. It was a movement that also had Jeffersonian roots, in that it longed for a simpler and agrarian America, where the yeoman farmer provided the American ideal. The rise of the cities with their huge immigrant populations and their alien religions were to be opposed, and the closing of the saloon became the ultimate goal of their movement.

The other major stakeholder in the Prohibition movement was government. Previously, government's interest in the beer industry, as well as other forms of alcohol, was as a source of revenue; but not in prohibiting its use. However, with the rise of the Prohibition movement, government's interest in alcohol was to change radically. This anti-alcohol movement demanded that government curb the use of alcohol. Early in the movement, it was the states that were the target of the demands of the Prohibition movement. Some states forbade the sale of distilled spirits such as whiskey and rum, while other states restricted the alcoholic content in beer from 4 percent to 2.1 percent (Clark, 1976: 33). Meanwhile, southern states such as Mississippi and Alabama banned the sale of alcohol completely and became known as "dry" states.

The Prohibition movement was not satisfied with the success it was having at the state level of government. The chief complaint that the Prohibitionists had was over the smuggling of beer, wine, and distilled spirits from "wet" states into "dry" states. With the outbreak of World War I and the accompanying anti-German sentiment, the Prohibition movement moved to established itself on the federal level. It gathered so much momentum that the prohibition question became the test issue for every political candidate. Those political candidates who wanted the individual to be free to choose whether they consumed alcohol were subjected to intense political pressure. The Prohibition era was certainly not one which tolerated "the right to choose."

Substitute Issues

The beer industry and its German owners were faced with an interesting dilemma in trying to stem the tide of Prohibition. Certainly, they could not condone either public drunkenness or the violence associated with alcohol abuse. Yet, in dealing with legislators who were faced with a public demand to do something about the alcohol problem, the beer industry was hoping to work toward some sort of compromise position.

This compromise position involved the portrayal of beer as the "healthy," all-American form of alcohol while banning the consumption of other forms of alcohol such as whiskey and rum. In order to achieve this status of being the "tolerated" form of alcohol, the beer industry engaged in various activities. First, the beer industry financed various displays of patriotism as well as submitting to the doubling of the excise tax on beer in 1898 to help finance the Spanish–American War. Second, the numerous brewing dynasties built restaurants that served only beer and wine. The buildings that housed these restaurants were often built as landmarks, such as windmills, gardens, and playgrounds. An example of this type of restaurant which was meant to be a socially acceptable alternative to the notorious saloons was Bevo Mill, built in southern St. Louis by the Busch family. Finally, the beer industry made endless presentations concerning the impracticality of imposing a ban on a product that so many individuals enjoyed consuming. It was perhaps the first industry to engage in the politics of "choice." Overall, the beer industry's strategy in dealing with the threat of Prohibition was a blend of economic, social, and practical reasoning. However, these arguments did not prevail, as they could not withstand the moral and religious fervor of the Prohibition movement.

Barriers to Entry and Exit

Throughout the late 1800s and early 1900s, the beer industry's ability to combat the prohibition issue was easily lost at the state level of government, especially in the southeast section of the United States. In the areas that were lost to the beer industry, the industry failed to distinguish its product from other alcoholic products. The key to access to the political process for the beer industry was to establish the legitimacy of beer as the healthy form of alcohol.

With the outbreak of World War I and its accompanying anti-German sentiments, the forces of Prohibition saw a golden opportunity to bring the issue to the federal agenda. The production of beer was labeled as a German and anti-American activity. Also, the beer industry's abandonment of its fellow producers of alcohol weakened the entire alcohol industry's ability to deal with the powerful forces that were pushing the Prohibitionist agenda. Even though the executive branch of the federal government (from Theodore Roosevelt to Franklin Roosevelt) was never sympathetic to the goal of prohibition, Congress was overwhelmingly in its favor. By 1919, the beer industry's ability to mobilize its economic and political power was completely negated, and the passage of the Volstead Act was assured.

Audience

The federal government was clearly the primary audience for regulatory activity during this second period of regulation of the beer industry. Obviously, the federal Prohibition law had catastrophic consequences for the beer industry. Those breweries that survived began making "near-beer"—nonalcoholic beer—as well as other malted beverages. Needless to say, sales of these products did not approach those of beer.

Nonetheless, the brewers had proved to be surprisingly maladroit in their public relations. They did not form political alliances with other producers of alcohol, nor did they provide sufficient support for politicians who were sympathetic to their survival. But above all, the beer industry failed to take seriously the political power which the Prohibition movement could bring to the political process. The alcohol industry, especially the beer industry, regarded Prohibitionists as mere fanatics who could be bought off eventually. But the outbreak of war and its resultant anti-immigrant sentiment, combined with the financial muscle of industry captains such as Ford, Carnegie, and Rockefeller, proved more than a match to the meager forces that the alcohol industry could muster.

THIRD PERIOD: TOLERANCE

Issue: Restoration of the Beer Industry

In 1933, the fourteen-year national experiment with Prohibition was ended with the repeal of the Volstead Act—but the beer industry that would be resurrected would be much different than the one that was buried with Prohibition.

Even before the passage of Prohibition, the beer industry had started to consolidate. In 1910, there were still more than 1,500 breweries that were small, local enterprises. In 1934, there were 756 breweries in operation in the United States. This number would be reduced to fewer than 200 breweries in 1959, with fewer than 100 operating by 1985. There are numerous reasons for this radical decline in the number of breweries and in the structure of the U.S. beer industry during this period from 1933 to 1985. The first major decline in the number of breweries from 1500 to 756 in the first few years after Prohibition can be attributed to the demise of those breweries that lacked the financial resources or substitute products to survive the period when they could not produce beer (Baron, 1962: 323). However, for the rest of the period, this consolidation of the beer industry was a result of "economies of scales," both in production and, especially, in the huge budgets that were needed for promotion and advertising at the national level. This national advertising made it possible for an increasing uniformity of taste which, in turn, permitted brewers to acquire other breweries and simply manufacture the same brand in various parts of the country; or even ship beer to all parts of the country, due to the advances in transportation. Thus, the beer industry experienced a great deal of vertical and horizontal integration.

The demographics of the U.S. population were also quite favorable to the beer industry during this period. For most of this period, the median age of the country was falling. Since the majority of beer is bought by the age group between 18 to 35, the age of the baby boomer was indeed a golden age for the U.S. beer industry. Beer sales throughout this period increased dramatically while the number of brewers decreased dramatically. Obviously, this is a situation where the firms that survived the initial "shakedown" found themselves in a lucrative position.

Stakeholders

Since the repeal of Prohibition, a new view of problems with alcohol has emerged that differs from either the colonial or the temperance views. This view holds that excessive drinking is a chronic disease known as alcoholism. For the first time in American history, the use of alcohol was viewed from its health consequences rather than solely as an economic or social problem. Neither the drinker nor alcohol is intrinsically evil, rather, the problem is inherent in a person's genes. According to this health perspective, most people can drink with no risk, but a minority cannot drink without succumbing to the disease of alcoholism. Thus, the problems of drinking can be cured by these individuals abstaining from alcohol rather than forcing an entire society to experience Prohibition.

But this new emphasis on the health aspects of alcohol did not preclude the traditional arguments that were used in the two earlier periods. These views were reflected in what can be termed the *alcoholic beverage control* movements. The vast majority of states established either an ABC (Alcoholic Beverage Commission) or LCB (Liquor Control Board). These boards or commissions were given the charge to shape the context in which drinking took place in order to minimize its harmful consequences.

Yet, it was the new health perspective that lies at the heart of such organizations as Alcoholics Anonymous. It has also found expression at the level of federal government with the establishment of the National Institute on Alcohol Abuse and Alcoholism (NIAAA), which was founded in 1971. The NIAAA sponsors research on alcohol abuse and alcoholism. Other medical organizations such as the American Medical Association, American Cancer Society, and American Heart Society also became involved in publicizing the health problems associated with the use of alcohol (Olson, 1985: 8).

Thus, the fifty-year period that followed Prohibition brought a new and different set of stakeholders for the beer and alcohol industry to engage in the public policy process. The emphasis of the new stakeholders, such as Alcoholics Anonymous and the American Medical Association, is on the possible negative health consequences. They are not ideologues, nor are their objections to alcohol in any way radical. Meanwhile, the traditional temperance organizations such as the Anti-Saloon League, with their moral and social objections to drinking, remained; but their strength and political clout were diminished.

Substitute Issues

Since the primary issue that brewers faced during this post-Prohibition era was acceptance or tolerance of its product, the beer industry once again embarked on a campaign to established its product as the alcoholic beverage of "moderation."

Another social trend seems also to have favored the beer industry during the re-establishment of beer drinking. With the advent of canned and bottled beer, beer drinkers were drinking the vast majority of their beer in the home rather than at a tavern. The beer industry sought to encourage this trend and a writer for *Brewery Age* took note of this development by commenting:

Those who prefer to drink their beer in taverns will always find that source open to them. But in our advertising to the typical beer drinker, we should encourage the development of home drinking and increased moderation and temperance. (*Brewery Age*, 1935)

The beer industry also wished to have its product associated with healthy activities, especially sports. In keeping with this theme, the beer industry formed a marriage with the newest form of mass communication—television—and sponsored large numbers of televised sporting events. Some of the substantial brewers such as Anheuser–Busch and Coors even bought their own baseball teams. The advent of Monday night football was made possible by the initial sponsorship of Miller Beer which used the opportunity to introduce to the public a healthy beer; namely, Miller Lite.

Once again, the beer industry was trying to separate itself from its other alcoholic cousins, especially wine and distilled spirits. No longer was the beer industry running saloons or other outlets for its product, but it was now diversifying into other activities where it could portray its product as a natural, all-American beverage.

Barriers to Entry and Exit

With the end of Prohibition also came the end of direct involvement of the federal government in regulating beer production and distribution. While the federal government imposed excise taxes on beer and other alcoholic beverages, it turned the regulation of the distribution and consumption of alcoholic beverages completely over to the states. Thus, the ability of the firms in the alcohol industries to enter the public policy process depended upon their ability to influence state legislators as well as the state beverage control commissions, which were usually controlled by governors.

The types of post-Prohibition era regulations that the alcohol industry faced can be broken down into four categories: (1) age restrictions, (2) where and how much a person can buy alcoholic products, (3) penalties for drunk driving, and (4) excise taxes. The rationale behind the first three types of measures was to "ration" the use of alcohol, while the fourth, excise taxes, performed a dual role of being "revenue enhancements" and rationing alcohol consumption by raising the price of alcoholic beverages.

What makes state regulation of the alcohol industry unique is the variety of regulation and the differences between states in trying to regulate alcohol consumption. A classic example of the multitude of different regulations is the various age restrictions that states imposed on alcoholic consumption. During the post-Prohibition era, every state in the United States had a minimum drinking age, ranging from eighteen to twenty-one. By 1985, three states had set the minimum age at eighteen, twelve set the limit at nineteen, two set the limit at twenty, and thirty-four (including the District of Columbia) set the limit at twenty-one. However, ten of the states that maintained twenty-one-year-old limits permitted beer sales to eighteen- or nineteen-year-olds. Once again, beer is perceived as the least dangerous of alcoholic beverages.

Another area where there is a variety of state regulation concerning alcohol consumption involves the places where someone can buy alcohol and how much and what type of alcohol someone can buy. Two states (New Hampshire and Pennsylvania) completely control the retail market for wine and distilled spirits, while some states permit the selling of beer and wine in supermarkets. The majority of states permit retail sales of beer, wine, and distilled spirits in privately-operated retail shops. It is also interesting to note that it is illegal for bars and taverns to sell beer or any type of alcoholic beverages to customers for consumption off-premises. The rationale behind all these restrictions is to control the sales of alcoholic beverages, in particular, to underage drinkers.

Another area where states have displayed a surprising degree of variety are the definitions they used to define drunk driving and the penalties they impose on drunk drivers. Once again, every state has declared that people should not drive while drunk; but in some states, a person with a blood alcohol content (BAC) of .08 percent would be considered a drunk driver, while in other states, a person's BAC would have to reach .1 percent to be considered a drunk driver. Hence, in general, to be considered intoxicated in most states, a person who has not recently eaten has to drink at least four to five ounces of alcohol within an hour. This level of alcoholic consumption is rare for the vast majority of Americans. Meanwhile, the penalties for drunk driving use a mixture of loss of driving privileges, fines, and, in extreme cases, jail time. Once again, the penalties for drunk driving vary significantly from state to state. However, as we will see, the trend in the next period of regulation of the alcohol industry will be for states to impose much stronger penalties for drunk driving.

The final measure that government can use to reduce the consumption of alcohol, in particular, beer, is the excise tax. An increase in excise taxes for alcoholic products obviously results in higher prices for these products. Research has shown that higher prices for beer can significantly reduce the amount that people drink (McGowan, 1992). These price-induced decreases in beer consumption have in turn been linked to declines in the incidence of drunk driving and alcohol related diseases (Olson, 1985: 40).

Yet, throughout this third period of regulation, the price of alcohol has been falling with respect to the price of other goods. A substantial part of this decline was due to federal and state taxes on alcohol not having kept up with the rate of inflation. Another curious aspect associated with alcohol excise taxes is that different forms of alcohol are taxed at different rates. Distilled spirits are taxed much more heavily than beer and wine. During the third period of alcohol regulation, liquor was taxed at 19 cents per ounce, wine at 6 cents per ounce, and beer at 1 cent per ounce. Once again, beer has been perceived by public policymakers as the "good" form of alcohol—thus, the other forms are taxed at a higher rate.

It appears that the beer industry did an extremely good job of reestablishing its political agenda after the repeal of Prohibition. Vital to promoting sales of its product, the industry was relatively successful in these two areas: (1) It was able to hold down excise tax increases, thereby holding down its prices, particularly as the baby-boomer generation was coming of age to drink beer; and (2) the beer industry was able to persuade legislators to permit sales of its products in many more locations than there were before Prohibition.

Audience

The end of Prohibition marked the end of direct regulation of the beer industry by the federal government. The period of more than fifty years after the repeal of Prohibition was, in many ways, the golden age for the alcohol industry, especially the beer segment of the industry. Sales boomed as a result of a number of factors, including: (1) demographics, (2) a much greater public tolerance of alcohol, and (3) weak and conflicting public policy measures that failed to hold down beer consumption.

The beer industry, as well as the wine and distilled spirits industries, had re-established their markets as well as their political legitimacy. The structures of these industries had also become much more oligopolistic. The beer and the distilled spirits industries had become quite concentrated. Figure 5.1 shows how, essentially, the beer industry had developed into a duopoly with Anheuser–Busch and Miller dominating the industry. The primary reason for this consolidation was the economies of scales in both production and advertising to establish a national presence.

Figure 5.1
1984 Market Share in the U.S. Beer Industry

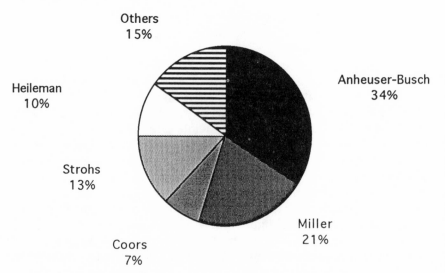

Source: Jobson's Beer Handbook.

However, this period of growth, tolerance, and lax regulation was about to change for the beer industry. The next section will examine the forces behind these changes and how the beer industry and the other segments of the alcohol industry tried to deal with these new developments in their relations with public policymakers.

FOURTH PERIOD: MADD MOVEMENT

Issue: Curbing Drunk Driving

In describing the first three periods of the relationship between the alcohol industry and government, policy measures involved a conflict of values. Many people who were usually inspired by fundamentalist religious principles viewed drinking as immoral or, at least, morally weak. Others viewed drinking as a sign of liberation or tolerance, and a means by which a person could relax and socialize. In the second period, the immoral point of view won over public policymakers, while in the first and third periods, the tolerance point of view prevailed.

However, starting in 1985, a third point of view developed. Nongovernment and nonreligious grassroots organizations such as MADD, Remove Intoxicated Drivers (RID), and Students against Drunk Driving (SADD) began to spring up to combat the problem of drunk driving. These groups did not advocate a return to Prohibition, nor did they view the consumption of alcohol as immoral. However, these groups did press public policymakers to enact statutes and impose penalties (such as jail sentences for repeat offenders, much more substantial fines, and lowering the BAC as to what would constitute drunk driving) that would make drunk drivers more responsible for their actions while they were driving under the influence of alcohol. None of these groups were viewed as radical by either the media or public, and their moderate point of view forced the alcohol industry to deal with a very different type of opponent.

Stakeholders

In the previous section, we saw how much of the drunk-driving issue was introduced by a variety of new stakeholders such as MADD, RID, and SADD. Other groups that have joined in with the MADD movement would be the traditional stakeholders who are involved in health organizations (American Medical Association, American Cancer and Heart Societies) and religious organizations who oppose any consumption of alcohol.

There is also one other major stakeholder that became involved in this prevention of drunk driving—the insurance industry. Drunk driving was a major contributor to the problem of traffic accidents, and the insurance industry was forced to pay the costs of the accidents. As a result, the insurance industry provided MADD, along with the other anti-drunk-driving organizations, with both financial and political support. Thus, the various segments of the alcohol industry were facing an opponent who could easily match them in both financial and political might at the state and federal levels of government.

The alcohol industry is not without allies during this era. Restaurant and tavern owners, as well as retail shops, that sell alcoholic beverages can be counted on to provide help to the alcohol industry, especially at the state and local levels of government. Other sources of support for the alcohol industry would include labor unions (especially those workers that are involved in the production and distribution of alcoholic products) and other businesses that derive sales from the sale and use of alcohol.

Substitute Issues

The issue of drunk driving poses a unique problem for the alcohol industry. Obviously, the industry could not make a case for drunk driving, nor could the alcohol industry portray the advocates of stricter drunk-driving laws as religious fanatics. The leaders of MADD and related groups have the ability of government to keep drunk drivers off the highways as their secular concern. While the groups are not in favor of Prohibition, the public policy measures which they advocate could have a detrimental effect on alcohol sales.

The alcohol industry has responded to various public policy measures advocated by MADD and related groups in two ways. First, the alcohol industry emphasizes the economic contributions the industry makes. If sales of alcohol are negatively affected by the passage of strict drunk-driving laws, then there would be severe economic consequences. Suppliers who produce agricultural commodities such as wheat, corn, and barley, as well as the producers of glass and aluminum, would suffer from a decrease in alcohol sales. Customers such as taverns and restaurants, as well as other producers, would lose sales on products with which they have traditionally experienced very high profits. Since these businesses are local by nature, they wield a great deal of power in state legislatures.

The theme of moderation is the other argument that the industry employs to derail public policy measures which could excessively discourage drinking. In response to the MADD movement, alcohol advertising has begun to emphasize the joys of moderate drinking. The alcohol industry has even begun to sponsor free meals at restaurants and taverns for those at a table who agree not to drink and be the designated driver. The industry has also agreed with proposals to ban "happy hours" as well as other promotional activities which involve the consumption of large quantities of alcohol. In others words, the alcohol industry has tried to make the argument that it can police itself—that another "prohibition" is not needed nor would it work.

Barriers to Entry and Exit

In the previous section, we saw how the alcohol industry as a whole has developed other issues to deal with the MADD movement. In reality, access to the public policy process differs greatly for each of the segments of the alcohol industry, as well as the level of government preparing to deal with the drunk-driving issue.

The majority of drunk-driving laws are being passed at the state level of government. For example, the lowering of BAC levels, as well as substantial fines and jail sentences for drunk driving, are the purview of state legislatures. In dealing with these measures, all three segments (beer, wine, and distilled spirits) of the alcohol industry have united with their other allied stakeholders in trying to lessen the consequences of these measures. It should be mentioned that the negative effect of these drunk-driving laws on the sales of distilled spirits is much more pronounced than it is on beer and wine sales (McGowan, 1992). It is also interesting to note that advertising for the beer industry has consistently stressed slogans such as "Know when to say when" and "Good friends don't let friends drive drunk." Hence, it appears that the beer industry has less to lose in the passage of drunk-driving laws. The passage of these laws might even help beer sales (McGowan, 1992).

At the federal level, the primary issue that faced the entire alcohol industry was the change in the legal age to purchase alcohol from eighteen to twenty-one years old for all states. While the MADD movement has conducted extensive campaigns to discourage underage drinking, it was the insurance industry that provided the impetus for the change in legal age for drinking. The insurance industry was able to assemble greater pressure on the federal level than the alcohol industry. This is because the insurance industry was stronger at the federal level in terms of political influence. Hence, the insurance industry was able to get a "states-rights" Reagan administration to pass a federal law that superseded state control over age limits.

The final issue that faced the alcohol industry was the increase in the excise tax rate for alcoholic products. It was pointed out previously that distilled spirits are taxed at a much higher rate than beer and wine. Yet, any proposed increase in the excise tax rate on alcohol is fiercely fought by the beer industry. While the other two segments of the alcohol industry are not in favor of excise tax increases, they know that their sales are not negatively affected by excise tax increases. Meanwhile, the beer industry is well aware that the majority of its sales are to the age group between eighteen and thirty-five, and this age group is much more sensitive to price increases because of excise tax increases (McGowan, 1992). In fighting excise tax increases, the beer industry has been much more successful at the state level while the federal government doubled the excise tax on alcohol in 1991. Once again, the beer industry has become a tempting target for revenue-starved legislators in the 1995 budget proposals.

Audience

With the start of the MADD movement, the beer industry once again had to face the regulatory activities of state governments. Throughout the MADD movement, the beer industry (as well as the rest of the alcohol industry) has experienced a relatively flat market for its product. One cause for this lack of growth is in demographics. As the baby boomers aged, the amount of alcohol which they imbibed has declined. The market for alcoholic beverages was further reduced with the raising of the legal drinking age to twenty-one throughout the United States (*Value Line*, February 21, 1992).

The MADD movement itself has promoted a much less tolerant view of alcohol use, and has forced public policymakers to enact various measures at the state level of government that have not only affected beer consumption, but also the structure of the brewing industry. The two primary weapons that state officials use to regulate the beer industry are the excise tax and the passage of drunk-driving laws. These approaches have a differential impact on the beer industry, and we will discuss them in the next section.

Throughout the period of 1985 to 1995, alcohol excise taxes have been raised by most states in order to raise revenue as well as to discourage the use of alcohol (Cook and Moore, 1994). The effect of these increases has had its most pronounced effect on beer sales (McGowan, 1992). Besides providing the impetus for a decrease in beer sales, this excise tax increase has led beer consumers to "trade down" from premium-priced products to popular-priced products over the past decade. This trade-down trend has served, in turn, to further consolidation in the beer industry (Figure 5.2).

When Figure 5.2 is compared to Figure 5.1, it is apparent that the spectacular growth in the Anheuser–Busch market share from

Figure 5.2
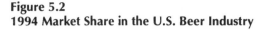
1994 Market Share in the U.S. Beer Industry

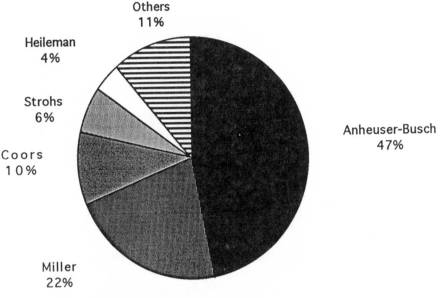

Source: Jobson's Beer Handbook.

34 percent to 47 percent has been accomplished at the expense of Stroh, Heileman, and Pabst. The primary reason why Anheuser–Busch was able to achieve this growth in market share is the economies of scale which it has achieved both in brewing and in its advertising and promotional activities. It appears that one of the unforeseen consequences of alcohol excise tax increases is a further consolidation of the brewing industry.

We have also commented on how the passage of stricter drunk-driving laws has created a less tolerant attitude toward the use of alcoholic beverages. In response to this trend, the beer industry has tried to portray itself once again as the alcoholic drink of moderation. For the large brewers such as Anheuser–Busch, Miller, and Coors, this campaign has been a bit too successful. This trend toward moderation, along with the aging of the baby-boomer generation, has opened the beer market to a new type of competitor—the micro-brewery. Figure 5.3 illustrates the explosive growth in the number of these firms in the past ten years.

Although micro-breweries currently account for a 1.5-percent market share, their sales have been expanding at an eye-popping rate of at least 50 percent annually. It is the only segment of the beer industry that experienced any growth for the past ten years. The typical consumer is between twenty-five and forty-five years

Figure 5.3
Growth in Micro-Breweries

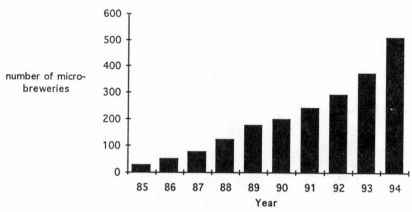

Source: Jobson's Beer Handbook.

old and affluent, with median income of $75,000, the majority having graduate school experience (Argus Research Corporation, 1993). However, these micro-breweries face their own problems with public policymakers. Many states have rigid regulations that separate the brewing, distributing, and retailing of beer and other alcoholic beverages. For example, Michigan has the "three-tier" system, which prohibits brewers from distributing their own beer, keeps distributors from owning a stake in either breweries or retail outlets, and forbids retailers from brewing or distributing beer ("Michigan's Lag with Microbreweries," 1994). However, many states, such as California, Massachusetts, Oregon, and Washington, are starting to loosen these requirements, so the future of micro-breweries appears to be quite bright.

Another segment of the beer industry that has benefited from this trend toward moderation is imports. In 1994, the imported beers reached their highest level in seven years, with nearly 5.5 percent of the U.S. malt beverage market. The leader among imported brands continues to be Heineken, with 23 percent of the import market; and Corona Extra from Mexico, its nearest competitor, with about half of Heineken's market share (*Jobson's Beer Handbook*, 1994).

CONCLUSION

As the brewing industry enters the twenty-first century, it is faced with a number of dilemmas; some new, while others are the same ones it has encountered throughout its history in the United States.

First, the brewing industry has to determine what its relationship will be with the rest of the alcohol industry. Should it join forces with the wine and distilled spirits segments of the alcohol industry in combating future public policy initiatives that would further restrict advertising and other promotional activities? Or should the beer industry try to portray itself as the alcoholic beverage of fun and moderation, distancing itself from its industry cousins? How does the brewing industry build additional tolerance for its product?

The second area of concern for the beer industry centers around the excise tax issue. It is these increases that posed the greatest public policy threat to increases in sales. Since the vast majority of states are searching for additional revenue to balance their budgets, how should the beer industry deal with ever increasing demands to raise alcohol excise taxes? Should the industry continue its dual argument that excise taxes are a regressive form of taxation that unduly targets middle-class working people who drink beer, and that these taxes put an undue burden on an industry that makes significant economic contributions not only in terms of sales, but in the contributions it makes to its suppliers and customers?

The final area of concern is how do multibillion-dollar firms such as Anheuser–Busch and Miller compete with small micro-breweries without being subjected to attack on antitrust grounds? While these beer giants seem to be gaining market share, this increase cannot be translated into profits. The highly profitable, high-premium segment of the beer industry is rapidly being taken over by the micro-breweries and import brewers. These brewing industry giants can take two courses of action: (1) Create new products to combat the micro-brewers and importers so that they can reclaim this lucrative part of the beer business; or (2) lobby state legislators to enforce existing legislation that separates the brewing, distributing, and retailing functions of the beer industry. The danger in successfully implementing either of the above policies is that these giants could be perceived as "crushing the small competitors," and there could be a public outcry for officials to initiate antitrust actions.

Overall, the future of the beer industry will involve frequent interactions with government, especially at the state level. The issues will center around availability and making beer drinkers responsible for their own actions. The issue of how to deter underage drinking will also pose some dilemmas for the beer industry, since the majority of its customers range between eighteen and thirty-five years old. How the beer industry deals with the MADD movement with its moderation theme rather than a prohibitionist mentality will no doubt determine how the industry will fare with society as a whole and its public regulators in the foreseeable future.

Chapter 6

THE BANKING INDUSTRY

In Chapters 4 and 5, the industries (cigarettes and beer) that were analyzed provided a consumer product of a controversial nature where technological change, competition, and consumer tastes determined the structure of the market and the size of the competitors that make up the industry. We also witnessed how various public policy measures also had an effect on the structure of these markets. While some of these public policy interventions were intended, many others were unintended consequences of public policy initiatives.

The commercial banking industry differs from these the two previous industries in that it provides services to its depositors and borrowers. First, commercial banks provide depositors with checking accounts and other transfers of funds while providing the accounting that accompany them. The second function of a commercial bank is to provide loans to business and credit-worthy borrowers. A bank's profitability is simply the difference in the interest rate it charges borrowers as opposed to what it pays depositors.

The basic problem that banks face, however, is that their liabilities are short term, while their loans are long term. Thus, if the public fears that banks cannot meet their deposit obligations, large withdrawals can occur. If these withdrawals are substantial enough, they could force the banks to default on their obligations in what is called a "run on the bank." This type of situation has occurred frequently in banking history.

All commercial banking activity (as well as other forms of banking) depends on the consent of the government. The history of banking is largely a chronicle of struggles between bankers seeking to maximize their profits and the government seeking to ensure the public of the banks' safety and to limit the power of these banks. Besides this conflict between government and the banks, the commercial banking industry has also been the subject of endless struggles between the federal and state governments over who should control commercial banking.

Both of these conflicts have been instrumental in molding the current structure of banking and the way it is regulated. They have colored the way the public views the banking industry. Finally, they have set the stage for banking's current dilemmas and future debates on the role of the banking industry in a deregulated financial-services industry.

As in Chapters 4 and 5, there will be a brief historical account of the various types of government interventions along with the banking industry's reaction to these interventions. While this chapter will focus on commercial banking, it will become readily apparent that it also applies to other forms of banking, such as savings and loans and investment banking. Table 6.1 summarizes the various episodes of involvement between the commercial banking industry and government. As in Chapters 4 and 5, the model of social and political analysis that was developed in Chapter 3 will be utilized in order to describe the interactions between government and the commercial banking industry throughout its history.

FIRST PERIOD OF REGULATION (1781–1863)

Issue: Banks as the Creators of Money

As the colonial economy developed, one of the major dilemmas facing it was the need to develop a money supply that could expand commerce. The traditional functions of money as a store of value, a unit of account, and a medium of exchange were either missing or the colonists were forced to use British money in order to pay for imported goods (Hildreth, 1968: 16).

The inadequacy of the barter system soon became apparent to the colonists when the British demanded payment in their pound sterling. What little money there was in circulation had to be used to pay for imported British goods. Thus, if the colonists wanted to develop their own industries (and the degree of specialization that they entailed), they also needed to develop a money supply so that both farmers and tradesmen could be free to produce a plentiful supply of the goods and services in which they had developed a specialty.

The question then became for the colonists: What would serve as money? Certainly, gold and silver often served as money. The prob-

Table 6.1
The Three Periods of Government Interactions with the Commercial Banking Industry

Time Period	Social Issues	Economic Issues	Political Issues
Colonial times to 1863	Safety of banks; industrial versus farming interests	Inflationary fears	State control over the banking system
1863 to 1913	Monetary control; banking failures	"Boom to Bust" economy	Federal control over the banking system
1913 to the present	Insuring savings	Ensuring growth; inflationary fears	Role of the Federal Reserve Bank
			The Glass-Steagall Act
			Deregulation

lem with this type of money is that it is bulky and subject to theft. One would need a safe place to deposit these precious metals. Those who left or deposited their gold or silver coins received a slip that entitled them to that amount of gold or silver. These slips could be used to pay another person who also had coins in the same place of deposit. This eliminated the need for physical withdrawals of gold and silver coins. Thus, banks became purveyors of deposits and made money by charging fees to act like an accountant for these transactions.

However, banks are not simply places of deposit, since they could lend out their depositors' money as well. The inducement that the bank gave depositors to have their money lent out was interest paid on that money. The bank, of course, would lend out these funds at a higher rate of interest to those who needed a loan to establish or expand a business. The risk to the bank was that the business could fail and be unable to pay back the loan; thus, the riskier the loan, the higher the rate of interest charged to the customer. Therefore, banks made their profits by charging a depositors' fee for transactions and charging interest on loans to customers.

In the United States, the history of banking began in 1782 with the founding of the Bank of North America in Philadelphia. By 1792, fourteen other banks were founded in twelve other cities. All these banks were oriented toward commercial customers by providing depository services and issuing notes as short-term loans to finance sales of commodities. They were subject to minimal supervision by the states in which they operated.

The federal government entered the banking arena in 1791 with the establishment of the First Bank of the United States at the urging of Alexander Hamilton, who was the Secretary of the Treasury. Hamilton had a variety of reasons for advocating the establishment of this national bank. First, he needed a place to deposit the tax receipts and to issue payments for the federal government. Hamilton's other desire was to create a strong federal presence in the nation's newly established banking affairs, designed along the familiar lines of the Bank of England, which was operated as a profit-oriented firm and a government institution which competed with the state-chartered banks (Pierce, 1991: 34).

Thus, two questions became the source of controversy during this earliest phase of the banking and government controversy: (1) What level of government would control the banks and, thus, the money supply?; and (2) To what interest group, rural versus urban, would these banks owe their allegiance?

Stakeholders

While both sides of this early banking controversy readily acknowledged the need to establish a banking system along with its ability to issue money, there was a great deal of difference on who would regulate the flow of its money and how much money would be issued.

Hamilton's primary concern with the state-chartered banks was their propensity to issue promissory notes without providing sufficient reserves to back up these notes. This situation caused a great deal of financial instability and inflation, and these conditions would create an obstacle for developing the type of industrial and urban economy which Hamilton was hoping to create throughout the United States. It was Hamilton's hope that his "central" bank would force state-chartered banks to back up their notes with sufficient reserves. This would force these banks to be much more conservative in their lending practices and in their creation of money. Hamilton's conservative monetary policy had the support of manufacturers, merchants, and most urban entrepreneurs. Clearly, the Bank of the United States was an urban northeastern institution and represented the interests of those with money (Hildreth, 1968: 95).

However, there was another set of stakeholders who had a much different monetary agenda; namely, the farming and rural interest, primarily in the South. During this early period of American history, the vast majority of Americans lived on the land. These farmers were involved in agricultural expansion and wanted greater availability of credit than the federal bank tolerated. Other opponents of federal banking regulations included proponents of states' rights, representatives of state-chartered banks, and state governments (Roussakis, 1984: 29).

The controversy over the control of the banking industry divided the newly established nation in many ways. Certainly, it pitted those in favor of a strong central government versus those who wished the new republic to be a loose confederation of sovereign state governments. It also developed into a sectional dispute where the Northeast—with its manufacturing interests—was in favor of tight monetary policy, represented by the Bank of the United States. Meanwhile, the South, whose economy was overwhelmingly agricultural, favored a loose money supply which should have been controlled by the states. This question of "loose" versus "tight" money is one that has been debated throughout American history.

Substitute Issues

Besides appealing to the economic interest of the various parties involved in the banking controversy, each side was able to appeal to an ideological aspect of their respective positions. In making the case for federal involvement in banking and, in turn, for a tight money supply, advocates painted a picture of a future America that was free of foreign interference—in particular, dependence upon British-manufactured goods. It was maintained that the struggling U.S. manufacturers needed to have a stable economy on which to base their investments.

Those groups in favor of a loose money supply and, hence, state control of banking pictured the newly created Bank of the United States as trampling down on the newly won freedoms from the British. Who would control the power of this new institution, especially since it appeared to be representing only the money interests? This scenario appealed to the American distaste of granting too much power to any one institution without establishing some sort of checks and balances.

Barriers to Entry and Exit

In the commercial banking industry, entry into the public policy process is primarily a function of what level of government is in position to exercise regulatory power over your bank. At the state level of government, capital requirements for obtaining a charter varied greatly, as did reserve requirements and any other supervision which might take place. However, some states did put in requirements that forced banks to meet other social requirements. For example, a Pennsylvania statute in the early 1800s required state banks to lend one fifth of their capital "for one year, to the farmers, mechanics, and manufacturers of their district" (Eccles, 1982: 45). This requirement demonstrates a concern that a bank take care of its own locale first (an early emphasis on community investment). It was the first of many such requirements that banks reinvest where they are obtaining their deposits. It is an issue that still troubles banking today.

During this period, there were no nationally-chartered banks, but the intent of both the First and Second Bank of the United States was to clamp down on the state-chartered banks, especially those banks in isolated locations, known as "wildcat banks." If a state-chartered bank was deemed to be extending too much credit and issuing too many notes, the federal bank would demand redemption of that bank's notes in the form of gold or silver payments. The impact of this demand from the federal bank was to reduce state-chartered bank reserves. This, in turn, forced the state-chartered banks to reduce their lending activities. While the federal bank could not stop entry into the commercial banking arena, it could curtail a state-chartered bank's activity and sometimes force the bank to exit the banking industry.

Audience

The banking system in the United States began as a dual banking system (i.e., state- and federal-chartered banks), and it is still operating in this manner today. During this early period of U.S. history, the two national-chartered banks (the First and Second Banks of the United States) were modeled after the Bank of England. They were to be the government's banker, but, just as important, they were to regulate the private state-chartered banks in the banking system.

However, both these national banks failed to have their charters renewed. The First Bank of the United States was in existence from 1791 to 1811, while the Second Bank of the United States was chartered in 1816—however, it also failed to have its charter renewed in 1836.

Criticism of the First Bank of the United States came from various quarters. Some critics attacked on grounds that the federal government had no right to charter a national bank. Agricultural interest denounced it for failing to pursue a policy of easy credit, while state banks opposed it for restricting its note-issuing ability. The primary reason why the First Bank of the United States failed, however, was that its supporters were hoisted on their ideological argument. The First Bank of the United States was capitalized at $10 million; however, three quarters of these funds came from foreign sources. Although the foreign investors could not vote their shares in the bank, there was a great deal of antipathy at having such a powerful public institution dominated by foreign concerns. Thus, critics of the bank could claim that the First Bank of the United States was actually an agent for prolonging U.S. dependence on foreign investment.

The Second Bank of the United States was chartered in reaction to the quick deterioration of economic conditions after the collapse of the First Bank of the United States. The bank's charter provided for essentially the same functions as those provided for in the first bank. It achieved a great amount of success, and by 1825, it controlled one third of U.S. banking assets. However, this success reinvigorated the same forces that led to the demise of the first bank. In 1832, President Andrew Jackson, who was elected as a representative of rural and state interests, vetoed the extension of the bank's charter. The following year, he removed all federal assets from the bank and deposited federal funds in various state banks. With these actions, Jackson effectively deprived the bank of its central banking power, and it went out of existence in 1841.

This was a period where state and rural interest triumphed over those forces which were seeking fiscal and monetary restraints. The primary policy audience or arena for banking issues remained at the state level of government. Yet, the struggles of this period are still with the U.S. banking system today. Should banks provide easy or tight credit? What is the responsibility of government to insure the stability of the financial system? What responsibilities do banks have to their local communities in terms of reinvestment and providing credit? Finally, what role should the states play in the banking system? We will see how these questions are brought to the forefront in describing the other periods of banking regulation.

SECOND PERIOD: THE RISE OF NATIONAL CHARTERS BANKS (1863–1913)

Issue: Federal Control over the Monetary and Banking System

Except for the two twenty-year periods when the First and Second Bank of the United States reigned in the behavior of state-chartered banks, chaos would be an appropriate description for both the state of banking and the resultant monetary system. There was a general lack of uniformity among states in banking laws and supervision. Some states even permitted "free banking," which basically allowed someone to open a bank if they met minimum requirements.

Meanwhile, equally chaotic conditions were present in the country's monetary system. There were some 1,600 state-chartered banks in operation by 1861, and each of these banks issued their own currency in different denominations (Roussakis, 1984: 29). While the notes of the majority of the northeastern banks were considered good, the notes of many southern and western banks were, at best, questionable.

With the coming of the Civil War, and the resulting inflationary pressures that resulted from financing, there was once again a sufficient public outcry to remedy the chaotic state of banking and money in the country. The battle of federal versus state control of the banking and monetary system was about to resume.

Stakeholders

The stakeholders during this second period of banking and government interaction were essentially the same as those that existed during the first period. However, there was a significant shift in the amount of power they possessed in determining the outcome of banking and monetary issues.

Those stakeholders that were in favor of stricter banking and monetary policy were primarily located in the northeastern part of the country. This is the section in which the manufacturing industries, as well as the stronger banks, were located. While the Northeast still had a substantial percentage engaged in agricultural activities, these interests were easily overwhelmed by the wealthy business interests in these states.

Meanwhile, those in favor of "wild cat" banking and state control over monetary activity were primarily located in the southern and western parts of the country. Obviously, during the Civil War, when the southern states seceded from the Union, their influence on any policy changes were minimal. Since the slavery issue was also connected with the states' rights movement, any argument in favor of the status quo which used states' rights as its basic premise was held in contempt.

Thus, at the beginning of this second period of banking and government relations, there was a dramatic shift in power to those forces which were in favor of federal control over the banking and monetary system. While this shift in power became somewhat less pronounced as the period progressed, in general, the ascendancy of the Northeast as the center of business interest in the country assured that the banking and monetary policies of the country would be conducted much more in tune to their interests.

Substitute Issues

As was pointed out in the previous section, the movement of having federal government play a major role in banking and monetary affairs gained public support with the coming of the Civil War and the resulting need to assure the public that the Union government could pay for the war's expenses. It was in this wartime atmosphere that the primary piece of legislation of banking monetary reform, the National Currency Act, retitled the National Banking Act of 1864, was passed. With this act, the federalist stakeholders obtained nearly all of the banking and monetary reforms that they were demanding. The National Banking Act established within the U.S. Treasury the Office of the Comptroller of the Currency to charter national banks that were authorized to issue national bank notes and to lay a 10-percent tax on all state-chartered notes. The U.S. Treasury also started to print greenbacks, which the government held as legal tender. All of these actions laid the groundwork for establishing a uniform currency in the United States.

Meanwhile, the banking portion of the National Banking Act returned the federal government to banking affairs in a much different manner than its two previous ventures. While the First and Second Banks of the United States involved joint ownership between government and private parties (most of whom were foreign interests), the newly established national banks were private, but regulated. They had minimum capital standards and reserve requirements, and the Comptroller of the Currency supervised and regulated all the activities of the national banks.

Those stakeholders trying to stem the tide of this federal assault on the pre–Civil War banking system had to portray these reforms as the work of greedy, big-city interests. The most famous spokesman for this point of view was William Jennings Bryan, with his famous "Cross of Gold" speech. In this speech, Jennings pleaded that debtors, primarily agricultural interests, be given some relief from the periodic retrenchment in the economy that was caused by a restrictive monetary policy. Once again, there was great concern that the rise of national banks would cause the demise of the local banks which, in turn, would cause the flow of more funds to the big financial centers. This would leave the rural areas without the benefits of funds to invest in these areas.

Barriers to Entry and Exit

The power of the federal government was greatly increased in the period of time after the Civil War. While the war was fought over the slavery issue, in many ways, it was also fought over the issue of whether states' rights or federal rights would be the driving force behind government. With the Union victory, the role of the federal government would be greatly expanded. This expanded role for the federal government provided an ideal setting for those business interests that wanted a stable and conservative monetary policy. Since the federal government had been the level of government which sided with these sentiments, it was only natural that legislation favor national regulation of banking, and that monetary policy would now be enacted.

Certainly, the farming interests and other interests which clamored for "easy" money and banking regulation suffered a severe blow with the passage of the National Banking Act. However, all was not lost. The key to their access in future policy debates over banking and money was to keep state participation in banking and monetary affairs. The farming and other stakeholders interested in less restrictive banking activities also made a strategic retreat in the area of monetary policy. They recognized the exclusive right of the federal government to regulate monetary policy in order to preserve a state's right to charter and supervise banks. Although the National Banking Act of 1864 made it quite difficult for state-chartered banks to operate, it did not rule out such a possibility. Hence, while advocates of local control of banking activity and "easy" money certainly had to make concessions during this second period of banking and government regulation, they still retained their access to the public policy process by enabling the states to preserve their prerogatives in the banking area.

Audience

At the conclusion of this second period of regulation of the banking industry, the federal government had clearly become the chief audience for the legislative action that determined banking and monetary policy. With the passage of the National Banking Act of 1864, the comptroller of the currency controlled the amount of money through the chartering and supervision of national banks. It appeared that the banking system had finally been out from under control of the federal government; in particular, the Treasury Department.

However, this triumph of federal control was to stay for only a relatively short period of time. Figure 6.1 shows the number of banks in the United States from 1860 to 1920.

Figure 6.1
Number of Banks in the United States: 1860–1920

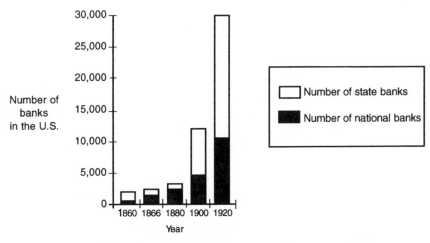

Source: Roussakis, 1984.

There are two striking features to Figure 6.1. First, while the National Banking Act of 1864 drastically reduced the number of state-chartered banks, this phenomenon did not last very long. By 1900, the number of state-chartered banks was double the number of federally-chartered banks. What accounts for the rise in popularity of state-chartered banks when their notes were taxed at a 10-percent rate? State-chartered banks soon realized that they did not have to issue notes to operate profitably. Instead, these banks realized that an alternative form of obligation, a check, could be used as money without all of the restrictions imposed by the U.S. Treasury. These state-chartered banks became banks of deposits and used these deposits to fund loans.

The other striking feature of Figure 6.1 was the spectacular rise in the number of banks throughout this period. This increase in banking activity was a direct result of the rapid economic development that took place during the later part of the nineteenth century. There was also an explosion of agricultural productivity which, in turn, fueled an unprecedented increase in the number of unit banks in farming regions.

By the end of the second era of regulation, the federal government did obtain some measure of control over the money supply, but the regulation of the banking system still remained primarily in the hands of the states. The same problem of booms and busts in economic activity still plagued the economy. The National Banking Act of 1864 was a victory of sorts for those who advocated a more conservative monetary and banking policy, but it did not contain the type of reforms needed to support a developing economy.

THE THIRD PERIOD OF REGULATION (1913–PRESENT)

Issue: Consumer Safety versus Deregulation

In 1908, a National Monetary Commission was established to recommend more fundamental reforms of the banking system, so that the financial panics that took place in 1903 and 1907 could be avoided in the future. Once again, the debates were centered around the old issues of states' rights versus federal domination, large banks versus small banks, and rural banks versus urban financial centers. The commission recommended a compromise proposal which resulted in the passage of the Federal Reserve Act of 1913.

The chief controversy surrounding the Federal Reserve Act was what type of central bank the federal reserve system would become. Regional interests opposed establishing a single central bank, and others feared that a central bank would be controlled by Wall Street interests. There was also disagreement about whether a central bank should be a private bank for bankers or government operated. The solution to all of these concerns was to placate every concern.

The central bank that resulted from the Federal Reserve Act was a coalition of twelve separate federal reserve banks weakly coordinated by the Federal Reserve Board in Washington. Each federal reserve bank had a federal charter but was owned by its member banks and was operated as a bank for banks. In fulfilling this role, each federal reserve bank was to function as a clearinghouse for its member banks' checks and to lend member bank funds in case of a sudden increase in demand for reserves by depositors.

The federal reserve system was also given the task of regulating the banking system. National banks were required to join the federal reserve system; however, it was optional for state-chartered banks. The federal system was given the power to regulate branching, bank mergers, deposit reserve requirements, and to limit the amount of interest paid on savings and demand deposits.

Finally, each federal reserve bank issued its own currency, called "federal reserve notes," and these notes became the basis for the money supply for the country. The federal reserve was to provide an "elastic" currency supply that would expand when the public was withdrawing funds from member banks and would contract when the public deposited currency with member banks. The federal reserve system was to make loans that were in accordance with safe banking principles, and they would not lend to a member who lacked sufficient collateral.

The first test of the federal reserve system was the stock market crash of 1929. During the three years following the stock market crash, banks failed at an alarming rate. There were 1,350 failures in 1930; 2,300 failures in 1931; and 1,450 failures in 1932 (Pierce, 1991: 44). The federal reserve system that had been created to prevent such a banking "meltdown" had failed miserably. Why was this system so unsuccessful?

The federal reserve system, particularly the New York Federal Reserve, did issue additional currency, made loans to member banks, and conducted open-market operations to pump money into the banking system, but these operations were not nearly enough to offset the withdrawals that banks were experiencing. Furthermore, as the monetary and banking crisis grew worse—which made existing bank loans look risky—federal reserve banks refused to make additional loans to troubled banks on the grounds that these banks were not a good credit risk. Hence, the federal reserve system was acting toward the banking crisis as a private bank would react, rather than as a central bank would act in times of dire monetary distress.

The New Deal banking reforms contained no grand new design but were, rather, a continuation of the trend to have the federal government stabilize the monetary system and rid the banking system of its worst abuses. These reforms still form the basis of U.S. banking regulation today.

The theme of all of these reforms was safety—to form a federal security net that would protect the individual depositor as well as the entire banking system. The primary vehicle for these reforms was the Glass–Stegall Act of 1933. In order to reassure individual depositors that their deposits were safe no matter what the condition of an individual bank, deposit insurance was enacted with the establishment of the Federal Deposit Insurance Corporation (FDIC). Even though state-chartered banks did not have to offer FDIC insurance, the benefits were so obvious that virtually all banks obtained it, and, thus, the federal government finally succeeded in bringing almost all banks under its regulatory control. FDIC insurance also allowed small banks to compete with larger banks, since depositors at small banks had no more to fear than those who had deposits at larger banks. However, since the vast majority of smaller rural banks had state charters, the Glass–Stegall Act did little to settle the controversy over the appropriateness of national versus state-charters for banks.

There were two other features of the safety net that the Glass–Stegall Act was to impose on the banking industry. First, banks were not permitted to pay interest on demand deposits, and the amount of interest that they were permitted to pay on time deposits was also regulated. Second, Glass–Stegall mandated that banks had to choose to be either a commercial bank or an investment bank. Since many of the failed banks had engaged in underwriting, dealing, and brokering corporate securities, it was thought that ordinary depositors should have the assurance that their funds were not being used to fund risky corporate ventures. Thus, commercial banks became known as retail banks, since they made loans to businesses using depositors funds while investment banks became underwriters of bonds and brokers of corporate securities.

Finally, the federal reserve system was transformed into an effective central bank. First, the regional autonomy of the individual federal reserve banks was drastically reduced with the real decision-making power delegated to the Board of Governors located in Washington. The federal reserve was instructed to act like a central bank during monetary crisis by relaxing or eliminating collateral for banks that were experiencing "runs." The federal reserve was to control the money supply by conducting "open-market" policies where the federal reserve bought or sold government securities, either to put money into the monetary system or to withdraw money from that system.

The reforms certainly achieved their intended result—the commercial banking system was made almost completely safe for any depositors who had less than $100,000. However, they also had a few unintended effects that have led to the current crisis in the banking system. First, the restraints placed on banks with respect to interest rates allowed even the poorest-run bank to be profitable. It was extremely difficult to lose money with these restraints. While the restraints protected bankers from competition, they cost depositors higher interest payments on their deposits. In general, these safety reforms produced a rather inefficient banking system. Second, since commercial banks and investment banks had very defined markets, there was no need for banks to offer any new services for depositors or customers. Lack of innovation was an unintended hallmark of post-New Deal banking.

The New Deal banking reforms worked quite well for the first twenty years following the conclusion of World War II. Bank failures averaged less than five per year during this period (Pierce, 1991: 50), and banking customers were generally satisfied with their regulated rates of return given the low inflation rates after the war. However, this golden period of well-regulated and well-protected banking ended in the late 1960s for two reasons. First, in order to finance the Vietnam War, the federal government started to run huge budget deficits. Since neither the President nor Congress wanted to raise taxes to pay for war, the result was a rising supply of money along with the resultant excess demand. In order to soak up this demand, the federal reserve system tightened the money supply by severely raising interest rates. Since deposit interest rates had ceilings, and as market interest rates rose above these ceilings, many customers withdrew their money to invest in treasury bills and other market instruments. While banks eventually received permission to raise interest rates on deposits, they had not only lost a considerable amount of funds, but were now forced to compete for the funds of depositors.

The other factor that changed the banking industry in the late 1960s was the introduction of computers, along with the other advances in databases and communication. These technological advances lowered the costs of issuing and purchasing commercial paper significantly. Traditionally, corporate customers turned to banks for loans, but now, with the new technology, corporations had the capacity to issue their own commercial paper at a significantly lower cost than banks. Large corporate firms no longer needed banks as a source of capital, as they could now raise the capital by themselves.

Thus, the commercial banking industry was being attacked on two fronts. First, depositors were fleeing the banking system in order to obtain higher interest rates on their funds. Second, the bank's role as a lender to large corporate firms was undermined by technology that permitted these firms to issue their own commercial paper as well as other financing schemes. Commercial banking was no longer benefiting from its regulated status; rather, the banking industry found it extremely difficult to compete with other financial intermediaries, simply because it had never been forced to compete until now.

Both commercial and investment banking industries now turned to the federal government to release them from the restrictions of the New Deal safety net. However, the old concerns of protecting the deposits of banking customers (as well as other issues, e.g., protecting the rural banking interests and providing funds for poor urban centers) remained as reasons to continue to regulate the banking industry. We will now examine how the various stakeholders view this still undecided controversy.

Stakeholders

The commercial banking industry has undergone a great deal of structural change in the past fifteen years. The number of commercial banks has diminished greatly. In 1984, there were 14,483 banks. This number was reduced to 10,715 in 1994 and had fallen below 10,000 in 1995 (Andrew, 1986: 84). Industry analysts have made predictions that the number of banks operating in the United States will decrease by one half ("Open Seasons on Banks," 1995: 48). This decrease in the number of commercial banks has also been accompanied by a dramatic increase in the value of the mergers and acquisitions of these various commercial banks. Figure 6.2 illustrates this phenomenon quite well. It also shows that the pace and value of these mergers and acquisitions has picked up greatly in the past five years. One reason for this increased merger and acquisition activity has been the gradual dismantling of the branching prohibitions by various state governments. Not only do most states permit statewide branching, but many states have entered into regional compacts which permit banks from neighboring states to own and operate branch banks in their states. This trend toward consolidation in the banking industry also points to a consolidation in the political power that the commercial banking can use in making its case for further deregulation at the federal level of government. The other stakeholders interested in deregulation of the financial services are the large and powerful investment banks, insurance companies, and brokerage firms. While these investment banks are not keen on having additional competition in their areas of financial services, they are willing to risk this competition in order to offer their clients the full range of financial services.

Though the forces that oppose further deregulation of the banking industry are varied, they are also quite powerful. First, the insurance industry opposes the entry of banks into the insurance business. Commercial banks desire to offer their customers a full

Figure 6.2
Value of U.S. Commercial Banking Mergers and Acquisitions: 1980–1995

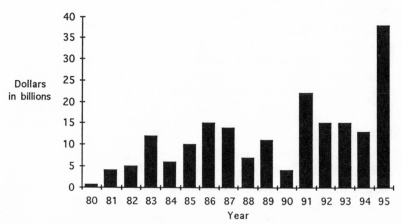

Source: The Economist, September 2, 1995.

range of financial services, including insurance. Meanwhile, of course, the insurance industry wants to be able to offer checking accounts and other traditional banking services to their customers. The aim of both industries is to free themselves from regulation while keeping other industries regulated. Hence, this is a contest between industries that can wield enormous economic and political power at both the state and federal levels of government.

The other forces against the deregulation of the banking industry are organizations that represent the poor urban and rural areas of the country. The fear of these groups is that as the commercial banking industry becomes more consolidated, their areas will either have no banks or, at most, one bank in their locales. Their concerns have great impact on state and federal officials who are concerned with the antitrust implications of this consolidation movement already taking place in the commercial banking industry prior to a full-scale deregulation of the banking industry.

Substitute Issues

The commercial banking industry's primary argument in favor of deregulation has been to "level the playing field" with other financial service organizations. Another argument of the commercial banking industry has to do with economies of scale. The changes in technology, in particular, the automatic teller machines (ATMs) and other advances in computerized operations, has enabled the operations departments of banks to handle increasingly large and distant transactions. In order for this technology to be cost effective, it demands that banks have a large number of transactions. The industry's final argument to buttress their case for deregulation involves foreign competition, in particular, with Japanese banks. In general, foreign banks have assets and deposits that are far larger than American banks (Channon, 1988: 124). We have seen how the banking laws have fostered the development of many state and local banks; however, these banks are by their very nature small, and are therefore in no position to compete with larger foreign banks should these foreign banks be permitted to compete in a local banking market. More and more, commercial banks are being permitted to merge in order to ensure that American banks can provide competition—not only in the American market, but throughout the world.

Meanwhile, opponents of banking deregulation have also supplemented their primary argument of "disenfranchisement" with one that emphasizes the loss of employment as a result of banking mergers. While banks argue that they become more efficient and can provide customers with cheaper services as a result of mergers, the downside of these economies of scale are the loss of jobs resulting from mergers and deregulatory activities. As banks become larger, it is somewhat ironic that they are able to downsize their workforce. Hence, state and local governments are becoming increasingly wary of banking mergers and acquisitions.

Barriers to Entry and Exit

During this period of interactions between government and the banking industry, the federal reserve system has been given the most regulatory powers over the industry. Since the members are actually the owners of the federal reserve system, they have had no problem in gaining access to any policy decisions that would affect the day-to-day operations of their banks. However, until all the restrictions on commercial- and investment-banking activities are removed with the repeal of the Glass–Stegall Act, Congress will still have a great deal to say about the future of banking in the United States. It is at this Congressional level that the opponents, particularly the insurance industry, have had the greatest success in preventing the banking industry from achieving its goal of being able to offer customers all financial instruments. The concern for the safety of depositors' assets is still a matter of great concern for many Congressional leaders.

Meanwhile, at the state level, the banks have been quite successful in having states repeal branching restrictions. Since the insurance industry is primarily regulated at the state level of government, the banking industry has petitioned the various state insurance regulatory agencies to keep the insurance firms out of those financial services which have traditionally been reserved for banks (such as taking deposits and writing checks). So, while the insurance industry is trying to prevent the banks from offering insurance by appealing to federal officials, the banks are appealing to state officials to protect them from incursions from the insurance industry.

Audience

Clearly, the primary arena where the battle over the complete deregulation of the banking industry has been taking place and will be taking place is at the federal level and, in particular, persuading Congress that the Glass–Stegall Act has outlived its usefulness.

The technology available to banks and consumers has made the necessity for banks to have physical branches more and more obsolete. As the issue of branches has become obsolete, so has the states' role in regulating the banking industry.

However, the issue has become: What is the role for banking in a deregulated financial services sector? It appears that banking will evolve the way so many other industries have; namely, an industry that becomes an oligopoly where four or five firms will divide what is left of the banking market. Currently, there are 10,450 banks in the United States ("Open Seasons on Banks," 1995: 48). The market for these banks, however, has changed drastically. Since 1980, banks' share of the overall loan market has been sliced in half when corporations found that they could raise money much more cheaply by offering commercial paper as well as medium-term notes. In addition, retail customers have also been abandoning the traditional commercial banks. Instead of going to their local bank to open up savings accounts or to buy a CD, consumers are taking their savings to mutual funds such as Fidelity or Vanguard . They are going for auto loans to the automobile companies themselves and financing mortgages through insurance firms, GE Capital, or other firms which have capital to lend.

The only way in which banks will be able to compete with these nonbank financial intermediaries is to achieve economies of scale that will enable them to spread the cost of this technology over a wider base of customers. This is the case made by banks to justify their many mergers and acquisitions. Banks need to be able to offer consumers mutual funds and IRAs as cheaply as possible. They also need to be able to develop computer systems that allow customers to do all of their banking without going to a branch. Clearly, the goal of the consolidation of the banking industry is efficiency. However, the problem for public policymakers is that while these changes in the banking industry are of benefit to the majority of consumers, they leave behind those individuals who have no access to the banking system either because they no longer live near a branch of a bank or they do not own a computer which will enable them to participate in electronic banking.

CONCLUSION

In the two previous industries (cigarettes and beer), we watched as the audience that would decide the eventual public policy measures which would regulate these industries changed from the federal to the state level of government. What makes the banking industry unique is that this evolution has proceeded in the opposite way. Banking's first period of government intervention took place at the state level of government, and the two federal interventions that were undertaken during the early development of U.S. banking were rejected. During the second period of banking regulation, the federal government took a much more active role, but the states still wielded enormous influence on how public policy would affect the banking industry. With the coming of the third period of regulation, technological advances, as well as other social forces, made state regulation of banking obsolete. The federal government has given the federal reserve system the power to regulate the banks, and this amounts to allowing the banks to regulate themselves so that they can compete in the new financial services industry.

One area where the banking industry is similar to the two previous industries that were analyzed is the manner in which new issues have been added for each of these industries. In the first two periods of regulation of the banking industry, the issues were the stability of the monetary system, the safety of deposits in the banks, and the accessibility of the banking system to everyone. While none of these issues were solved completely, there were attempts made to satisfy the various stakeholders that were involved with these issues.

During the third period of regulation, another issue was added to this mix—the efficiency of the banking system. The primary focus of public policymakers has been to deregulate the banking industry so that its costs could be lowered in order for the banking industry to compete against other segments of the financial service industry. Though deregulating the banking industry has certainly lowered the cost for certain consumers, the concerns for assuring the safety of bank deposits as well as providing access to banking services have once again become much more problematic. Clearly, public policymakers are faced with the dilemma of having a banking system that either achieves greater efficiency (lower costs) but less equality (access), or produces greater equality but less efficiency. How public policymakers balance this tension between equality and efficiency will become the chief dilemma of public policy and the banking industry as they approach the twenty-first century. In Chapter 7, the chemical industry will be used to show how our model developed in Chapter 3 can be used to analyze a controversial manufacturing industry.

Chapter 7

THE CHEMICAL INDUSTRY

The chemical industry, much like the cigarette industry, has been subjected to intense scrutiny by public interest groups and public policymakers. What makes this all the more interesting is that, for the most part, the chemical industry has a large sales volume in industrial products—that is, it rarely sells its products and services directly to the consuming public, but rather sells products to other firms both within and outside of the chemical industry.[1] In addition, much like the cigarette industry, the chemical industry has been a major contributor to the positive side of the balance of payments problem for the United States.

As Taylor and Sudnick note:

The chemical industry is second only to the oil industry in the complexity of its operations and in the ramifications of its influence on modern society. Hundreds of other industries, from pulp and paper processors to movie producers, rely on materials supplied by chemical manufacturers, and the relationship between the oil and chemical industries has become increasingly close in the years since World War II. No one company and no single country dominates this diverse and amorphous industry. Today virtually every industrial nation and many developing countries have established some form of domestic chemical manufacturing, although the United States and Western Europe remain the major exporters of most materials. (1984: 18)

Table 7.1 provides a view of this relationship for the chemical industry over time and over different issues. Although the discussion to follow deals with the U.S. chemical industry, it must be made clear that the time periods suggested in Table 7.1 and the specific issues and concerns have developed worldwide. The United States has probably led the world in the development of concern for the

Table 7.1
Four Periods of Government and Chemical Industry Interaction

Time Period	Social Issues	Economic Issues	Political Issues
Transformation of the Industry Worldwide: 1770 to 1850	None, as national level issues such as self-sufficiency were prominent	Trade barriers and existence of too many competitors	Individual nations developing a competitive chemical industry capability
United States: 1850s to 1913	Rising expectations	Intense merger activity and growth	Federal involvement, particularly in the form of antitrust activity
Worldwide: 1913 to 1962	Employee safety, wages, and working conditions	Continued concentration of the industry; economies of scale; and diversification into new products/processes	Government involvement: war restrictions; oversight for quality and timely delivery
Worldwide: 1962 to present	The "Environmental" Movement	Tremendous worldwide price competition, especially in basic chemicals	Governmental legislation and involvement in industry affairs reaches new levels

environment and in specific legislation and public outcry for preservation of the environment. In other parts of the world, this level of interest and government and societal activity has lagged that of the United States, but it has developed nonetheless. In some ways, one could argue that the pace of societal and government involvement in the chemical industry in the United States has set the tone for similar developments worldwide.

This chapter will be somewhat different in its approach than that of the three previous industry explorations. In Chapters 4 through 6, the thrust of the analysis was centered on a specific industry's relationship with government and society over time and over changing and evolving issues. Those particular chapters explored how issues and industry involvement in those issues changed over time. In this chapter, we shall concentrate on the development of relationships between the chemical industry, public interest groups, and government during the period 1962 to the present. However, the greatest focus will be on the maneuverings and battling over a specific issue—the passage of a toxic waste legislation that was to become known as "Superfund." This particular legislative battle provides us with a situation to assess the detailed political strategies and tactics of several key stakeholders, individual members of the chemical industry, and the trade association for the industry. This will serve to highlight aspects of the model introduced in Chapter 3.

SUPERFUND: PREHISTORY

There is some debate over precisely when society in general became aware of the environmental damage being caused by industrial activity.[2] A major force in the development of this awareness can be traced to the publication of Rachel Carson's *The Silent Spring* in 1962. In that widely read book, later critically examined on nationwide television, society was alerted to the dangers of unregulated chemicals in our environment. Incidents of contamination that have occurred around the world since then seem to bear out her early warnings (e.g., the Minamata, Seveso, Bhopal, and Sandoz incidents discussed in Mahon and Kelley, 1987). The chemical industry attempted to derail pollution as an issue, in some cases attacking those who argued for pollution as an issue, noting that "those opposed to chemical pesticides are a motley lot ranging from superstitious illiterates and cultists to educated scientists." (*Chemical Week:* 30). Monsanto published a parody of *The Silent Spring* entitled *The Desolate Year*, which, in a writing style similar to Carson's, portrayed a world dominated by malaria and cholera without the benefits of pesticides ("A Look Back at History," 30). When all else fails, denial is a tactic that is often used by industry and firm alike, and the chemical industry is no exception. The industry argued, much like the tobacco industry would argue, that "there is no conclusive scientific evidence that pesticides damage the ecosystem and that their role in increasing food production is a proud example of the industry's contribution to progress" ("A Look Back at History," 30).

Despite their attempts to dismiss it, this issue would not go away. The industry realized that inconsistent regulations were being developed in various state legislatures and at the federal level in various executive departments (e.g., Department of Interior, Department of Health, Education and Welfare, etc.) and was concerned over the potential jurisdictional disputes and costs that were likely to arise from such duplicative efforts. A report prepared for the Committee on Public Works and Transportation of the U.S. House of Representatives addressed the problems of hazardous wastes and toxic substances in some detail:

In recent years, several episodes of environmental contamination by toxic substances have occurred in which health is threatened, products condemned, and resources destroyed or declared off-limits. The most notorious of these include mercury in Lake St. Clair, PCB's in the Hudson river, PBB's in Michigan, kepone in the James River,[3] carbon tetrachloride in the Ohio river, and HEXA-OCTA in the Louisville, Kentucky sewers and in the Ohio river. These episodes have been nationally newsworthy, and stories of ill workers (kepone), condemned fish (mercury, kepone), destroyed cattle and possible health hazards (PBB's), sewage treatment breakdowns (kepone, HEXA-OCTA), and drinking water warnings (carbontet, HEXA-OCTA), are generally well known. To these episodes must be added uncounted local ones of varying seriousness; these sometimes contaminate fish or shellfish, pollute streams, and cause wells to be condemned. (Blodgett, 1979: 25)

One should not get the impression that these incidents are confined to lakes, rivers, and streams. In August 1978, the national news media began reporting the leakage of hazardous chemicals from disposal sites in the abandoned Love Canal site in Niagara Falls, New York.[4] At least eighty-two different chemical compounds were identified, eleven of which were actual or suspected carcinogens. This was to lead to one of the largest relocations of families from contaminated areas in U.S. history, at immense cost to state and federal governments in terms of money and human misery.

If the past does serve as a predictor for the future, then the chemical industry had grave reason for concern. During the period 1970–1980, there was a tremendous increase in the regulation of the industry. Some of the increased regulation, while attributable to strong public interest lobbies, was also a reflection of the industry's loss of public confidence and the perceived need for increased protection of the environment. Some examples of incidents that contributed to this loss of confidence included but were not limited to the following:

- Elizabeth, New Jersey: Fire broke out in April 1980 at a dump that had been used by the former Chemical Control Corporation for highly explosive wastes. Catastrophe was averted when winds blew toxic clouds away from populated areas. Cost of clean-up was estimated at $10 to $15 million.

- West Point, Kentucky: There is an abandoned site known as the "Valley of the Drums," which contains 17,000 drums of unknown contents. Chemical leakage from these drums has been detected in streams feeding the Ohio River.

Earl Harbison, in remarks made at the Chemical Industry's Strategic Planning Conference in 1979, pointed out the impact of these incidents, noting that: "Opinion research undertaken for Monsanto showed that the public continued to identify the chemical industry as the *prime* contributor to air and water pollution problems. For example, 71 percent said that waste from chemical plants is the greatest pollution hazard; it is ahead of all other industries (1979).

Business Week also noticed the problems with the chemical industry's public image, stating that "The chemical industry now ranks lowest in image of 13 industries surveyed by New York pollster Yankelovich, Skelly, & White, Inc. The 'gap between the chemical industry and the one ranking second-last is quite large,' says Laurence D. Wiseman, a Yankelovich vice-president" ("Cleansing the Chemical Image," 1979: 73). Yet, the industry was not able to stave off the growing activity by public interest groups and the federal government in the establishment of new regulations and oversight. Let us briefly review the legislation of this period in order to understand the political and social context that the industry found itself in the late 1970s.

In 1969, the National Environmental Policy Act was passed. Its stated purposes were to declare a national policy which would encourage productive and enjoyable harmony between man and the environment, to promote efforts which would prevent or eliminate damage to the environment and biosphere, and to establish a Council on Environmental Quality. The practical impact of this legislation was that if a company wanted to build or substantially alter an old site, it would have to prepare an "environmental impact statement" explaining how the proposed change would affect the environment.[5]

In 1970, two key events occurred. The first was the first-ever "Earth Day." This day brought together environmentalist groups, public interest groups, and common citizens to celebrate the earth and to raise concerns about what industry was doing to it. When the chemical industry attempted to participate in Earth Day activities, their representatives were jeered by the participants.

The second event was the passage of the Clean Air Act (with key amendments in 1977). This act established an intricate system of federal and state regulations and enforcements designed to enhance the nation's air resources. Under the act, the Environmental Protection Agency (EPA) was established which brought together fifteen different federal offices dealing with pollution under single management. The EPA enforces environmental protection policies, recommends policies to the President, sets national ambient air quality standards for pollutants (e.g., sulfur dioxide, lead, and carbon monoxide), and could also set national emission standards for hazardous pollutants (e.g., asbestos, benzene, and vinyl chloride). The chemical industry is now receiving the consistency in regulation and oversight that it earlier thought would be helpful, but still cannot shake its view that the problem is a technological one, and that industry is the best provider of solutions to this problem. However, as *Chemical Week* noted,

By the end of 1971, concern for environmental protection reached an unprecedented level and *governmental action increasingly influenced corporate policy*. Dow and DuPont began to emerge as the most referenced companies in relation to environmental issues. The magazine's [*Chemical*

Week] focus on technological solutions to environmental problems was being displaced by management, public relations, legal, and political concerns. In response to all of this, industry remained consistent in its view that pollution is a problem it can solve through its own technological prowess. ("A Look Back at History," 1994: 31, emphasis added)

However, the march of legislation continues onward, and the chemical industry continues to object and resist, noting that the environmental report prepared by Ralph Nader's group is "inflammatory, lacks objectivity, is illogical in its conclusions, and the writers are naive" ("A Look Back at History," 1994: 34). In 1972, Congress passed the Federal Environmental Pesticide Control Act; the Federal Insecticide, Fungicide, and Rodenticide Act; the Federal Water Pollution Control Act; and the Marine Protection, Research, and Sanctuaries Act all of which impact on the chemical industry.

In 1976, Congress enacted the Toxic Substance Control Act (TSCA) over bitter industry opposition.

EPA writes the rules, plays against you, keeps score, and makes arbitrary decisions. . . . After four years of debate, Congress seems determined to add one more regulation (TSCA) to the already 27 health and safety regulations we must answer to. This will make the EPA a chemical czar. No agency in a democracy should have that authority. . . . Environmentalists have decided that the law is the only way to settle and they've set up the NRDC (National Resources Defense Council), EDF (Environmental Defense Fund), and the Center for Law in the Public Interest. This could tie us up in court for decades. ("A Look Back at History," 1994: 34)

The most complex and far-reaching of the environmental laws was the TSCA. It was meant to give the federal government control over chemicals not already regulated under other laws. It also gave the EPA a first-strike authority with respect to clearing an agent before it entered the market, as well as the power to control existing chemicals if they were shown to be unreasonably hazardous. In addition, the 1976 Resource Conservation and Recovery Act (RCRA) was passed, and it created a federal hazardous materials disposal program for land disposal of discarded materials. It was a multifaceted approach toward solving the problems associated with the 3 to 4 billion tons of discarded materials generated each year and the problems resulting from the anticipated 8-percent annual increase in the volume of such wastes.

Finally, in 1977, Congress amended the Federal Water Pollution Control Act with the passage of the Clean Water Act. This act established national goals and authorized the EPA to adopt effluent standards and a national permit system. The national goals included prohibition of toxic pollutant discharges, elimination of discharges by 1985, and the development of "fishable" and "swimmable" water by July 1, 1983.

It is against this backdrop of two decades of challenge and change that the industry began to prepare for a significantly new environmental initiative—the regulation and cleanup of existing hazardous waste sites; or, as it came to be called, Superfund.

Issue: Cleanup of Hazardous Waste Sites

The beginnings of Superfund can be traced back to a variety of government and industry actions. Starting in 1973, the petroleum industry approached Congress on the issue of oil spills. The petroleum industry wanted federal legislation in order to achieve a dollar limit on liability and to obtain release from the numerous state regulations in effect (the legislation was never passed, and surely Exxon wishes that it had been after their problem in Valdez). This initial interest of the industry on the issue of oil spills spurred Congressional action and thought on the entire issue of oil spills and hazardous wastes.

Superfund can also trace its legislative roots back to the RCRA of 1976. The General Accounting Office (GAO) released a report on December 19, 1978, on the administration of RCRA:

that shocked industry and made public debate and controversy over the recently proposed hazardous waste rules even more heated.

The report said money should be available to pay claims resulting from disposal operations, to clean up resulting damages, and to prevent further contamination.

The fund would be supported by fees assessed on the disposal of hazardous wastes, but in developing the fee schedule, "an effort should be made to reflect the degree and duration of risk posed by specific wastes," the GAO report noted.

Inadequate disposal practices in the past have caused harm to humans and the environment many years after the sites have closed, the report said. In many cases, site ownership was transferred or relinquished, making legal liability difficult to establish and causing clean-up costs and remedial costs to be passed on to taxpayers. A federal fund is needed to address the liability problem, the report stressed. ("An Analysis of the Resource Conservation and Recovery Act," 1980: 708)

According to Philip Cummings (interview) and Curtis Moore (interview, counsels for the Committee on Environment and Public Works in the U.S. Senate), meetings were held starting in late 1978 between Congress, the EPA, and the Manufacturing Chemists Association (the industry's trade association, later to rename itself) to discuss a possible bill for hazardous waste clean-up. Mank, of the

EPA, recalled that Stauffer, Dow, Monsanto, Olin, Union Carbide, and Allied Chemical Corporations were represented at these meetings where the EPA laid out the government's position and asked the industry for their input on this issue (1981). At that time, according to Cummings, Moore, and Mank, the Manufacturing Chemists Association's position was that the government should foot the entire bill for clean-up from general funds. Later, this position was modified to suggest a three-way split among the industry, the federal government, and state and local governments. Finally, the industry said that they thought they could contribute 40 percent of the total cost. Edmund Frost, general counsel and vice president of the industry trade association, reportedly stated that "we are all but at agreement on this." Then, according to personnel both in Congress and the EPA, the industry simply disappeared. They would no longer participate. It is not clear why the industry withdrew at this time, but it might be reflective of the changing attitude and strategy within the industry's trade association.

Stakeholders

The list of stakeholders involved in this issue is shown in Table 7.2. It is a very large list, and many of these stakeholders entered and left the debate as the issue unfolded and approached resolution. Some of the key players, however, are noted here.

No discussion of the hazardous waste issue would be complete without the inclusion of the members of the chemical industry itself. Since the industry had been in a constant battle with government and environmental groups over the twenty years preceding this proposal, many of the firms had developed sophisticated boundary-spanning units to deal with these issues and problems (generally in the public affairs function) that reflected the views and interests of the corporation's top management and the competitive political rivalry within the industry as a whole. Some of the larger firms that played a role in this issue were Allied Chemical, Dow, Du Pont, Monsanto, Rohm and Haas, and Union Carbide.

Allied Chemical and Dow had unique reputations within the chemical industry at this time, as well as in their relationships with Congress and the EPA. *Chemical and Engineering News* (June 8, 1981) referred to these two companies as "hardliners." Staff members of Congressional Committees in Congress, and staffers in the EPA noted that during the battle over Superfund, these two firms were "the stormtroopers of the industry." These general impressions were also supported within the industry trade association's

Table 7.2
Stakeholders in the Superfund Issue: An Illustrative, and Not All-Inclusive, Listing

Business Entities	Governmental Entities, Environmental groups, and Selected Individuals
American Fertilizer Institute	President James E. Carter
American Mining Congress	Environmental Protection Agency
Association of American Railroads	Department of Commerce
Business Roundtable	Department of Health and Human Services
Chemical Manufacturers Association	
Chemical Speciality Manufacturers Association	House Ways and Means Committee
The Fertilizer Institute	House Interstate and Foreign Commerce Committee
National Association of Manufacturers	House Subcommittee on Transportation and Commerce
The Petroleum Institute	House Subcommittee on Water Resources
Individual firms and Individuals	Senate Environment and Public Works Committee
Allied Chemical	Senate Finance Committee
Dow Chemical	
DuPont	Senate Committee on Commerce, Science and Technology
Hooker Chemical	
Monsanto	Individuals and Associations
Olin	Representative James J. Florio
Occidental Petroleum	Senator Jesse Helms
Rohm and Haas	Senator Edmund Muskie
Union Carbide	Senator Robert T. Stafford
Robert Roland	Senator Jennings Randolph
Vincent Gregory, Jr.	Senator John C. Culver
Irving Shapiro	National Governors Association
William Stover	National Wildlife Federation
	Audubon Society

membership. Dow Chemical was one of the clear leaders in political action committee spending during this period, and their president, Paul F. Ofeffice was a member of the trade association's executive board during the Superfund issue. Finally, Dow's environmental manager served as chairman of the Environmental Management Committee of the trade association.

Du Pont spent time on traditional public relations activities, but at this period was devoting increasing amounts of time and manpower to environmental analysis and forecasting. Du Pont, at the time, did not have a political action committee in its government affairs department, nor did responsibility for legislative lobbying reside there. Du Pont also had a very activist-oriented CEO—Irving Shapiro. Du Pont tried to make public affairs a strong point within the firm, embracing an advanced view of the world and the need for understanding the external environment in a philosophy that stated:

Corporate reputation is not, in our judgment, nebulous goodwill. Rather it is based on clear perceptions by influential groups of basic corporate characteristics. First, it is the practical utility and value of a company's products. Second is a company's contributions to the national quality of life—social worth and benefit of business. Third is the fairmindedness and ethical behavior of company management. (Du Pont, 1975)

More than any other chemical firm at this time, Monsanto tried hard to persuade the general public that chemicals are not all bad. It had been conducting an extensive public relations program entitled "Chemical Facts of Life" for several years. A familiar refrain in their advertising was that "Without chemicals, life itself would be impossible." Monsanto was also recognized within the industry as having the most sophisticated grassroots operation. So involved in grassroots organizations is Monsanto that they were subjected to a series of articles in the *St. Louis Post-Dispatch* several years prior to the Superfund issue. Several Monsanto executives were quoted as saying that they were pressured to join the firm's political action committee (PAC). One executive noted that contribution to the PAC was to be considered a "cost of employment." During the Superfund debate, Louis Fernandez, Monsanto's vice chairman, served as chair of the trade association's Superfund Committee.

Another large chemical firm, Rohm and Haas, had often taken moderate stands on legislation affecting the chemical industry. Part of this positioning is a consequence of Vincent Gregory, Jr.'s (the chairman of the firm) view of the firm in a broader societal context.

Union Carbide staked out their relationship with the external environment through the use of issue managers who concentrated on issues of vital importance to the corporation. The guiding philosophy at Union Carbide has been "come and let us reason together" (Menzies, 1978: 87).

In addition to these individual firms, it is important to understand the changes that were taking place in the industry's trade association as Superfund became an issue demanding attention. In June 1979, the Manufacturing Chemists Association (MCA) changed its name to the *Chemical Manufacturing Association* (CMA). This change involved a great deal more than just a name change. The Manufacturing Chemists Association was formed in 1872 when a small band of oil or vitriol (sulfuric acid) producers banded together. In the past, the MCA's unofficial motto was "quiet excellence," and the group's lobbyists worked inconspicuously behind the scenes. According to William Stover (1981), vice president of CMA, "The industry was getting beaten up, and the MCA was not a forceful voice in Washington." Certainly the period immediately preceding this name change offers ample evidence of the ineffectiveness of the MCA.

The industry brought in a new president, Robert A. Roland, who had twenty years of experience with the National Paint and Coatings Association fighting similar battles in Washington. Roland quickly moved to demonstrate that business would not be conducted as usual. He reorganized CMA, increased dues revenue by 88 percent, and developed an entirely new committee and staff organization.

The change in faces at the CMA over the last year or so has been dizzying, several insiders there say. Among the fifty-four professionals in the office, only six have been there for ten years or more.

"We're an association, not a chemical company," one executive explains. "Some second career people who worked well in the corporate world did not do so well in that of the trade group," he says. (Feare, 1980: 11)

This growth in staff was particularly evident in the technical department and in the office of general counsel, areas that would reflect the association's new aggressive stance. Edmund B. Frost, vice president and general counsel who came to CMA in 1978, observed that "CMA will bring no frivolous cases and it will not move out of spite. It will not fight for the sake of a fight, but neither will it hesitate to sue when it thinks the general interests of the chemical industry are damaged and there is a chance of winning in court" (Feare, 1980: 12).

Thus, as the Superfund debate unfolded, the industry participants were somewhat divided in their views of government regulation, and the trade association was headed by a new individual and team, determined that the industry would no longer be a scapegoat and willing to battle on issues in the courtroom and in the legislature.

As the issue unfolded, it would also assume new meaning for President Jimmy Carter. The issue reached a crucial stage just prior to the elections in 1980. Domestically, President Carter had been doing poorly at that time. Although the Camp David Accords between Israel and Egypt were a notable international achievement, he had no clear successful programs and actions on the domestic front. The public's attention was drawn to the embassy hostage drama in Iran being played out in nightly news shows (which, incidentally, is how *Nightline* got its start). As the elections drew near, the Superfund issue became one of increasing importance to Carter and the administration as a potential domestic policy success that could be used in the re-election campaign.

Other stakeholders involved in this issue included Hooker Chemicals, Olin Corporation, the Fertilizer Institute, the National Association of Manufacturers, the National Governors Association, the media, petroleum firms, the American Petroleum Institute, the insurance industry, environmental organizations, labor unions, individual congressmen, the American Mining Congress, and the Business Roundtable. Many of these stakeholders were involved in the issue for very different reasons. For example, the National Governors Association saw the issue as one of federal cost transfer; that is, if they did not get involved, it was likely that the federal government would pass on some or all of the costs to the states for clean-up. The American Mining Congress was interested because early discussions of hazardous waste disposal proposed taxing mining wastes. As the debate unfolded, these concerns were dropped from consideration, and the mining interests withdrew from the discussion. The insurance industry became involved when the Senate introduced the Post Closure Liability Fund (PCLF) into the legislation. This aspect of the legislation proposed the establishment of a fund to pay for any problems with a site after its closure. In order to qualify for the fund, the site had to be maintained in strict accordance with the law and then monitored for leaks after closure. If no leaks occurred during a certain time frame, the federal government would pay for clean-up and repair of the site through the PCLF.

Barriers to Entry and Exit

As the debate over Superfund unfolded, the barriers to entry and exit into the political contest altered. Throughout the debate, it was clear that major chemical companies and the CMA could not exit the contest unless they were willing to forego any substantive impact on the legislation. There were companies that the CMA and the industry wished not to be engaged—for example, Hooker Chemical Company—but Congress forced (and Hooker wanted) involvement. In any political contest, it is difficult for the individual citizen to be heard, as the mechanism for his or her voice is through an organized group like a public interest group.

As the legislation was defined more clearly, barriers to entry were raised as other industries were no longer impacted by the legislation and, therefore, were not considered as necessary to the debate (e.g., the American Mining Congress). The petroleum industry would like to have exited this debate, but it was their push for legislation that triggered the interest in chemical wastes and hazardous waste sites. This was a particularly troubling issue for firms that had both chemical and oil interests. The oil industry was in support of federal legislation and was willing to make major concessions on key issues like liability, but the chemical industry was not willing to make such concessions. This legislation effectively divided the industry and served as a barrier to entry and exit for both industries.

As the legislation unfolded, the positions of the CMA and the executive branch, reflected in their respective leaders—Robert Roland and President James Carter—hardened and made it difficult for withdrawal and compromise. They, too, were effectively precluded from exiting this debate.

THE LEGISLATION UNFOLDS AND SUBSTITUTE ISSUES ARE OFFERED

Congressional hearings began in March 1979 on the Comprehensive Environmental Response, Compensation, and Liability Act (CERCLA, or, more commonly, Superfund), and among the first topics pursued was the toxic situation at Love Canal in New York. Hooker Chemical Company testified and several revelations of their activities in California, along with the generally emotionally charged issue of Love Canal, proved damaging to the firm and to the industry as a whole.

The press was not silent on this issue and played a key role in keeping the issue of hazardous wastes before the public during the entire debate over Superfund. In an editorial entitled "Who Pays for Poison?" the *Washington Post* noted:

By now, companies such as Hooker ought to realize that times have changed. Instead of waiting to be pushed, they should voluntarily disclose all they know about their past and present dumps, and shoulder responsibility for cleaning up the problems—residues that they know or had reason to know about. That would put them in a stronger moral position from which to ask for public help if the problems exceed their resources. It wouldn't be bad public relations either. (April 12, 1979: 16)

   This brought an immediate response from Robert Roland, president of the CMA, that laid out the industry's first attempts to redefine and substitute a new issue for the one currently in favor (clean-up of hazardous waste sites). On April 21, 1979, he responded:

One of the things that we must all realize in discussing the solid-waste disposal problem, including toxic or hazardous wastes, is that it is not just the problem of the chemical industry. It is a result of society's advanced technology and pursuit of an increasingly complex lifestyle. The *Post's* editorial implies that a more positive public posture by manufacturing companies would engender a more positive public response if the solution to the problems exceed the resources. I think it is manifestly clear from testimony given recently that such will clearly be the case, with estimates of a Superfund to stabilize and secure existing hazardous dump running to the tune of almost $50 billion. (Roland, 1979: 15)

   Later in the Superfund debate, Roland would observe that "The administration's bill unfairly singles out the chemical and related industries to bear a disproportionate burden of the clean up costs. In doing so, it fails to adequately reflect the society's responsibility for resolving a problem which everyone helped create and for whose solution everyone should help pay" ("Bill Proposes Hazardous Waste Clean Up Fund," 1979: 27). Supporting these themes and proposing an additional way of looking at this issue was Bruce Davis, President of Hooker's Industrial Chemicals Group in his testimony before Congress. He urged that any "ultrafund" proposals (as the industry referred to Superfund) must address four key questions: (1) What would be the exact use of the ultrafund? (2) Should the ultrafund be comprehensive in its coverage? (3) Which sites should be covered by legislation? (4) What would be the fund size and method of funding?
   Davis addressed the third and fourth questions in his testimony. He argued that the clean-up of hazardous waste sites should actually be the clean-up of abandoned hazardous waste sites and not just hazardous waste sites in general. Davis also noted that "Because the problem is truly a national one, we feel that a fund should be comprised of public as well as industry funding. In fact, in view of the national scope of the problem, substantial Federal funding appears to be appropriate" (U.S. Congress, Senate, May 18, 1979).
   The industry's attempts to redefine the issue and shape the debate to come should be clear as they pursued a strategy to simultaneously expand and narrow the issue. Roland raises a number of issues that could be substituted for the issue of hazardous waste site clean-up. He first argued that it is a solid waste disposal problem and not just a toxic waste problem. As a result, it is not just a

chemical industry problem, but a problem of all industries. This is a very clear tactic—broaden the definition of the issue and bring in other stakeholders with different personal agendas to confuse the issue or make the issue so complex that it defies analysis and easy solutions. If this did not work (and it did for only a short period of time), then Roland argued that it is the result of society's advanced lifestyle and advanced technology—that is, society in its demands for new products and technologies has contributed to the development of hazardous wastes and should therefore bear the burden of clean-up costs. Again, the attempt is to broaden the issue and make all of society responsible, thus making it a general problem that should be resolved with federal funds and not just industry funds. This position was supported by Davis's testimony. This particular substitution of an issue attempt did not work as industry representatives were repeatedly asked who benefited financially from products and services that produced a toxic byproduct? The answer was evident—industry profited from these activities and did not absorb the hazardous waste costs associated with these profits.

Davis's final point was an interesting attempt to offer a substitute issue that narrowed the issue at hand. His argument was that the focus of clean-up should only be on those sites that have been abandoned and for whom it would be difficult to assess responsibility. These sites, he and others in the industry argued, were a fraction of the total sites and would cost far less than the federal government was suggesting. For those sites where responsibility and ownership was clear, hold those individuals and firms responsible for hazardous waste management and clean-up.

The industry's strategy in dealing with legislation introduced in both the House of Representatives and Senate was clear to John Doyle, minority counsel for the Subcommittee on Water Resource in the U.S. House. It was "to try and get legislation to as many committees and subcommittees as possible, complicating the legislation, increasing the number of hurdles necessary for passage, and hopefully killing the legislation" (Doyle, 1981).

At the end of 1979, *Chemical Week* cautioned the industry about the future, and argued that the industry, Congress, and the EPA were about to enter the "eye of the 'Superfund' storm" ("CPI Wants Superfund Bill Cut Down to Size," 1979: 44).

THE AUDIENCE AND THE FINAL PUSH FOR ACTION

It should be clear from the discussion thus far that the arena for resolution of the hazardous waste issue was the national legislature, and that the audience consisted of the U.S. Congress, individual Senators and Representatives, and their associated committees and subcommittees. This audience was selected by the executive branch of government when it decided to press for legislation in this area, and the chemical industry was placed in the position of responding to the issue in an already selected arena. As noted in Chapter 3, though, it is not just the Congress that is being appealed to in these contests—it is society as a whole. All the stakeholders in this drama attempted to appeal to the general public in hope that the general public would agree with their position and take action in support of that position. The chemical industry clearly tried this in their arguments that it was a societal problem, and that it should only focus on abandoned waste sites. The government (with the help of the press) kept the pressure on the main issue—the cleanup of hazardous waste sites around the nation. This argument went even further to note that the chemical industry had not cleaned up sites in the past when it had the opportunity and could not be trusted to this task in the future without external oversight and pressure. The action desired from all stakeholders was to have the general public write or call their Congressman with their position on hazardous waste site legislation. As such, every tactic and strategy should be viewed in relation to its likely impact on both Congress and the general public.

The opening of the CMA's campaign against Superfund began in earnest on March 7, 1980 with the release of a summary of a study the CMA conducted on hazardous waste sites around the country. CMA President Roland noted that the study

confirms our belief that the size of the Superfund problem is not as great as the Environmental Protection Agency has estimated, and that state agencies are acting in this area in a responsible manner to handle their own problems.

The hazardous waste disposal problem is manageable at the state level, and it precludes the need for massive new intervention.

The Association opposes Superfund legislation because it would create an unnecessary bureaucracy and squander the nation's resources at a time when sound fiscal management is imperative. (CMA News Release, 1979)

Note again the attempt to substitute new issues and to appeal to both the general public and Congress simultaneously. Roland is putting three new issues on the table for debate. The first is the debate in this country since its founding of states rights versus federal government rights. Roland is arguing that we do not need more federal involvement, as it can be and is being handled at the state level. This is potentially appealing to the general public that is tired of increasing federal involvement and can be appealing to federal legislators as well. After all, if the regulation of such sites is being carried out effectively at the state level, is there a need for federal intervention? The second issue is one of fiscal responsibility, and it appeals to the general public and Congress. Given the state's actions, do we need to spend scarce additional funds on a federal bureaucracy that is unnecessary? The third issue is to question the need for a new bureaucracy and set of legislation when existing bureaucratic procedures and legislation that covers this problem already exists. It is a subtle argument with great appeal for elected officials, as it allows them to oppose new or changed legislation on the grounds that existing legislation is sufficient to cover the problem. One may recall the struggle in the recent past by the National Organization for Women (NOW) to get a constitutional amendment for women's rights. A powerful argument, used at both the state and federal legislative level, was that the Bill of Rights and the Civil Rights Act already guaranteed equality and rights for women.

This summary report was attacked quite harshly and in detail by the EPA. Among other things, the EPA accused the CMA of releasing a report that "is both inaccurate and has been circulated by CMA in a self-serving attempt to scuttle proposed Superfund legislation." The EPA response went on to address each and every point in the CMA document. More important, from a public reaction and relations standpoint, the EPA circulated a copy of its response to all committees in the House and Senate that were dealing with the legislation and asked CMA for a copy of the full survey (not just the summary that was provided).[6] In all instances, the CMA refused to provide the material, raising doubts as to the accuracy of the study and as to whether it was performed at all. While all this was going on, the explosion at a chemical dump in Elizabeth, New Jersey (discussed earlier) occurred, raising both media interest and general public concern.

At this time, a difference in political strategy surfaced within the chemical industry. The industry had succeeded in stopping the bill in Representative Florio's (a prominent and outspoken supporter of this legislation) subcommittee. Union Carbide, Olin, Du Pont, Rohm and Haas, and Monsanto wanted to compromise on the size of the funding and receive other concessions. When the bill went to full committee, a compromise did occur. According to *Chemical Week:*

The first crack in the chemical industry's opposition to Superfund began at about 4 P.M. on May 13, when Vincent L. Gregory, Jr., chairman of Rohm and Haas, and Kenneth Davis, the company's Washington representative, visited Representative James J. Florio (D., NJ), chairman of the House Subcommittee on Transportation and Commerce. Gregory and Davis ex-

pected to continue an argument with Florio over the form of HR 7020. . . .
Florio told Gregory and Davis that he understood the industry's position
and that he was willing to support amendments on funding and liability,
which were major points of concern. By midnight, the revised bill was ready,
and on May 13, the Commerce Committee moved swiftly to adopt the measure, easily overcoming attempts to toughen it. ("Superfund Compromise
Wins 'Grudging' Nod," June 18, 1980: 63)

These "cracks" in the industry's position were not public knowledge in May. The compromise noted involved the use of funds for
remedying failing or orphan sites and the removal of third-party
liability. In addition, this particular bill would not change liability
laws to make it easier to recover damages for injuries and, where
several companies were found responsible for damages, courts could
apportion the costs among them rather than hold one firm liable
for all damages. This compromise did not meet with unanimous
approval with CMA, as *Chemical Week* noted: "But such suppport
for HR 7020 appears to have caused serious dissension within the
chemical industry. One company official says there has been 'blood
in the streets'" ("Superfund Compromise Wins 'Grudging' Nod," June
18, 1980: 63).

Some of the dissension centered around the view of some members of the CMA that any compromise was a sign of weakness, and
a signal to the public interest groups, Congress, and the executive
branch of government that the industry was admitting to some
degree of guilt and culpability on this issue. Those favoring the
compromise argued that the industry's position that they were not
responsible for dumping

appeared to antagonize many congressmen, who were being pressured as
a result of media coverage of hazardous-waste-sites. In additon, Union
Carbide's representative, Jeremiah Kenney, points to the EPA's "skillful,
two-pronged campaign" in the media and in direct lobbying to push for
Superfund. And, congressional sources say the chemical industry "stonewalled" on the Superfund making it difficult, even for sympathetic congressmen, to work out an acceptable compromise. ("Superfund Compromise
Wins 'Grudging' Nod," June 18, 1980: 63)

The compromise passed by a full committee vote of 21 to 3 and
was placed on the calendar for consideration by the entire House.
In the Senate, a new wrinkle arose which, from the chemical
industry's perspective, might influence the outcome. Senator
Edmund Muskie (D., ME) left the Senate to accept President
Carter's appointment as Secretary of State. Muskie was considered by many to be a leading figure on environmental issues, and
as one staffer noted, "Muskie's loss (to Secretary of State) changed

for all time the deliberative aspects of this and all future bills." The industry was very concerned that the Senate, out of respect for Muskie, would pass Superfund. Fortunately for the industry, this did not occur.

The strains within the CMA in terms of holding a united front were beginning to erupt into the public arena at this time. Mosher points out that

The Chemical Manufacturers Association, which has fought every proposal, undoubtedly has contributed to the slow pace of legislation. And it has contributed to some ill will in Congress, even among opponents of Superfund legislation.

"Those who have stonewalled the legislative process have also made it very difficult for those of us who wanted a reasonable bill," Representative Edward R. Madigan (R., IL) said during the debate on the Florio bill. . . .

A considerable segment of the chemical industry is coming to believe that if Congress doesn't act this year, it will soon. Officials of many chemical companies are putting pressure on the Chemical Manufacturers Association to abandon its hard-line position against any legislation. If regulation is inevitable, they want to have a voice in shaping it. "I think society will demand some level of federal effort to clean up waste sites like Love Canal," predicted Jerry Kenney, Union Carbide Corporation's Washington representative. "Politically, the chemical industry is not going to escape without paying a fee." (1980: 855, 857)[7]

A FINAL ATTEMPT AT REDEFINING THE ISSUE

The chemical industry brought immense pressure to bear on the House of Representatives to have Florio's bill referred to the Ways and Means Committee. This was another attempt to redefine the bill, but in a way that made sense procedurally within the House of Representatives. The industry successfully argued that Superfund's financing constituted revenue raising for the government, and was therefore under the jurisdiction of the Ways and Means Committee. The industry believed that they would get a better deal from Ways and Means. John Doyle (1981) noted that "Ways and Means was especially sensitive and knowledgeable of industry needs." William Stover (1981), vice president of the CMA, was especially pleased at the time, noting: "We were delighted to see it go to Ways and Means. We thought we would get a more balanced view there that would limit the bill to 'orphan sites' and hang the wrongdoer. If you can't find the wrongdoer, then use federal money."

The Committee considered the bill, and on June 17, formally voted, 20 to 15, on HR 7020. In a major blow to the industry, the Committee doubled the size of the fund from $600 million to $1.2 billion, and raised industry's contribution from 50 percent to 75 percent. According to several observers, the CMA had bipartisan support within the Committee for a $900 million Superfund. CMA decided that it could defeat this proposal and did not go with the compromise. Unfortunately, according to congressional sources, a "key congressman took a walk," and Representative Downey's amendment to double the size of the funding and increase the industry's level of contribution was passed in less than four minutes. Even with this defeat, there was still optimism within the industry:

Chances of a final, compromise legislation reaching President Carter's desk before Congress adjourns in October are slim. But the chemical industry's opposition to a Superfund is crumbling.
    The Chemical Manufacturers Association is granting what is called "grudging approval" to HR 7020 and is seeking a similar measure from the Senate. ("Superfund Compromise Wins 'Grudging' Nod," June 18, 1980: 63)

Other comments from industry members demonstrate the size of the rift within the industry and the growing thrust for compromise on this issue:

Rohm and Haas's Davis says his company unequivocally supports HR 7020. "It would have saved lots of aggravation if we had gotten this measure months ago," he says. And Du Pont's Washington representative, John Klocko, says the Commerce Committee's markup of Florio's bill was the turning point for Superfund, because the industry decided it could get improved legislation it could live with.
    Companies that were pushing for a compromise—particularly Rohm and Haas, Olin, Monsanto—appear to have won their point. ("Superfund Compromise Wins 'Grudging' Nod," June 18, 1980: 63)

This support for compromise caused serious dissension within the CMA. Within the councils of CMA, Allied, Dow, and Du Pont were still urging the membership to help kill any Superfund legislation. As these battles were being played out within the CMA, the legislation was moving through the Senate. In late June, the Senate Environment and Public Works Committee approved a $4.1 billion fund for clean-up and to compensate victims of toxic waste sites. This was significantly different from the Florio bill, and the CMA reacted predictably:

We haven't stopped a goddamn thing in that committee," said CMA President Robert Roland before the bill passed, "but we have indications that a lot of people will support us on the floor." The current House version is "a more reasoned approach," Roland added, calling the Senate committee product yesterday, "impractical, unnecessarily broad and punitive." Any fund financing by the industry is "still repugnant," he said. (Omang, June 28, 1980)

The industry was beginning to realize that its political strategy on this issue was not producing desired results and that their positioning and tactics on this issue were hurting:

Lobbyists for the Chemical Manufacturers Association have already stumbled badly over the Superfund. For months, after the Administration first proposed it more than a year ago, the industry refused to consider and compromise.

The industry already has suffered for its miscues. For example, chemical lobbyists urged sending the Commerce Committee bill to Ways and Means. Some claim this was a tactic to delay the bill, but CMA's Roland says that the industry wanted the fee scrutinized as a tax. In any case, the strategy backfired. Ways and Means, under pressure to come up with $1.2 billion in revenue to conform with the fiscal 1981 budget resolution, voted to triple the original fee.

Industry's best chance for derailing the Superfund now is delay. ("Closer to a Cleanup Superfund," July 14, 1980: 30)

Irving Shapiro, in an address to the nation's lieutenant governors, kept the pressure on for a compromise; especially in regard to abandoned waste sites. Although the speech was not widely publicized, it served as a signal of Shapiro's position on Superfund and where Du Pont was likely to go on this issue:

Nonetheless, the chemical industry is willing to pay its fair share to make the environment safe from these orphan dumps. To that end, we support a Federal "Superfund" to help the states clear up abandoned disposal sites. Presently there are three such bills in Congress and Du Pont believes that the best of these to be the bill sponsored by Congressman Florio of New Jersey—HR 7020. The Florio bill addressed the primary problem of providing funds today to clean up inactive waste sites. (Shapiro, 1980: 8)

With the end of summer approaching, and the Congressional and Presidential elections in November, the pace of legislation began to slow in the Senate. In the Senate, the Finance and the Commerce Committee sought jurisdiction over the bill, but the request of the committee was to be denied. The industry continued to maintain pressure on the legislation, with a focus on the Senate where the bills being considered were considered far more threatening. The St. Louis Post-Dispatch reported that

The chemical and oil industries have begun a well-organized and well-targeted campaign to dramatically change a Senate bill.

The chemical company campaign include what Congressional Quarterly, in a report published this last week, termed a "highly sophisticated computerized mailing" by St. Louis based Monsanto Company to its 40,000 shareholders.

"There's been no groundswell of public support to offset the massive campaign being waged by the chemical industry," said a staffer for the Senate Environment Committee. "Unless people are sitting near a chemical dump, they don't write. As a result, the lobbying is very lopsided now."

"This campaign is much more sophisticated, much more effective than a postcard campaign," said Curtis Moore, minority counsel for the Senate Environment Committee. "It speaks of a high degree of knowledge of how the Senate operates. It shows awareness that a single contact from a personal friend, or a single letter from the right kind of organization may be worth more than a hundred postcards.

The campaign is effective because instead of flooding Capitol Hill with letters from housewives, the letters are from engineers, lawyers, and architects—"the people who influence policy," Moore said. ("Superfund Stalls in Senate," September 14, 1980: 1, 7k)

The Senate Finance Committee, who obtained jurisdiction over the Senate Superfund bill, did not want to bring the bill to a Committee vote or to allow the bill to go to the Senate floor for action. There were several reasons for this reluctance. Some senators were opposed on ideological grounds, while others were concerned with the legal precedent that would be set, and yet others were concerned over the impact this legislation might have on small firms. The media maintained pressure for action now rather than later. The *Washington Post,* in an editorial entitled "Running out the Clock," observed that

Time is running out on one of the more important pieces of legislation before Congress this year. The legislation would create a fund—nicknamed Superfund—for dealing with emergencies caused by spills and leaks for oil and hazardous chemicals. Though no one publicly disputes the need for such a fund, it is being delayed to death by a massive lobbying campaign waged by the oil and chemical industries.

Enactment has been frustrated by splintered congressional jurisdiction—three or more different committees on each side of the Capitol—and by a determined lobbying campaign against any but the weakest versions of the bill. With so many different committees in the act, there are almost endless opportunities to kill the legislation through inaction without anyone's saying to come out and vote against it, and this is precisely the chemical and oil lobbyists' strategy.

The present arena is the Senate Finance Committee, which finally held hearings last week after two months of delay. Senators outdid each other in extolling the importance of the bill but then solemnly noted the complexity and momentousness of its precise administrative details and funding mechanisms. These matters can be worked out on the floor and in the House-Senate conference, however; the committee's job is to take prompt enough action so that final passage is possible in the remaining few days of the session. If this committee and other key members of the leadership continue to vacillate, no amount of rhetoric will hide the fact that the Senate let the chemical industry pressure it into running out the clock on a bill that would serve everyone's best interest. (1980: 24, 28)

The CMA then made a critical credibililty blunder. CMA President Roland, appearing on ABC's September 11 edition of *Nightline*, stated that "In testimony before the Senate Finance Committee on S 1480, we indicated once more that we support 7020—HR 7020—the Florio bill on the House side. The breakdown would be 75 percent industry and 25 percent government. It would be $1.2 billion" (Ember, 1981: 17). The CMA appeared to be sending out mixed signals, and even though Roland sent out a letter the next day stating that he had been misquoted, the industry's supporters were dismayed, and proponents of the legislation were pleased to use this to damage the CMA's credibility.

On September 23, the House voted to consider HR 7020 as reported by Ways and Means (the $1.2 billion; 75–25 percent split). David Stockman, then a representative in the debate over the bill, referred to the bill's creation of the EPA as a "czar" in the hazardous waste area. He offered two amendments to the bill, the first of which would have gutted the bill and removed all industry contributions. This amendment was rejected. His second amendment would have required the administrator of the EPA to define "hazardous waste site" within 120 days of enactment of the law, and subjecting that definition to Congressional review and one House veto, was also rejected. The House passed the legislation by a large majority—351 to 23—and it was sent to the Senate for consideration.

Roland, after the passage of the bill in the House, observed that "the bill, although not perfect, represents a conscientious bipartisan effort to address the problem realistically and to establish adequate protection for the public and the environment" (*Environmental Reporter*, September 26, 1980: 729).

As Congress adjourned for the election recess, the media kept the Superfund issue alive. The *Washington Post*, in an editorial entitled "Last Days for Superfund," continued to focus on the Senate Finance Committee and its delaying actions:

However, the measure is now stalled in the Senate, in the Finance Committee to be precise. So far, Finance Chairman Russell Long and his committee have refused to indicate what changes they would like to see in the existing Senate bill, or even to agree to act in time to allow final action on the bill during the post-election lame-duck session. Senator Dole and others have further hurt the bill's chances by threatening to use Superfund as the vehicle for the controversial tax cut should it be taken up on the Senate floor. These senators and others regularly proclaim their support for

some kind of Superfund. But after months of delay, their actions—or failure to act—tell the real story.

The Finance Committee owes it to the rest of Congress—and to the public—to let Superfund be voted by the full Senate before the end of this
year. (September 24, 1980: 26)

The *New York Times* also applied pressure and noted in an editorial entitled "While Poisons Fester":

Finally, the House has approved "Superfund" legislation to clean up abandoned hazardous waste sites for oil and chemical spills. The only barrier
now is the Senate, where, alas, there is no sign that Russell Long is prepared to allow the "Superfund" bill to reach the floor for a vote. If the
Finance Committee fails to act, the nation will lose a precious opportunity
to defend against toxic hazards that are becoming increasingly common.

Diehard proponents of one bill or another threaten to block final action
unless their versions prevail. That would be the worst outcome of all. Either legislative approach would be far better than no bill at all (HR 7020
or S 1480). Congress has stalled long enough. Poisons are festering. So is
injustice. The nation is waiting. (September 26, 1980: A34)

In spite of this strong rhetoric and the fact that Superfund was
becoming "one of the best spectator sports now being played on
Capitol Hill" (Ember, 1980), the chance for passage was seen as only
50–50. The Finance Committee was given a deadline for action by the
Senate. The Finance Committee had to report back to the full Senate
by November 1 or lose jurisdiction over the legislation.

This slowing of momentum was not lost in the White House. President Carter contacted legislators directly and asked if his administration could work for a compromise. This work, at the urging of
several senators, took the form of meetings among key actors. These
meetings were apparently helpful in moving the industry to accept a
compromise. However, in yet another change in political strategy and
tactics, the industry apparently decided that Reagan would win
the Presidential election and that they would get a better deal from
him, so any further compromises would be unnecessary. The prevail-
ing mood at this time was, in the words of White House aide Robert
Maher, that "Superfund is dead for now, but we think we can get a
compromise when Congress comes back" (Shabecoff, 1980: 20).

FINAL RESOLUTION

The Presidential and Congressional elections on November 4, 1980
dramatically altered the power structure and stakeholder positioning around Superfund politics. The Republican Presidential candidate achieved a landslide victory, and the Republican Party made

significant gains in membership in the House. More important, the Republicans achieved control of the Senate, where the Superfund legislation was being delayed. The election of Ronald Reagan, with his avowed philosophy of reduced government intervention in business and individual affairs, must have been a bright spot for the CMA and member firms. Further good news arrived with the announcement by Senators Byrd and Baker (outgoing and incoming majority leaders) that the Senate would not consider controversial legislation in the lame-duck session beginning November 12. The forecasts for passage of Superfund were poor. Omang predicted at the time that "another Carter environmental goal, the so-called 'Superfund' to finance cleanup of toxic waste dumps apparently is dead. Both situations are products of the new Republican strength in the Senate" (1980: A1). At this point, the CMA was positive that Superfund was dead for this Congressional session. " 'The question is whether the Senate wants to take up something as time consuming and controversial as this is going to be,' he [Roland] said. 'I would say that they have other more important budget matters to take care of'" (Omang, 1980: A1).

Once again, the overconfidence of the CMA and industry would lead them to make critical errors in judgment. Congressman Florio and CMA President Roland had a meeting on November 14, 1980. Aides to both individuals agree on the following facts: (1) Florio wanted the CMA to issue a statement clearly in support of HR 7020; and, if the CMA would do this, then (2) Florio would guarantee delivery of the Senate in support of HR 7020. Roland stated that he could not make such a commitment without the approval of the CMA executive board or at least the executive committee of that board. Roland also stated that the CMA would probably not agree to such a statement of support, as it was opposed to HR 7020, and that Roland doubted Florio could deliver the Senate, since he could not deliver his own subcommittee. It is disputed, however, as to whether Roland said that the industry felt it could get a better deal from the incoming Republican administration. According to Ember, "Florio left the meeting enraged and held a press conference to announce that Roland had reneged on his deal to support his $1.2 billion bill. Florio tells *Chemical and Engineering News* that Roland did make the statement about industry's getting a better deal next year. Roland, through CMA spokesman Jeff Van, insists he never made that comment" (1981: 18).

Whether Roland made these comments about the incoming administration to Florio is unimportant. Two points stand out that further damaged the industry and the CMA's credibility. First, the CMA did, given previous comments to the press and others, appear to reverse its position in regard to HR 7020. Second, influential senators such as Baker, Dole, Domenici, and Moynihan believed that the CMA could make a statement like this, and it put the Republicans in an untenable public position. To fail to act now would make it appear that they were in the industry's hip pocket. Later, when asked about this statement, Roland, while denying that he made it, acknowledged that the political climate in 1981 (after the new administration took office) would be more favorable to business. He insisted that the CMA has not "reneged on a thing" because it always opposed the House bill as too "radical" ("Toxic Cleanup Suffers a Reversal," November 15, 1980: A26). This continued hardline approach to compromise caused great tension within the CMA, and Florio's actions spread that tension further:

But Representative James J. Florio (D., NJ) apparently sensed that the Chemical Manufacturers Association would not support his bill (HR 7020) and would try instead to put the bill over into the next Congress, hoping for a better deal. So Florio created sufficient publicity over the issue to tip the balance in favor of passage of a Superfund bill. "If you're going to cut a person off at the knee," says one industry source, dismayed at CMA'a handling of Florio, "at least you shouldn't do it publicly." ("Superfund Finale Wrenches CMA," December 3, 1980: 16)

All the publicity and controversy caused the incoming administration to request a position paper from the EPA addressing two questions: (1) Why does the bill have to pass now? and (2) How would the Reagan administration pass it? The EPA's response highlighted four points, and it emphasized the political and not the substantive nature of the issue. The four points were as follows:

1. The passage of the bill next year would require a great deal of rebattling over the same issues and prevent the development and progress of the Reagan legislative program.
2. Any Superfund bill would affect industry–government relationships. Passing Superfund now would make it a Carter versus Reagan bill.
3. If passage is delayed until next year, Reagan would have to use "chips" to get congressional support. ("Chips" are promises of support for individual congressmen's legislation or appointments or other political favors.)
4. The current Superfund can be made acceptable to a broad spectrum of the industry.

Senior Republican congressional members accepted the position laid out in the EPA position paper but were skeptical about getting industry support. Without this support, Republicans were reluctant to push for passage.

More public pressure was brought to bear on the Senate Finance Committee to release S 1480 in mid-November. The *New York Times,* the *Washington Post,* and the *Boston Globe,* as well as other major newspapers, released articles dealing with chemical industry political action committee contributions in the 1980 elections to Finance Committee members. No impropriety of any kind was suggested, but the circumstances at this time did not portray these members in a favorable light. The total of the contributions to the Finance Committee was $300,000, the maximum of which—$73,950— was given to incoming Senator Charles Grassly (R., IA), who defeated an outspoken sponsor and supporter of Superfund, Senator Culver. Yet these figures are not particularly large contributions.

In spite of these revelations, the CMA attempted to remain aloof and somewhat neutral. William Stover, vice president of CMA said, "I feel sure that the new power figures in Washington are not going to permit the Congress to move ahead with major precedent-setting legislation. Our support or lack of support at this time is really beside the point" (Roeder, November 17, 1980: 20). The reaction to this pressure by the Finance Committee was immediate. The next day, in an unusual move, "The Senate Finance Committee washed its hands of the controversy over a 'Superfund' to clean up chemical dumps yesterday, reporting without comment a $4.2 billion bill that is certain to be either killed or significantly amended on the Senate floor" (Omang, November 18, 1980: 24).

Almost immediately, compromise legislation was introduced to bring the Senate bill into alignment with the House passed legislation. The industry continued to oppose the legislation, but Shapiro (of Du Pont) publicly broke with the industry and argued for rational legislation dictated by the facts of the situation. Senator Moynihan, commenting on the industry position, noted, "I have to say that I can't imagine a greater disservice that the business community can do to President Reagan than to signal its expectation of what his administration will be like by withdrawing support for this legislation. In the annuals of corporate cynicism, I have not encountered anything as brazen" (Shabecoff, 1980: 20).

After Shapiro's public break, support within the CMA began to erode. Rohm and Haas and Union Carbide announced support for hazardous waste clean-up legislation in the current Congress. This was the type of support that the Republican leadership was looking for—they could count on the support of the largest (Du Pont) and the third-largest chemical firm (Union Carbide) for support of the Superfund.

Shortly thereafter, the Senate worked out a compromise bill that closely matched the House bill and passed the legislation by a floor vote of 78 to 9. *Chemical Week* attempted to analyze the industry's performance on this issue in an article entitled "Superfund Finale Wrenches CMA." In this analysis, it was pointed out that the CMA did not cover itself with glory during the debate over Superfund and may well have sown the seeds for future problems within its own membership and in its dealings with Congress:

Caught unprepared by the wave of support for the compromise bill, CMA found itself alone in support of a $600 million Superfund bill approved months ago by the House Commerce Committee. "From my standpoint, CMA did not negotiate with us in any real sense," says an aide to Senator Stafford. The aide maintains that, as debate progressed, the Chemical Specialities Manufacturers Association moved itself away from the CMA's position. In short, he says, "CMA did not serve itself well."

Nevertheless, CMA has antagonized a number of congressmen by underestimating political realities and presenting no unified position on Superfund. An aide to a Republican congressman, sympathetic to industry, says that the industry was "disorganized" when the House was considering Superfund. He recalls there were "too many people supposedly speaking for the industry, too many points of view, and too great a reluctance to make concessions." Another source says: "Had [CMA] been more constructive, this wouldn't have been so bitter at the end." ("Superfund Finale Wrenches CMA," December 3, 1980: 16)

EPILOGUE

Although the chemical industry lost the battle over Superfund, it was not the end of their battling over the issue. Although there is great public and media attention to controversial legislation, attention to the actual implemention of legislation is greatly reduced. The implementation of regulations is highly technical and usually quite boring to the general public. Reagan did not really support Superfund, and he appointed as the head of the EPA Anne Burford Gorsuch. Gorsuch hired Rita Lavelle to head the branch of the EPA charged with the implementation of Superfund. Action in implementation of the Superfund was very slow in coming. In December 1982, environmental and industry groups jointly filed a lawsuit against the EPA for failure to implement the law. For example, the legislation allowed for the government to clean a site and then pursue compensation for the clean-up afterwards. The EPA decided instead to pursue negotiations with those involved with the site and, while in negotiation, no clean-ups were pursued. Rita Lavelle and other top EPA aides were fired in early 1983 amidst claims of wrongdoing with Superfund monies. Lavelle was later convicted of perjury and sentenced to serve six months in jail. Gorsuch resigned her position as administrator of the EPA in March. Reagan then brought in William Ruckelshaus to head the EPA. Ruckelshaus had been the first administrator of the EPA. He was brought in to fix the EPA, improve its credibility, and to reduce the negative press associated with the administration and the EPA.

In 1986, Superfund came up for reconsideration and extension. The debate over this legislation never reached the level of controversy that the original bill generated, and the amendments (Superfund Amendments and Reauthorization Act of 1986; or, more commonly, SARA) were passed with industry support. One of the major changes in the SARA legislation was the inclusion of broad-based taxes to support the clean-up of toxic wastes (e.g., a tax on domestic oil, a tax on imported oil, and a tax on fuel to be used to treat leaking underground storage tanks). It is just possible that the industry learned from its earlier experience with Superfund and applied these lessons to SARA, with improved results, less controversy and alienation of congressmen and staffers, and reduced media and general public interest. One thing that the industry did learn was the need to maintain a united public front and prevent cracks in the industry position that hurt their credibility in the original Superfund debate. One observer of the SARA debate noted member companies' representatives, who normally struck side deals with legislators to help their firm, disappeared: "They (individual company representatives) spoke to us all the time; but they never delivered. Every time they tried (to make a deal) they were reeled in real fast. . . . CMA would get wind of it, the CEO would be called by the president of the CMA and told to call that lobbyist in and get him off the streets and stop talking this way. Lobbyists . . . were placed on short leashes very quickly" (Kelley-Judge, 1988: 167). A legislative aide also observed this change in CMA and industry behavior, noting that "The CMA has only gotten better through adversity in the political process. It has had so many fights that it had to become effective. It's a matter of a learning curve that they've gone through" (Kelley-Judge, 1988: 194).

CONCLUSION

Unlike Chapters 4, 5, and 6, this chapter allowed us to analyze one specific issue faced by an industry and the unfolding of that issue over time. We were able to clearly see the attempts by the industry to redefine the issue and offer substitute issues for consideration, both from substantive and procedural standpoints. The stakeholders involved in the issue remained fairly constant, with some departing the scene as the issue was redefined and no longer of interest or impact to them. The audience, in this case, was preselected by the government in its initial proposal of the legislation, and the chemical industry was forced to fight its battle in the legislative arena.

This particular situation saw the intersection of two elements in the contextual situation of the CMA and the executive branch of government—specifically, the White House. The reorganization of the CMA brought in new leadership and a willingness to be more forceful and confrontative in representing the industry's position. This realignment of the trade association followed nearly twenty years of increasing government intrusion and regulation of the industry. Superfund was the first opportunity for the revitalized CMA to flex its political muscle and provide leadership to the industry.

At the White House, Superfund legislation took on a new meaning for President Carter as the Iranian hostage crisis gripped the nation's attention. Although Carter achieved an international triumph with the Camp David Accords (peace between Egypt and Israel), there were no strong and notable domestic programs that he could point to as a legacy of his administration. As a consequence, Superfund took on a personal meaning that became even more important after the Presidential election and Carter was not returned to office.

The nature of events leading up to Superfund's consideration posed a set of entry and exit barriers for the chemical industry as a whole, for specific firms within the industry, and for related industries. The barriers to entry for the petroleum industry have already been discussed, and the specific entry and exit barriers for individual firms have been noted.

The audience was twofold—government and the general public. The media played a major role in keeping this issue alive at critical junctures during the debate, and both the government and the industry attempted to mobilize the public to support their position.

Ultimately, the industry lost on the issue of hazardous waste sites. The industry had ample opportunity to win on this issue, but it frequently made blunders at key moments in the debate, and the leadership of the industry did not accept a compromise when compromises were available and achievable. What is extraordinary about this issue is that the industry still had an opportunity to prevent passage of the legislation almost to the very end of the controversy. A willingness to compromise earlier could have led to a better result for the industry.

The Superfund issue raises in clear relief the difficulties of developing and executing an industry-wide political strategy with powerful, individual industry members and facing a well-organized opposition and a media interest in keeping the issue alive. In fairness to the chemical industry, this was the first attempt to develop and execute an industry-wide political strategy. Since this issue, the chemical industry has improved its political strategy and tactics, reducing the controversy surrounding the renewal of Superfund, and, more recently, achieving very favorable publicity for its responsible care program.

Finally, the evolution of the chemical industry's political strategy and tactics over the course of eight years (1979–1986) suggests that the industry can learn from previous mistakes and political and social battles and improve its ability to deal with them and achieve success in the nonmarket arena.

NOTES

1. This highlights another flaw in Porter's Model and in most other approaches to strategy in that one can find little advice in the strategy literature as to how to deal with a competitor or rival that is simultaneously a major supplier and a major customer. These relationships abound in the chemical industry and in the high-technology field.

2. Parts of this section are built on Mahon, 1982, 1983.

3. The pollution of the James River and other problems with Hopewell, Virginia, are documented in the Harvard case entitled "Allied Chemical." This case is excellent reading for those trying to understand how organizations can respond to social and political issues.

4. Unfortunately for Hooker Chemical Company, their name was forever associated with the problems at Love Canal. What was buried in the media frenzy over Love Canal, and rarely reported anywhere, was Hooker's warnings about the toxicity of the site and their attempts to prevent building on the site by the Love Canal school board. In addition, the fact that the burial of the toxic chemicals was carried out in accordance with the law and with the best methods *at that time* has been obscured. Hooker Chemical Company did not, however, acquit itself as honorably in toxic locations in the State of California (Mahon, 1982).

5. An unintended consequence of this act was to make it extraordinarily difficult to build a new factory or plant in the chemical and oil refining industry. As a result, the industry elected to expand existing sites, in some ways contributing to increased degradation of the environment in existing areas—but still maintaining the purity of the environment elsewhere.

6. By law, executive agencies are prohibited from lobbying activities— but there are many ways around this that can be utilized by a creative agency. For example, the EPA detailed staffers to work on key House and Senate committees and subcommittees as this legislation unfolded. When this legislation was completed, most of these staffers returned to the EPA.

7. Kenney was seen by many as the "Dean of Chemical Company Washington Representatives," and his speaking out carried a great deal of clout. He was summoned back to Union Carbide's Corporate Headquarters in New York to explain his position—especially since Union Carbide was pub-

licly supporting the CMA's position at this time. In a tense and lengthy meeting, Kenney convinced top management that Union Carbide and the rest of the industry needed to move on this issue if they were to have any say on how it would be resolved. After this meeting, Union Carbide became more active in pressing for moderation and compromise.

Part Three

CONCLUDING
THOUGHTS

Chapter 8

CONCLUSION

The focus of this book has been centered on the impact of political and social action and changes on the evolution of industry and on the patterns of strategic action by individual actors within an industry to deal with these changes and challenges. The argument has been that the current literature has, for the most part, ignored the impact of political and social changes on the environment in which an industry operates. Part of this ignorance is explained by the domination of certain models and paradigms that have captured managerial and research interests. These models and paradigms have driven out serious research in the political and social realm and have led managers to a false sense of security. As noted earlier, the general thrust of existing models lulls practitioners into believing that they are prepared for most of the contingencies that an organization will face. This is simply not true, and the changes and challenges to industries and individual firms from the political and social arena are likely to increase at an accelerating rate requiring managers and organizations to deal with political and social forces in a national and global setting. More important, such changes have a dramatic impact on the success of individual firms within an industry. No modern manager can afford to ignore the need for political and social strategies and tactics. It is such knowledge and skills that we believe are crucial now and will become even more crucial in the future.

In this analysis, we have looked at four different industries: tobacco (cigarettes), beer, banking, and chemicals. The debate in each of these industries has raged in intensity and rhetoric over the years and has been focused on very different specific issues and problems. In some instances (as in the cigarette and chemical waste industries), the debate has moved to the international level, involving different political systems and cultures. Yet, at one level, the debate is the same—much of it around the political legitimacy of the industry being addressed. We tend to forget that in order for an economic entity to exist, it must have some degree of political and social legitimacy. This legitimacy focuses simultaneously on the legitimacy of the particular product or service and on the legitimacy of the marketplace and its ability to provide fair and equitable results. As societal belief in the value of an industry's product or service erodes, the political and social system begins movement to question and investigate that particular industry or specific product or service. If the social and political system finds problems, it reacts with social movements (protests, calls for boycotts and bans, etc.) or legislation and regulation that can restrict the exercise of discretion of managers within the industry and can, in extreme cases, destroy the industry through said regulation and outright bans on the products or services. There are many voices that enter into this debate over legitimacy and the rules by which an industry will operate. Certainly, government and opponents of the industry will be clearly heard, especially in the form of public interest groups who purport to represent the will of the general public. If the industry's voice is not well represented, if the voice is fragmented, or if no voice arises at all, the industry will be doomed to adjust to whatever the political and social system deems necessary. Such a surrendering of influence in an evolving debate runs counter to the basic tenets of democracy. We believe that managers and organizations need to enter into this debate on an ongoing basis and use the tools and techniques of political strategy and tactics to counterbalance the skills in this area that have been developed and honed to a fine edge by public interest groups and other stakeholders.

The techniques used in competitive industry political dynamics and the analysis of the same are not alien to the general manager's background and experience. The techniques and approaches utilized, however, need some translation for their utility to be appreciated by managers. The analysis of the four industries in this text have been oriented toward that end. In these remaining sections, we shall review the industries selected and raise what we believe are the critical lessons that managers can take from each of these experiences.

THE CIGARETTE INDUSTRY AND POLITICAL AND SOCIAL CHALLENGES

Tobacco has been an industry subject to controversy and criticism from its very founding. Indeed, the context within which the debate over tobacco has evolved is demonstrated in the three waves discussed earlier.

In the first wave, the major issue was an economic-based issue—competitiveness in the marketplace for cigarettes. The development of the industry was led by a few individuals, and the firms they established dominated the business and prevented new competitors from entering freely and easily. Political intervention took the form of trust busting and legal dissolution of what was seen as a monopoly. There were several stakeholders involved in this particular debate, and what is important to understand about their involvement is that they supported the existence (or the breakup) of the status quo for different reasons; that is, stakeholder support or opposition is not always based on a unified position but, rather, on individual stakeholder perceptions of what they believe the contest is about and what they will get out of (or keep) in the resolution of the issue or problem. For example, the Southeastern Congressional Delegation was concerned with employment of farmers in their states and the flow of tax receipts. Customers were more concerned with the availability and pricing of the product and less with where the product was grown. The state governments were not heavily involved in this issue, which made the management of the problem easier for the tobacco firms—they could focus their efforts on the executive branch of government. Figure 8.1, utilizing the model developed in Chapter 3, lays out the first wave of tobacco–government–societal involvements.

Note that the industry tried to redefine the issue in such a way as to make political action (legislation or regulation) unnecessary, and to drum up widespread public support. They tried to argue that the industry is a natural monopoly because of the economies of scale necessary to manufacture and advertise the product. Some economists supported this proposition. In addition, the industry argued that the economic contributions of the industry to the entire economy were of sufficient impact to warrant no change in the industry structure. Although these arguments undoubtedly limited the amount and frequency of attack on the industry, they were not sufficient to win on this issue; thus, the industry saw major players dismembered. In hindsight, one of the reasons the industry did not win may have been a consequence of their redefinition activities. The arguments about natural monopolies and about the industry's contribution to the entire economy were somewhat technical and not terribly appealing to either the general public or to the media at large. The redefinitional activities were not oriented to engaging the general public and having that public enter the debate on the side of the industry. In fairness, the use of the general public to bring pressure on government was not a recognized tactic at this time. As a consequence, the issue was resolved around a base of technical issues by the executive branch of government. Barriers to entry and exit in this debate were very low.

Figure 8.1
Cigarette Industry: First Wave

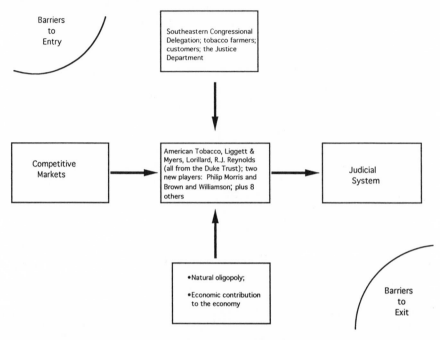

The substance of the issue was technical, and the only barrier to entry was understanding the nature of the issue and gaining recognition as a legitimate party to the government's lawsuit under the antitrust law.

The second wave added a new issue for the industry to confront. After the breakup, the industry did quite well financially. Starting in 1964, however, the health hazards of cigarette smoking were raised for consideration. This issue added a new mix of stakeholders that the industry needed to deal with in some fashion. This new issue, and the key elements involved in it, are shown in Figure 8.2.

Although the executive branch of government, through the Surgeon General's office, raised this issue, Congress became far more involved in it than with the previous issue of competition. Unlike the competition issue, with its technical- and jargon-laden debate, smoking and health was an easy concept for the average citizen to understand. The potential impact on every smoker could be easily explained and made clear. Unfortunately for the tobacco firms, this period also marked an upward interest in the public in improving its own health, and the debate over the health and safety of tobacco was one more extension of this concern. In addition, powerful public interest groups (such as the American Heart Association and the American Cancer Society)

Figure 8.2
Cigarette Industry: Second Wave

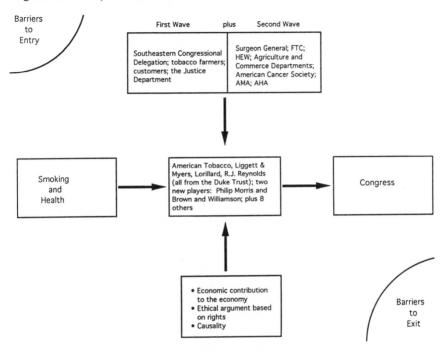

and representative groups (such as the American Medical Association) became involved and found a receptive audience to this issue and concern. These groups had a very different image and reputation with the general public than Congress, the executive branch, or the industry. As such, their presence in the debate demanded a different industry response to this issue than had been used in the past on previous issues.

The industry had also changed, with the two clear leaders being PM and RJR. These two firms, much to the presumed chagrin of the government, essentially formed a duopoly within the industry, cornering almost 73 percent of the cigarette market. These results raise another important point about political and social strategies. Although the industry lost the competition issue earlier to antitrust action, they won in another sense. The implementation of regulation and legislation is far less interesting than the establishment of such legislation and regulation. The enactment of regulation and legislation is often accompanied by extensive media coverage and lively debate among the interested stakeholders. Implementation, on the other hand, does not have the glare of media attention, and the development of specific operating rules and procedures is accomplished between industry and the regulating or oversight body. As a consequence, the antitrust activities of the turn of the century had little real impact on the operation of the industry.

The industry responded with the traditional arguments offered earlier—the economic contribution of the industry to the economy as a whole and that the industry, through excise taxes, contributed significantly to the financial well-being of state governments—but these arguments were not sufficient to appeal to the general public and to offset the arguments of the powerful interest groups noted earlier on the specific issue of health. Much of the industry's arguments did not directly address the issue of health. In order to respond to these concerns, the industry made powerful attempts to redefine the issue and switch the fundamentals of the issue to something else. The first argument was centered on an ethical argument based on rights guaranteed to individuals in the Constitution of the United States. Any ban on products, or dramatic increases in taxes, violated free speech rights of the industry and violated the rights of their customers in that they are being singled out for special punishment—higher taxes on products that they legally use. This is a very powerful symbolic argument, appealing to the general sense of fair play and the rights of citizens in this country to make free choices. The second argument was based on causality. The industry argued that there were no specific statistical links to smoking and health problems. Therefore, without such specific and readily agreeable links, why single out the cigarette industry for special and onerous treatment? Unlike the arguments in the competition debate, free speech and causality were arguments that the industry could make understandable by the general public. The industry was able to interject into the debate the fundamental notion of fairness—was the industry being treated fairly in the discussions over smoking and health? To many, the answer was no; the industry was being unfairly singled out, with questionable research, for further punishment and restrictions.

The lowering of the technical nature of the arguments over cigarettes also lowered the barrier to entry in the political debates. Since the arguments were now over the impact of smoking on health (and not on technical competitiveness issues) more stakeholders, individuals, and groups could enter into the contest. Each of these brought in a different set of assumptions as to what the problem was, and had a different set of solutions to resolve any difficulties. This involvement of an expanded set of actors did help to confuse the situation and probably limited even more drastic action that was contemplated at the time. The cigarette industry players, of course, could not exit the debate at this time, but some of the smaller firms could achieve "free-rider" results by allowing PM and RJR to carry the industry's standard in the debate.

The ultimate actions produced mixed results, and many of them were clearly unintended by Congress. This was especially true of the banning of advertising and the label warnings. The banning of television and radio advertising served as a tremendous barrier to entry for new competitors in the cigarette industry, as they could not inform the general public of their existence in a cost-efficient manner. Such a ban also lowered the incentives for improving cigarettes, as such an improvement could not be advertised in an efficient manner. The ban also removed the requirement for broadcasters to provide equal time for nonsmoking advertising. Finally, the banning of electronic advertising was a tremendous financial boon to the industry, as the monies previously spent in such advertising went directly to the bottom line as sales did not decrease anywhere near the level of advertising costs. Label warnings would later be used successfully by the industry to win court cases over the use of their products. The industry was able to successfully argue that the individuals were warned of the potential dangers of smoking and were, therefore, at least partially culpable in their own physical problems.

The third wave in this industry is curious in that it builds upon the previous concerns over smoking and health and extends them to the nonsmoker. That is, unlike the previous wave, where the issue of smoking and health was quite different from the issue of competition, this issue, the impact of smoking on the nonsmoker, built on the previous concerns and extended them to a new stakeholder—everyone who sat near a smoker. This new issue broadened the potential impact of smoking to a much larger segment of the public. Now, everyone, smoker or not, could have adverse health impacts. This was a very effective challenge to the industry and eroded their argument based on the rights of the smoker. The rights of the smoker made sense when just the smoker was impacted by cigarettes, but now the health of innocent bystanders was affected by the smoker. New stakeholders entered into this debate, representing both the smoker and nonsmoker (ASH, GASP, STAT). The nonsmoking activist groups considered themselves crusaders against an evil empire, and their battling is based on ideological grounds. Ideological grounds are extremely difficult to counteract, as the basis for support of the ideology is based on fact, emotion, and belief (values/morality). The involvement of these groups in the debate, along with the continued involvement of previous groups, has raised the rhetoric and intensity of the debate. For the anti-smoking groups, no amount of legislation or regulation will suffice—what is necessary for them is the complete elimination of smoking as a product choice and as an individual act. Figure 8.3 lays out this new industry political landscape.

In addition to these new, more ideologic-based interest groups, academicians, economists, and health care specialists have entered into the fray. Academicians and economists have offered insights into the impact of taxing mechanisms on the frequency of cigarette sales and on the contribution of cigarette sales tax to government revenues. The health care specialists, much like the ideological interest groups, have begun to advocate much stronger measures of control and elimination of the product.

The ideological interest groups have turned the industry's argument of the "rights of the smoker" on its head, arguing for the "rights of the nonsmoker." This has had a dramatic impact on the battle for the support of the general public. The industry also continued with its traditional rights arguments and economic arguments (contribution to the economy) but with two new wrinkles. In these days of heightened and intensive international trade, tobacco is a net, positive contributor to the country's balance of trade. Therefore, tobacco is needed

Figure 8.3
Cigarette Industry: Third Wave

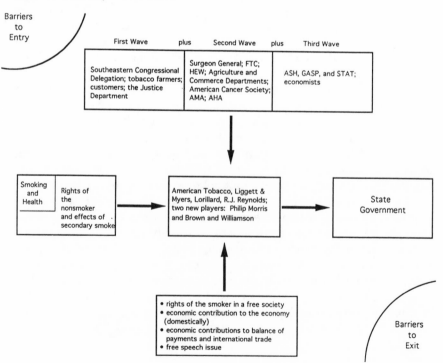

to assist the United States in its global competitiveness. The second new wrinkle has been an attempt to make bans on smoking a civil rights issue by arguing that such bans are really a form of discrimination. If society is opposed to discrimination on the basis of race, gender, age, and religion, how can it support a new form of discrimination based on personal habit? This clever redefinition of the issue merited at least passing attention from such organizations as the American Civil Liberties Union (ACLU) and the NAACP. However, this redefinition, while clever, has not caught on with the general public, nor has it addressed directly the new concern—the impact of smoking on the nonsmoker.

Of equal concern with the substantive nature of this issue is the new challenges to the industry's political competitiveness across multiple arenas. Previous issues and problems have been combined to one or two arenas. Now the industry is forced to defend itself in the federal legislative arena, in the state and local arena, in the judicial arena, in the federal regulatory arena, and in the general media and public arena. The industry is faced with guerrilla warfare on a variety of fronts; and it is gradually, incrementally, and slowly losing. If ever there was an industry with a need for both an end-game marketing and production strategy and an end-game political and social strategy, it is the tobacco industry. The question is no longer whether cigarettes are going to be banned; but when they will be banned and what role the industry will have in shaping both the nature of the ban and its implementation. In addition, over time this issue will migrate beyond the borders of the United States and become an international issue.

THE BEER INDUSTRY

Much like tobacco, beer has enjoyed a great deal of controversy during its life. We have carefully separated out our discussion of the alcohol industry to focus on beer, as the competitive industry and political dynamics change when either distilled liquor or wine is discussed. However, much of the analysis of this industry is applicable, with modifications, to those two products as well.

The first wave in beer dealt with the issue of the availability of beer for the consuming public. The key debate in this issue lay in the development of a healthy industry, the rights of individuals to brew beer at home, and how each of these was to be taxed. The stakeholders, given the context of the times, were rather limited in number. Substitute issues offered dealt with the need to develop a native industry and with beer as a healthy form of alcohol. The framing of this issue in an industry political framework is shown in Figure 8.4. In both a competitive and political sense, barriers to entry and exit in this political debate were virtually nonexistent.

Figure 8.4
Beer Industry: First Wave

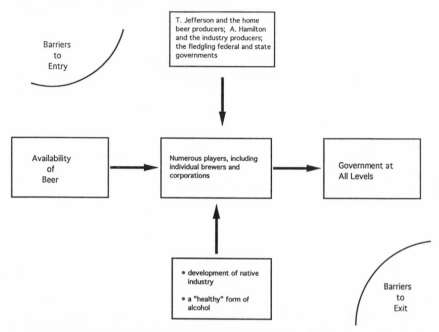

Although the brewers did not avoid eventual taxation on this issue, they did set the precedent, still firmly in place today, that beer should be taxed at a much lower rate than other alcohol products.

Unlike tobacco, the availability of beer was, and still is, an issue that was to never go completely away. Over time, the issue of who shall be allowed to drink beer and where beer shall be obtained has been raised again and again. In the second wave of interest with this industry, the legality of drinking any alcoholic beverage assumed center stage. This movement against alcoholic beverages had been growing for some time, and the rapid growth and consolidation of the beer industry around German beer caused further concern. It was the Germans, and their taste for lager beer that they brought to America. More important, they brought large-scale urban breweries to America that soon displaced the individual, at-home brewer. These additions to the industry fundamentally changed the competitive dynamics of the industry.

Along with the rise in concern over the use of alcohol was growing unrest in urban areas. This unrest was linked by interest groups (religious and others like the "know-nothings") to the drinking of beer, and leaders of the industrial revolution (e.g., Rockefeller and Ford) provided money for these groups to organize and oppose alcohol. The

Figure 8.5
Beer Industry: Second Wave

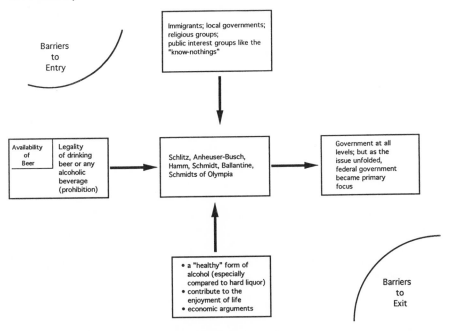

movement started at the state and local level, and achieved some success there. It was quickly realized, however, that the fastest way to eliminate alcohol was through the actions of the federal government. Figure 8.5 lays out this issue using the model introduced earlier.

The battle lines were drawn. On one side were ideological groups opposed to alcohol in any form, supported by leaders of industry (who thought drinking was not good for business). On the other side was the entire alcohol industry. The beer industry attempted to derail these concerns by redefining the issue as one of enjoyment of life. Beer contributed to the enjoyment of life, and it was a healthier form of alcohol with broad economic impacts. The beer industry hoped to distance themselves from the harder forms of alcohol and work out a compromise, but they were unable to distinguish their product from other alcoholic drinks in the eyes of the general public.

The anti-alcohol groups were aided by the advent of World War I and the rising anti-German sentiment. Since Germans made beer, and we were at war with them, producing beer was an un–American activity and should be prohibited. In many ways, the Prohibition movement seized on the changed context to redefine the issue in such a way as to achieve their desired result—the nationwide banning of alcohol (including beer). The beer industry (and the entire alcohol industry) deeply underestimated these interest groups and the power of the emotional and patriotic appeal they would make to the general public. This appeal, combined with the financial muscle of Carnegie, Ford, and Rockefeller, proved too much for the industry, and they were legislated out of existence with the passage of the Volstead Act.

The third wave centered around the restoration of the beer industry after World War I and the repeal of the Volstead Act. When beer was prohibited, this was the start of a major consolidation of the industry that continues to this day. With the repeal of Prohibition, new concerns arose over the health aspects of alcohol—for the first time, drinking was viewed as a potential disease and not as an economic or social issue. Notice the similarity with tobacco here—migration of the issue to one of health concerns. New public interest groups and health-related interest groups entered into a discussion of the problem and potential solutions, including the old issue of availability of beer and alcohol. These groups were not ideologically based and offered compelling arguments over the health consequences of beer. This political scene is laid out in Figure 8.6.

The beer industry dealt with this issue in a variety of ways. The advent of bottling and canning allowed beer to be a contributor to the

Figure 8.6
Beer Industry: Third Wave

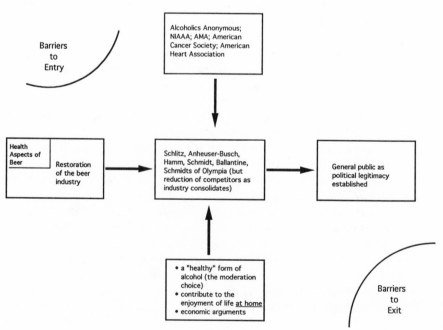

enjoyment of life at home rather than at a tavern. The industry continued to emphasize its healthy aspects (as compared to other alcohol choices) and economic contributions to society. The audience in this situation had also changed dramatically. When the federal government exited the Prohibition era, it left regulation of alcoholic beverages entirely up to the states. Thus, the beer industry had to aim its efforts at state legislatures, beverage control commissions, and the executive branch of government (e.g., the governor). New regulations and legislation were developed that limited the access and availability to beer and other alcoholic beverages, and to have an impact on drunk driving.

Therefore, exit and entry into the competitive political dynamic was altered. Oversight at the state level meant that any variety of stakeholders and actors could enter into a political contest in fifty different arenas. The entry barrier was effectively eliminated, and the beer industry had, much like tobacco, to worry about attacks from a near-infinite number and variety of sources. Exit barriers were also nonexistent. Groups could enter and leave the fray at will, further contributing to the assessment of and response to the strategic political problem or issue.

The fourth and final wave, as we have noted, is the development of the drunk-driving issue. This issue, building off of earlier concerns over availability and health, was led by new groups that the beer and alcohol industry had never seen before. These groups were not advocating a return to Prohibition, nor did they see drinking as immoral. Rather, they were concerned with the impact of drunk driving on innocent victims—much like the impact of smoking on the nonsmoker. Their moderate viewpoint and clear concern with a visible issue—the impact of drunk drivers—created new problems for the industry (Figure 8.7).

The issue of drunk driving brought another powerful actor into the debate—the insurance industry. The insurance industry had legitimate concerns with this issue, as they were involved in insuring the drivers of vehicles and the owners of establishments that serve alcohol. Any measures that would reduce the incidence of drunk driving (and, therefore, the financial liability of the insurance industry) were seen as a good thing. As in earlier times when Rockefeller and Ford provided support, this set of stakeholders received financial support from the insurance industry to deal with the drunk-driving issue.

This particular issue poses some unique problems for the industry—they cannot come out in support of drunk driving, but neither can they sit back and admit that their product is the root cause of drunk driving. The beer industry attempted to steer away from this issue by emphasizing again their economic contributions to society. The industry did, however, emphasize the use of beer in moderation,

Figure 8.7
Beer Industry: Fourth Wave

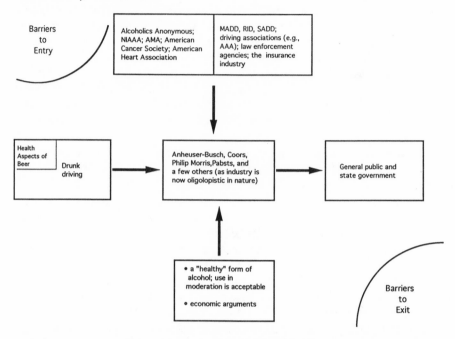

especially in their advertising and promotional campaigns. The beer industry has even joined forces with the MADD movement to produce advertisements encouraging the use of moderation in the drinking of alcohol. By these actions, the industry is tacitly arguing that it can self-regulate, and that additional legislation and regulation is not necessary. So far, this subtle manipulation of the issue (to one of self-regulation), along with visible support of efforts to limit drunk driving, seems to be working.

THE BANKING INDUSTRY

The previous two industry examples have dealt with consumer products and with industries that are in themselves somewhat controversial. The banking industry was chosen for investigation next because it is an example of a service industry—an industry that is important and in which every individual has an interest or stake. In addition, the nature of some of the issues in this industry are quite different. For example, the confidence of the public in a specific bank is very important to that bank's survival, as an erosion of confidence can lead to a run on the bank and the inability of the bank to meet depositor

Figure 8.8
Banking Industry: First Wave

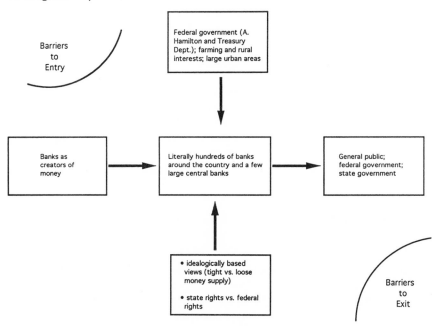

demands. In order to narrow the discussion to a manageable portion, the focus was on the commercial banking industry.

The first major issue confronting banks and the new American society was centered on banks as creators of money (Figure 8.8). As trade in goods increased throughout the land, barter as a form of exchange became unacceptable as a form of payment. Although gold and silver were recognized forms of payment virtually everywhere, their bulk and the temptation for robbery made them unrealistic as long-term alternatives for payment. Payment in an easily transportable and recognizable form was becoming a necessity. The establishment of money (in bills and coins) met this need, but questions arose as to who would manage the money supply and oversee the entire monetary system, and as to which major segment of society (urban or rural interests) would be dominant.

This was an early indication of the battles that continue to this day over states versus federal government rights reflected in the dispute between rural and urban interests. As we noted in the tobacco issues earlier, there was an ideological aspect of this debate in the arguments over a tight versus loose money supply. The arguments for a centrally controlled tight money supply painted a picture of an America free from foreign interests and, more specifically (and emotionally), from British manufactured goods. On the opposite side, proponents of a loose money supply with dispersed control argued that the central government would be a substitute for the British and trample the newly won freedoms.

Although there were few barriers to entry and exit in the political debates on this issue, the location of banks as major providers of local financing made them an obvious target of pressure from the community. This local involvement, in turn, fed into the concerns of the loose money supply advocates, as it enhanced their position and provided them with a potential power base to bring pressure on the federal government.

The audience for this issue was diffuse, and both supporters of loose money and tight money attempted to influence the different audience members to their advantage. The general public was wooed by all sides in the debate. The federal government, as the establishing agency for the national banks, was the target of intense activity to not renew these banks (and they did not) and to pursue a loose money supply. The state governments were also pressured to develop flexibility and loose money supplies to spur investment and growth in their jurisdictions. The key to movement of this issue to the purview of state governments (and, therefore, a loose money supply) was the election of President Jackson. Not only did he veto the extension of the charter of the Second Bank of the United States, but he removed all federal funds from that bank and placed them in state banks. This issue ended with the victory of those seeking loose money and state oversight of the banking system.

This resultant victory led to chaos in the banking system since each state developed its own set of laws and regulations, as well as differentiated levels of supervision and oversight. This widespread lack of uniformity caused enormous problems with the monetary system, as many banks simply issued their own currency in different denominations. Many of these currencies were not uniformly recognized, so the goal of a single, uniformly recognized form of payment was not achieved. This led to sufficient and widespread public outcries for reform (Figure 8.9).

The stakeholders in this issue were the same as earlier, but the relative power shifted dramatically. The states-rights supporters' credibility was hurt by the debacle over slavery, and the state governments' interest in this issue was diluted by the Civil War. The stakeholders with the greatest power in influencing the one target audience—the federal government—were urban areas; in particular, the northeast section of the country where manufacturing and strong banks were located. Substitute issues around states rights versus fed-

Figure 8.9
Banking Industry: Second Wave

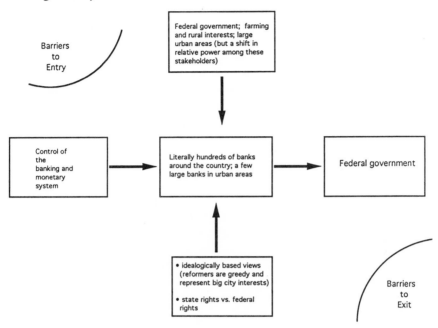

eral rights were offered, but did not attract a significant basis of support. Every individual could experience directly the difficulties with loose money supplies and different currencies. In addition, the argument of greedy industrialists and reformers representing big cities at the expense of rural areas was offered, but it also proved insufficient in the prevention of national oversight and control.

The barriers to entry were raised during this time for rural interests and for representatives of states rights. The Civil War forever altered the power of states in debates with the federal government, and the rural interests were associated with slavery and the South. As a result, their influence and legitimacy as a stakeholder in the issue was limited. All was not lost, however, as the states kept their rights to charter and supervise banks. The states did lose control of the monetary system.

The third wave was a qualitatively different issue, with an expanded set of stakeholders. The early focus was on the prevention of disasters, like the great Depression, and the protection of deposits in banks. One of the outcomes of this period was to compel banks to choose between commercial activity and investment activities (a debate that is being revisited once again as this book goes to press). As the federal reserve system and other legislation asserted control over the banking system, the issue of deregulation versus consumer protection rose to the center stage (Figure 8.10).

This issue of deregulation that would allow banks to reenter investment activities was opposed by new and large stakeholders. These stakeholders (financial supermarkets and the insurance industry) have developed products and services that will be threatened by bank involvement. In addition, representatives of the poor urban and rural areas are opposed to such changes. There concern is that as deregulation unfolds, there will be consolidation, and they will be left without financial institutions that will service their needs. Since consolidation has been taking place already, and in other industries has resulted in reduced service to rural and smaller areas (e.g., airlines), this was not an argument that could be easily dismissed.

The only audience that could accomplish deregulation was the federal government and it has become the focus of activities. Substitute issues have been offered. One argument is that the banking industry needs a "level playing field," and that deregulation would accomplish that goal. Another argument or issue in favor of deregulation is to strengthen banks against foreign competition, and to improve the efficiency of operations. Arguments against deregulation include con-

Figure 8.10
Banking Industry: Third Wave

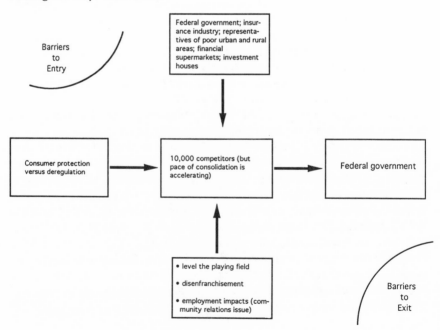

cerns over disenfranchisement and the loss of employment in smaller and rural communities. The debate on this issue involving very powerful stakeholders is so intense and the stakes are so high that as of this writing, the issue of deregulation has not been resolved.

THE CHEMICAL INDUSTRY

This industry is another addition to our studies in that the industry is primarily a supplier to other industries—that is, most chemical products are utilized in a variety of other products and not sold directly to an individual member of the public at large. Like the tobacco industry, however, the chemical industry contributes enormously to the U.S. balance-of-payments situation.

Unlike the previous three studies, the focus in this industry was on a single issue and how that issued was resolved over the course of approximately two years. This narrowing of our conceptual lens to a single issue and how it was debated and resolved improves our understanding of the dynamics of the model introduced in Chapter 3.

The history of the industry was relevant in that it sets the stage for our understanding of the context in which the industry entered the debate on the issue of hazardous waste sites. The focus on a single issue allows us to draw into sharper contrast the specific political strategies and tactics discussed throughout this book, and to see the interplay of individual and industry political strategies on an issue of great political and economic salience to the chemical industry, to other related industries, and to the government as a whole.

The specific introduction of legislation to deal with hazardous waste sites was the culmination of a period of ten years of heavy regulation and investigation into the operation of the chemical industry (Figure 8.11). This concern with toxic wastes (and how to deal with these sites) was a natural and predictable outcome of the stream of legislation and public debate that preceded it around issues such as worker safety, clean water and air, and the protection of the environment as a whole embodied in the establishment of the EPA.

The events leading up to consideration of the clean-up of toxic wastes or, more commonly referred to as Superfund, also served as an indicator of the ferocity with which the debate would be pursued by the two principal stakeholders in the debate—the chemical industry and the White House. The chemical industry, as represented by the CMA, was fed up with what they saw as a singling out of their industry, their products, and their processes for special and detailed federal oversight and legislation. Robert Roland, the newly appointed President of the CMA, reorganized, significantly raised dues, and promised that the CMA would no longer be passive in its response to legislation and

Figure 8.11
Chemical Industry

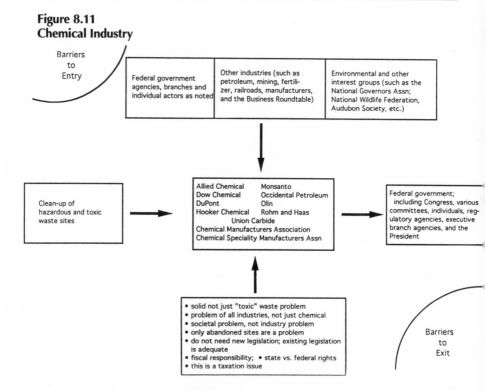

Barriers
to
Entry

| Federal government agencies, branches and individual actors as noted | Other industries (such as petroleum, mining, fertilizer, railroads, manufacturers, and the Business Roundtable) | Environmental and other interest groups (such as the National Governors Assn; National Wildlife Federation, Audubon Society, etc.) |

| Clean-up of hazardous and toxic waste sites | Allied Chemical   Monsanto
Dow Chemical   Occidental Petroleum
DuPont   Olin
Hooker Chemical Rohm and Haas
Union Carbide
Chemical Manufacturers Association
Chemical Speciality Manufacturers Assn | Federal government; including Congress, various committees, individuals, regulatory agencies, executive branch agencies, and the President |

- solid not just "toxic" waste problem
- problem of all industries, not just chemical
- societal problem, not industry problem
- only abandoned sites are a problem
- do not need new legislation; existing legislation is adequate
- fiscal responsibility; • state vs. federal rights
- this is a taxation issue

Barriers
to
Exit

regulation. Several individual firms within the industry (e.g., Dow and Allied) were also disturbed by the increasing federal presence in day-to-day operations of the business. As such, Superfund arose at the precise time that the chemical industry decided to stiffen resistance and reorganize to better combat federal legislation and what they saw as unnecessary and onerous intervention.

As the debate over Superfund unfolded, President Carter's interest and involvement with it grew as a consequence of other unrelated events. The most important event was the seizing of the U.S. Embassy in Tehran, Iran. This event, occurring late in the Carter Presidency, overshadowed his success in obtaining peace between Egypt and Israel. The hostage crisis was in the news every day, and it raised questions about the President's leadership. This event, combined with a rather weak record domestically, left the President in a potentially weakened condition as Presidential elections grew near. Superfund provided an opportunity for him to reassert his leadership, demonstrate domestic policy success, and perhaps provide the news media with another story to run in place of the hostage tale.

The issue was defined from the beginning as the clean-up of hazardous waste sites in order to protect the general public at large. The issue was emotionalized in the press by several incidents that captured the general public's interest. The CMA engaged in a vigorous campaign to redefine this issue and the industry's role and responsibility in it. The industry offered a dizzying array of redefinitions to this issue, many of these redefinitions building upon previously advanced definitions. The industry's first set of arguments was an attempt to expand the impact of the issue and involve virtually every other industry in the clean-up debate. The CMA argued that it was a solid waste problem and not just a toxic waste problem. The argument here was that the entire problem of solid waste disposal needed to be addressed, and that it was an issue that went far beyond the chemical industry, impacting every citizen. Even if it is only a "toxic waste" issue, it is a problem of all industries—not just the chemical industry—because all industries generate toxic wastes. In an adroit move, the industry then attempted to argue that the issue was a societal problem. Society demanded new products and benefited from them, so they should pay for the clean-up of these waste sites—that is, the chemical industry was an innocent victim here in that it was merely responding to the public's demand for new products and services. Unfortunately, these new products and services generated hazardous wastes. Note that these three redefinitional attempts had two common themes—to move the financial burden of clean-up beyond the chemical industry alone and, ideally, to society, with no payments or contributions from the industry at all; and to broaden the debate and potential number of stakeholders that could become involved in the debate. The industry hoped that such a broadening of the issue would significantly raise the stakes and inhibit major changes.

When these efforts did not succeed, the industry turned to redefinitional attempts to narrow the issue. They argued that the real problem was with abandoned waste sites and not a general problem. The solution was to leave clean-up of sites to those who currently owned and maintained them. In the situation where ownership could not be verified, then the government should clean the site (with federal, not industry, funds). This issue of abandoned sites should be a smaller physical problem (in terms of number of sites) and cost less than other proposals. The industry also offered the traditional argument in issue tactics—no new legislation is needed because existing legislation and oversight is more than sufficient. This is just an attempt to establish a new bureaucracy that is wasteful and unnecessary.

When these attempts failed, the industry tried yet another spin on redefinition. The industry attempted to place this issue as an issue of states' rights versus federal oversight. They argued that the states were doing a fine job in oversight here, and that federal government actions were an intrusion into the operation of state government oversight and, therefore, unwarranted. As in the cigarette industry, where attempts were made to keep the issues at the federal level to allow the industry to focus its efforts, the chemical industry attempted to argue that the establishment of federal oversight was fiscally irresponsible and to cloak the debate in broad economic principles and priorities for national government priorities and spending. Finally, when all else failed, the industry attempted to redefine the issue as a taxation issue. This redefinitional attempt had little meaning for the general public (because of its technical complexity), but it was an argument that was perfectly suited to the arena in which the issue was engaged. Congressional committees and the House and Senate carefully defended their prerogatives and, labeling the issue as one of taxation, guaranteed that the House Ways and Means Committee would not only assume oversight, but that the House would grant that committee the right to consider the legislation.

When every other issue redefinition attempt failed, the industry still attempted to redefine the issue as one too complicated and controversial for consideration by the lame-duck Congress. All attempts by the industry failed, and the legislation establishing Superfund was passed by the lame-duck Congress and signed into law by President Carter. When the legislation came up for renewal in 1986, the industry did a much better job of managing the issue, and the law was extended with much less acrimony and public attention. Superfund is once again up for renewal as this book goes to press.

CONCLUDING COMMENTS

It is the belief of these authors that the experience of these four industries and firms within those industries (and numerous others) are illustrative in the understanding of the impact of political and social action on industry competitiveness. The impact on competitiveness is not just within the industry (i.e., one competitor against another) but also on the competitiveness of the industry against industries outside of the United States. Political and social action can impose external costs that damage individual firm and overall industry competitiveness. However, what specific lessons can be drawn from these experiences? There are several lessons, and some of the more important ones are noted in the next paragraphs.

First, each industry has particular issues that they have to deal with over time. This is shown clearly in each of the industries addressed in this book. More important, the seeds for a subsequent issue can be found in the previous issues that the industry has faced. For example, in the cigarette industry, the issue of competitiveness has never completely gone away and is revisited with every new wave.

When the industry confronted the issue of smoking and health, it was relatively easy to identify the migration of that issue to one of concern for the health and safety of the nonsmoker long before that particular issue was ever raised. Yet, the industry seemed surprised by the spin on the issue concerned with the health of the nonsmoker. In the chemical industry, the same phenomena occurred. The industry dealt with legislation on clean air and water, toxic substances, and so on, yet seemed surprised by the introduction of legislation to deal with toxic waste sites. The same thing happened in the beer issue with the migration of the issue from one of health for the drinker to the impact of the drinker on others (drunk driving). Why is it that leaders in industries miss these trends? In part, it is because of an unwillingness to invest in monitoring and understanding political and social processes and to develop strategies and tactics to respond to these changes in a consistent fashion over time.

Second, new issues do not necessarily substitute for previous issues—the introduction of a new issue for an industry does not necessarily drive out the old or previous issue, but adds to it. Much like the layering of an onion, an issue can have multiple layers that an industry has to respond to over time. Each layer adds new complexities and stakeholders that need to be addressed. Certainly, the experiences of the cigarette, beer, banking, and chemical industries bear this out.

Third, industries, firms, and executives need to find better ways to carry their arguments to the general public. Often, the industry response is to avoid direct confrontation on the issue and to pursue redefinitional attempts instead. Although redefinitional attempts are a reasonable strategy, they are not successful in battles with stakeholders that have defined the issue clearly and simply, and they pursue their position with ideological fever. Clear and simple definitions work with the general public; complex and technical responses do not. The issue of nuclear power is a case in point. As that industry unfolded, societal concern arose over the safety of nuclear plants (and Three Mile Island provided a visible symbol of that concern). Still, the industry continued to respond to these concerns with technical arguments and with a redefinitional attempt (the industry will provide cheap power and relieve the United States from its dependence on foreign oil). The industry underestimated the power of the appeal to safety. Therefore, it is crucial for executives to assess the appeal of a given issue; and, if it is widespread, then attempts at issue redefinition are generally doomed to failure. Thus, the issue needs to be confronted head on.

Fourth, certain issues arise that prevent industries and related industries from forming a united front. The tax issue on alcohol, for example, split the distilled spirits, wine, and beer manufacturers.

Rather than pursuing a common political strategy, the alcohol industry fragmented into narrower parochial interests. The same problem was evident in the chemical industry's battle over Superfund. A natural ally—oil—could not enter as a credible actor in the Superfund debate because of the oil industry's long-term public stand on seeking federal legislation around oil spills. Executives must look at specific issues and consider what impact the definition of the issue or problem has on potential alliances in the political and social arena.

Fifth, defeat on an issue in a specific arena is not necessarily a long-term defeat and can result in positive outcomes for the industry in another arena. Look at the cigarette industry's defeat on the issues concerning warning labels and limitations on advertising in the legislative arena. The warning labels required by law have served to date as a fairly good defense in liability suits, as the industry has argued that the consumer was adequately warned. The limitation on advertising raised a new, powerful barrier to entry and provided the industry with monopoly-like conditions. The enormous cash flow generated from the movement of funds previously allocated to advertising to the bottom line has allowed the larger firms in the industry to go on a spending and acquisition binge. The chemical industry lost on Superfund but won a reprieve in the manner in which it was administered. Therefore, a key lesson here for individual firms and industries is that the administration and implementation of legislation and regulation is just as important, if not more so, than the passage of the legislation and regulation.

Sixth, the role of the media in keeping an issue alive and before the general public cannot be underestimated or understated. The media has played a crucial role in the cigarette, beer, and chemical industry issues. The media has not played as key a role in the recent banking debates, perhaps owing to the technical and complicated nature of the issue surrounding deregulation in this industry. This would suggest that strategies to keep the issue from expanding and gaining media attention are worthy of investigation by individual firms and by the industry as a whole (Mahon, 1989).

Seventh, one individual can make a difference in the outcome of a given issue. Certainly, President Andrew Jackson had an impact on the banking industry's evolution; and in the chemical industry, Irving Shapiro's actions were crucial to the passage of Superfund. Related to this notion of one individual's having an impact is the importance of maintaining a united industry front when dealing with political and social issues. The media, public interest groups, Congress, regulators, and the general public look for inconsistencies in individual firm and industry positions. The management of a political or social issue across an industry to present a unified and consistent position requires both skill and practice.

Eighth, corporate and industry political strategy and activity is not a discrete process. Firms and industries cannot enter into the political and social arena on only one or two issues or problems over the course of several years. To be successful, corporate and industry political activity has to be a continuous process. Involvement in political and social arenas also demands the recognition that the concern should be rightly placed with long-term considerations and not just focused on the specific issue at hand. To put it another way, remember that it is a war, and the outcome of a single battle is not necessarily the end or defeat. This is particularly true in political contests where yesterday's enemies are today's allies and friends.

Finally, the need for industries and individual firms to develop their skills in political and social strategy should be unquestioned. Public interest groups are becoming better managed, more international (e.g., Greenpeace), and more adroit at bringing their arguments to the public arena for resolution. As noted earlier, an industry or firm that does not wish to play in this game will be compelled to accept outcomes over which it has had no input or voice. This gradual erosion of managerial discretion should be of great concern to any business leader. It will continue until business executives decide that skills and abilities in political and social strategies are important. Until that time, firms and industries will continue to be blindsided by political, regulatory, and social action, and they will see their attempts to deal with such problems and issues rebuffed.

[] [] []

BIBLIOGRAPHY

Ackerman, R. W. *The Social Challenge to Business*. Cambridge: Harvard University Press, 1975.

Allen, C. A., and Mahon, J. F. "The Politics of Health Care in Massachusetts." *Case Research Journal* 6 (1987): 37–58.

Allison, G. *The Essence of Decision*. Boston: Little, Brown, 1971.

"An Analysis of the Resource Conservation and Recovery Act." *Chemical Regulation Reporter*, August 22, 1980, 705–718.

Andrew, K. *The Bank Marketing Handbook*. London: Woodhead Faulkner Limited, 1986.

Andrews, K. *The Concept of Corporate Strategy*. Homewood, Ill.: Dow Jones–Irwin, 1971.

———. *The Concept of Corporate Strategy*, rev. ed. Homewood, Ill.: Richard D. Irwin, 1987.

Annual Survey of the Cigarette Industry, 1947–1994. *Business Week*.

Ansoff, I. "The Changing Shape of the Strategic Problem." In *Strategic Management: A New View of Business Policy and Planning*, edited by D. E. Schendel and C. W. Hofer, 30–43. Boston: Little, Brown, 1979.

———. *Corporate Strategy*. New York: McGraw-Hill, 1965.

Argus Research Corporation. "Private Label Analysis—Industry Report." New York: Argus Research Corporation, August 3, 1993.

Bachrach, P. "Corporate Authority and Democratic Theory." In *Political Theory and Social Change*, edited by D. Spitz, 257–273. 2nd ed. New York: Atherton, 1967.

Bachrach, P., and Baratz, M. S. "Two Faces of Power." *American Political Science Review* 56 (1962): 947–952.

Bain, J. S. *Industrial Organization*. Rev. ed. New York: John Wiley & Sons, 1968.

Baron, D. *Business and Its Environment*. Englewood Cliffs, N.J.: Prentice-Hall, 1993.

———. "Integrated Strategy: Market and Non-Market Components." *California Management Review* 37 (2; 1995): 47–65.

Baron, S. *Brewed in America: A History of Beer and Ale in the United States.* Boston: Little, Brown, 1962.

Bass, F. M. "A Simultaneous Equation Regression Study of Advertising and Sales of Cigarettes." *Journal of Marketing Research* 6 (1969): 291–300.

Bauer, R. A. "The Corporate Response Process." In *Research in Corporate Social Performance and Policy*, edited by L. E. Preston, 99–122. Greenwich, Conn: JAI Press, 1978.

"The Beer Industry." *Value Line Reports*, August 19, 1994, 2.

"The Beer Industry." *Value Line Reports*, May 19, 1995, 13.

Belluck, P. "Cipollone Case Strikes the Tobacco Industry." *Wall Street Journal*, June 4, 1988, 1.

Berger, P. *A Sociological View of the Antismoking Phenomenon, in Tollison Smoking and Society.* Lexington, Mass.: Lexington Books, 1986.

Berry, J. M. *The Interest Group Society.* Boston: Little, Brown, 1984.

Berton, L. "Big Six's Shift to Consulting Accelerates." *Wall Street Journal*, September 12, 1995, B1, B2.

Bigelow, B., Fahey, L., and Mahon, J. F. "Corporate Political Strategy: Influencing the Rules of the Game." In *Contemporary Issues in the Business Environment*, edited by D. Ludwig and K. Paul, 125–142. Lewiston, N.Y.: Edwin Mellen Press, 1992.

———. "Issues Management: A Theory Based Strategic Perspective." In *Proceedings of the Fourth Annual Meeting of the International Association for Business and Society*, edited by J. Pasquero and D. Collins, 175–180. San Diego: The Association, 1993a.

———. "Political Strategy and Issue Evolution: A Framework for Analysis and Action." In *Contemporary Issues in Business Ethics and Politics*, edited by K. Paul, 1–25. Lewiston, N.Y.: Edwin Mellen Press, 1991.

———. "A Typology of Issues Evolution." *Business and Society* 32 (Spring 1993b): 18-29.

"Bill Proposes Hazardous Waste Cleanup Fund." *Chemical and Engineering News*, June 25, 1979, 27.

Blau, R., and Harris, R. "Strategic Uses of Regulation: The Case of Line-of-Business Restrictions in the U.S. Telecommunications Industry." In *Research in Corporate Social Performance and Policy*, edited by J. E. Post, 161–190. Vol. 13. Greenwich, Conn.: JAI Press, 1992.

Blodgett, J. E., ed. *Compensation for Victims of Water Pollution.* Report prepared for the Committee on Public Works and Transportation, U.S. House of Representatives. Washington, D.C.: U.S. Government Printing Office, May 1979.

Boddewyn, J. "Political Resources and Markets in International Business: Beyond Porter's Generic Strategies." In *Research in Global Strategic Management*, edited by A. Rugman and A. Verbeke, 57–86. Vol. 4. Greenwich, Conn.: JAI Press, 1993.

Bosch, F. A. J. Van Den, and de Man, A. P. "Government's Impact on the Business Environment and Strategic Management." *Journal of General Management* 19 (Spring 1994): 50–59.

Carson, R. *The Silent Spring.* Boston: Houghton Mifflin, 1962.

Caves, R. E. *American Industry: Structure, Conduct, Performance.* 2nd ed. Englewood Cliffs, N.J.: Prentice-Hall, 1967.

Chafee, E. E. "Three Models of Strategy." *Academy of Management Review* 10 (1; 1985): 86–98.

Chandler, A. "Government versus Business: An American Phenomenon." In *Business and Public Policy,* edited by J. Dunlop, 1–11. Cambridge: Harvard University Press, 1980.

———. *Strategy and Structure.* Cambridge: MIT Press, 1962.

Channon, D. F. *Global Banking Strategy.* London: John Wiley & Sons, 1988.

Chappell, V. G. "The Economic Effect of Excise Taxes on Tobacco Products." *Tobacco International* 186 (16; 1984): 14–16.

Clark, N. *Deliver Us from Evil: An Interpretation of American Prohibition.* New York: W. W. Norton, 1976.

"Cleansing the Chemical Image." *Business Week,* October 8, 1979, 73.

"Closer to a Cleanup Superfund." *Business Week,* July 14, 1980, 30.

CMA News Release. Washington, D.C., March 7, 1979.

Cobb, R. W., and Elder, C. D. *Participation in American Politics: The Dynamics of Agenda Building.* Baltimore: Johns Hopkins University Press, 1972.

"The Concentration of the Cigarette Industry." *Business Week,* January 18, 1985, 90.

Congressional Budget Office. "The Tobacco Industry." Spring, 1987.

Cook, J., and Moore, P. "This Tax's for You: The Case for Higher Beer Taxes." *National Tax Journal* (September 1994): 559–573.

"CPI Wants Superfund Bill Cut Down to Size." *Chemical Week,* October 3, 1979, 44.

Cummings, P. Interview by author. Washington, D.C., January 8, 1981.

Dahl, R. A. "Business and Politics: A Critical Appraisal of Political Science." In *Social Science Research On Business: Product and Potential,* edited by R. A. Dahl, M. Haire, and P. F. Lazarsfeld, 3–44. New York: Columbia University Press, 1959.

———. "The Concept of Power." *Behavioral Science* 2 (1957): 210–215.

Davis, P. "No. 1 Mattel Drops Bid to Take Over No. 2 Hasbro." *Providence Journal Bulletin,* February 3, 1996, A1.

Department of Health and Human Services. *A Report of the Surgeon General: The Consequences of Smoking.* Rockville, Md.: Department of Health and Human Services, 1994.

———. *A Report of the Surgeon General: The Health Consequences of Smoking.* Rockville, Md.: Department of Health and Human Services, 1988.

———. *A Report of the Surgeon General: The Health Consequences of Smoking.* Rockville, Md.: Department of Health and Human Services, 1986.

———. *A Report of the Surgeon General: The Health Consequences of Smoking.* Rockville, Md.: Department of Health and Human Services, 1985.

Dill, W. R. "Strategic Management in a Kibitzer's World." In *From Strategic Planning to Strategic Management,* edited by H. Ansoff, R. Declerck, and R. Hayes, 125–136. New York: John Wiley & Sons, 1976.

Doyle, J. Interview by author. Washington, D.C., January 6, 1981.

"Drinking Patterns." *Brewery Age*. Washington, D.C.: Beer Institute, 1935.

Du Pont. *Public Affairs Department Manual*. Wilmington, Del.: Du Pont, May 1975.

Eccles, G. S. "The Politics of Banking." Unpublished Ph.D. diss., The Graduate School of Business, University of Utah, 1982.

Edelman, M. *The Symbolic Uses of Politics*. Urbana: University of Illinois Press, 1964.

Elber, L. "Getting to the Heart of TV Violence." *Boston Globe*, September 20, 1995, 84.

Ember, L. "Chances Only 50-50 for 'Superfund' Legislation." *Chemical and Engineering News*, September 20, 1980, 29.

————. "Industry's Superfund Lobbying Goes Awry." *Chemical and Engineering News*, January 5, 1981, 17–19.

Emerson, R. M. "Power-Dependence Relations." *American Sociological Review* 27 (1962): 31-41.

Epstein, E. M. "Business Political Activity: Research Approaches and Analytical Issues." In *Research in Corporate Social Performance and Policy*, edited by L. E. Preston, 34–56. Greenwich, Conn.: JAI Press, 1980.

————. *The Corporation in American Politics*. Englewood Cliffs, N.J.: Prentice-Hall, 1969.

Eyestone, R. *From Social Issues to Public Policy*. New York: John Wiley & Sons, 1978.

"Facts and Figures for the Chemical Industry." *Chemical and Engineering News*, June 8, 1981, 22–58.

Fahey, L., Mahon, J. F., and Bigelow, B. "A Political Strategy Perspective on Product and Market Strategy." In *Proceedings of the Third Annual Meeting of the International Association for Business and Society*, edited by Sandra Waddock, 96–103. Leuven, Belgium: 1992.

Feare, T. "Can CMA Remove the Tarnish?" *Chemical Marketing Reporter*, July 28, 1980, 8–14.

"Finding the Right Chemistry." *The Economist*, September 2, 1995, 67–68.

Fleisher, C. S. "Public Affairs Management Performance: An Empirical Analysis of Evaluation and Management." In *Research in Corporate Social Performance and Policy*, edited by J. E. Post, 139–167. Greenwich, Conn.: JAI Press, 1993.

Freeman, R. E. *Strategic Management: A Stakeholder Approach*. Marshfield, Mass.: Pitman, 1984.

Fried, V. H., and Oviatt, B. M. "Michael Porter's Missing Chapter: The Risk of Antitrust Violations." *Academy of Management Executive* 3 (1; 1989): 49–56.

Friedman, M. "The Social Responsibility of Business Is to Increase Its Profits." *New York Times Magazine*, September 13, 1970, 32, 122ff.

"The Future of the Brewing Industry." *Value Line Reports*, New York, February 21, 1992.

Galambos, L. *The Public Image of Big Business in America: 1880–1940*. London: Johns Hopkins University Press, 1975.

Galbraith, J. *Designing Complex Organizations*. Reading, Mass.: Addison-Wesley, 1973.

Garraty, J. *The American Nation*. New York: Harper and Row, 1966.

Getz, K. A. "Selecting Corporate Political Tactics." In *Corporate Political Agency: The Construction of Competition in Public Affairs*, edited by B. M. Mitnick, 242–273. Newbury Park, Calif.: Sage, 1993.

Ghemawat, P. "Sustainable Advantage." *Harvard Business Review* 64 (5; 1986): 53–58.

Gonzales-Herrero, A., and Pratt, C. B. "How to Manage a Crisis Before— or Whenever—It Hits." *Public Relations Quarterly* 40 (Spring 1995): 25–29.

Hamilton, J. L. "The Demand for Cigarettes: Advertising, Health Scare and the Advertising Ban." *Review of Economics and Statistics* 54 (1972): 401–411.

Harbison, E. "Image Is a Problem, but There Is Still Time to Act." Remarks made at the Chemical Industry Strategic Planning Conference, Wilmington, Del., May 23, 1979.

Hardy, C. "The Contributions of Political Science to Organizational Behavior." In *Handbook of Organizational Behavior*, edited by J. W. Lorsch, 96–108. Englewood Cliffs, N.J.: Prentice-Hall, 1987.

Harris, J. E. "On the Fairness of Cigarette Excise Taxation." Proceedings of the Conference on the Cigarette Excise Tax. *Institute for the Study of Smoking Behavior*, Harvard University, 1987, 106–111.

Hay, T. M., and Gray, B. "The National Coal Policy Project: An Interactive Approach to Corporate Responsiveness." In *Research in Corporate Social Performance and Policy*, Vol. 7, edited by L. E. Preston, 191–212. Greenwich, Conn.: JAI Press, 1985.

Hildreth, R. *Banks, Banking, and Paper Currencies*. New York: Greenwood Press, 1968.

Hilgartner, S., and Bosk, C. L. "The Rise and Fall of Social Problems: A Public Arenas Model." *American Journal of Sociology* 94 (1; 1988): 53–78.

Hillman, A. "The Choice of Corporate Political Strategies: The Role of Institutional Variables." Paper presented at the Annual Meeting of the Academy of Management, Vancouver, B.C., Canada, August, 1995.

Hoberg, G. "Risk, Science, and Politics: Alachlor Regulation in Canada and the United States." *Canadian Journal of Political Science* 23 (2; 1990): 257–277.

Holton, R. "Business and Government." In *The American Business Corporation*, edited by E. Goldston, H. Morton, and G. Ryland, 57–75. Cambridge: MIT Press, 1973.

Jackson, M. *The World Guide to Beer*. Philadelphia: Courage Books, 1986.

Jacobstein, M. *The Tobacco Industry in the U.S.* New York: Columbia University Press, 1908.

Jennings, D. F., and Lumpkin, J. R. "Insights between Environmental Scanning Activities and Porter's Generic Strategies: An Empirical Analysis." *Journal of Management* 18 (4; 1992): 791–803.

Jobson's Beer Handbook. Annual Review of the Beer Industry. New York: Jobson Publishing, 1984–1995.

Keim, G. D., and Baysinger, B. "The Efficacy of Business Political Activity: Competitive Considerations in a Principal-Agent Context." *Journal of Management* 14 (2; 1988): 163–180.

Keller, J. J. "Abortion Issue Prompts AT&T to End Its Support for Planned Parenthood." *Wall Street Journal,* March 26, 1990, A3B.

Kelley-Judge, P. *Trade Associations and Political Strategy.* Unpublished DBA dis., Boston University, 1988.

Kingdon, J. W. *Agendas, Alternatives, and Public Policies.* Boston: Little, Brown, 1984.

Klein, H. "Commentary." In *Strategic Management: A New View of Business Policy and Planning,* edited by D. E. Schendel and C. W. Hofer, 144–151. Boston: Little, Brown, 1979.

Krebs, R., and Orthwein, P. *Making Friends in Our Business: 100 Years of Anheuser–Busch.* St. Louis: Anheuser–Busch, 1953.

"Last Days for Superfund." *Washington Post,* September 24, 1980, 26.

Lenn, D. J., and Mahon, J. F. "Corporate Political Strategy in the Multinational Corporation: A Framework for Analysis." In *Managing in a Global Economy V, Proceedings of the Fifth International Conference of the Eastern Academy of Management,* edited by E. Kaplan and R. Pieper, 214–217. Berlin: Eastern Academy of Management, 1993.

Letwin, W. "The Past and Future of the American Businessman." In *The American Business Corporation,* edited by E. Goldston, H. Morton, and G. Ryland, 17–38. Cambridge: MIT Press, 1973.

Levin, G., and Sandler, A. "Mattel–Hasbro Deal Dead, Not Forgotten." *Variety,* February 12, 1996, 76.

Lindblom, C. E. *The Policy Making Process.* Englewood Cliffs, N.J.: Prentice-Hall, 1968.

"A Look Back at History in the Making: Framing the Issues." *Chemical Week* 155 (7; 1994): 26–53.

Mahon, J. F. "Corporate Political Strategies: An Empirical Study of Chemical Firm Responses to Superfund Legislation." In *Research in Corporate Social Performance and Policy,* Vol. 5, edited by L. Preston, 143–182. Greenwich, Conn.: JAI Press, 1983.

———. "Corporate Political Strategy." *Business in the Contemporary World* 2 (1; 1989): 50–62.

———. "The Corporate Public Affairs Office: Structure, Behavior, and Impact." Unpublished DBA diss., Boston University, 1982.

———. "Shaping Issues/Manufacturing Agents: Corporate Political Sculpting." In *Corporate Political Agency: The Construction of Competition in Public Affairs,* edited by B. M. Mitnick, 187–212. Newbury Park, Calif.: Sage, 1993.

Mahon, J. F., Bigelow, B., and Fahey, L. "Political Strategy and Issue Evolution: Toward a Framework for Analysis." In *Proceedings of the First Annual Meeting of the International Association for Business and Society,* edited by D. Wood and W. E. Martello, 156–167. San Diego: International Association for Business and Society, 1990.

Mahon, J. F., and Cochran, P. L. "Fire Alarms and Siren Songs: The Role of Issues Management in the Prevention of, and Response to, Organizational Crises." *Industrial Crisis Quarterly* 5 (1991): 155–176.

Mahon, J. F., Fahey, L., and Bigelow, B. "Corporate Political Strategy." In *The Portable MBA in Corporate Strategy,* edited by L. Fahey and R. Randall, 142–167. New York: John Wiley & Sons, 1994.

Mahon, J. F., and Kelley, P. "Managing Toxic Wastes—After Bhopal and Sandoz." *Long Range Planning* 20 (4; 1987): 50–59.

Mahon, J. F., and Vachani, S. "Establishing a Beachhead in International Markets: The Direct and Indirect Approach." *Long Range Planning* 25 (3; 1992): 60–69.

Mahon, J. F., and Waddock, S. A. "Strategic Issues Management: An Integration of Issue Life Cycle Perspectives." *Business and Society* 31 (1; 1992): 19–32.

Mank, A. Interview by author. Washington, D.C., January 8, 1981.

March, J., and Simon, H. *Organizations*. New York: John Wiley & Sons, 1958.

Marcus, A. A., and Irion, M. S. "The Continued Viability of the Corporate Public Affairs Function." In *Business Strategy and Public Policy: Perspectives from Industry and Academia*, edited by A. A. Marcus, A. M. Kaufman, and D. R. Beam, 267–282. New York: Quorum Books, 1987.

Marcus, A. A., Kaufman, A. M., and Beam, D. R. (Eds.). *Business Strategy and Public Policy: Perspectives from Industry and Academia*. New York: Quorum Books, 1987.

McGowan, R. A. *Business, Politics and Cigarettes: Multiple Levels, Multiple Agendas*. Westport, Conn.: Greenwood Press, 1995.

———. "Multiple Segments, Multiple Measures: An Analysis of the Relationship between the Alcohol Industry and Government." In *Research in Corporate Social Performance and Policy*, Vol. 13, edited by J. E. Post, 119–140. Greenwich, Conn.: JAI Press, 1992.

———. "Public Policy Measures and Cigarette Sales: An ARIMA Intervention Analysis." In *Research in Corporate Social Performance and Policy*, Vol. 11, edited by J. E. Post, 151–180. Greenwich, Conn.: JAI Press, 1989.

McGowan, R. A., and Mahon, J. F. "Collaborating with the Enemy: Tobacco, Alcohol, and the Public Good." *Business in the Contemporary World* 7 (4; 1995) 69–92.

Menzies, H. "Union Carbide Raises Its Voice." *Fortune*, September 25, 1978, 86–88.

"Michigan's Lag with Microbreweries." *The Detroiter*, February 1994, B-1.

Mitnick, B. M. *Corporate Political Agency: The Construction of Competition in Public Affairs*. Newbury Park, Calif.: Sage, 1993a.

———. "Organizing Research in Corporate Social Performance: The CSP System as Core Paradigm." Paper presented at the 1993 Annual Meeting of the International Association for Business and Society, San Diego, March, 1993b.

Moore, C. Interview by author. Washington, D.C., January 8, 1981.

Morison, S. E. *The Oxford History of the American People*. New York: Oxford University Press, 1965.

Mosher, L. "Love Canals by the Thousands—Who Should Pay the Costly Bill?" *National Journal*, May 24, 1980, 855–857.

Murray, E. A., and Isenman, A. W. "The Concept of Strategy Formulation as a Negotiation Process." Paper presented at the Annual Meeting of the Academy of Management, San Francisco, August 1978.

Narayanan, V. K., and Fahey, L. "The Micro-Politics of Strategy Formulation." *Academy of Management Review* 7 (1982): 25–34.

Nichols, W. *Price Policies in the Cigarette Industry*. Nashville, Tenn.: Vanderbilt University Press, 1951.

Olson, M. *The Logic of Collective Action*. Cambridge: Harvard University Press, 1965.

Olson, S. *Alcohol in America: Taking Action to Prevent Abuse*. Washington, D.C.: National Academy Press, 1985.

Omang, J. "Senate Committee Sends 'Superfund' Bill to Floor." *Washington Post*, November 18, 1980, 24.

———. "Senate Unit Wants Industry to Pay for Chemical Damages." *Washington Post*, June 28, 1980, A5.

———. "Shifts on Hill May Help Alaska Lands Bill, Doom Toxic Superfund." *Washington Post*, November 8, 1980, A1.

"Open Seasons on Banks." *Fortune*, August 21, 1995, 43–52.

Otsuka, R. "Merger May Be Only Hope for Daiwa Bank." *Reuters North American News Wire*, Tokyo, November 3, 1995.

Parisi, A. "Who Pays? Cleaning up the Love Canals." *New York Times*, June 8, 1980, sec. 3, p. 1.

"Passive Smoking as an Issue." *Congressional Search Service*, April 14, 1994, 231–238.

Pettigrew, A. M. *The Politics of Organizational Decision Making*. London: Tavistock, 1973.

Pfeffer, J., and Salancik, G. R. *The External Control of Organizations: A Resource Dependence Perspective*. New York: Harper and Row, 1978.

Pierce, J. L. *The Future of Banking*. New Haven: Yale University Press, 1991.

Porter, M. E. *Competitive Advantage: Creating and Sustaining Superior Performance*. New York: The Free Press, 1985.

———. *The Competitive Advantage of Nations*. London: Macmillan Press, 1990.

———. *Competitive Strategy: Techniques for Analyzing Industries and Competitors*. New York: The Free Press, 1980.

———. "How Competitive Forces Shape Strategy." *Harvard Business Review* 57 (2; 1979): 137–145.

Post, J. E. *Corporate Behavior and Social Change*. Reston, Va.: Reston, 1978.

Post, J. E., Murray, E. A., Dickie, R. B., and Mahon, J. F. "The Public Affairs Function in American Corporations: Development and Relations with Corporate Planning." *Long Range Planning* 15 (1982): 12–21.

Reidy, C., and Shao, M. "Mattel Gives up Bid for Hasbro: 'Scorched Earth' Response Cited." *Boston Globe*, February 3, 1996, 28.

Roeder, E. "18 Panel Senators Got Chemical Industry Money." *Boston Globe*, November 17, 1980, 20.

Roland, R. "Toxic Scapegoats." *Washington Post*, April 29, 1979, 15.

Roussakis, E. N. *Commercial Banking in an Era of Deregulation*. New York: Praeger Publishing, 1984.

Rugman, A. M., and Verbeke, A. "Environmental Change and Global Competitive Strategy in Europe." In *Research in Global Strategic Management*, Vol. 2, edited by A. M. Rugman and A. Verbeke, 3–28. Greenwich, Conn.: JAI Press, 1991.

"Running Out the Clock." *Washington Post*, September 15, 1980, 24.

Russo, M. "On Collective Strategy in the Public Policy Domain." In *Advances in Strategic Management*, edited by W. Lamb, 353–374. Greenwich, Conn.: JAI Press, 1993.

Schattschneider, E. E. *The Semi-Sovereign People*. New York: Holt, 1960.

Schuler, D. A., and Rehbein, K. "The Filtering Role of the Firm in Developing Corporate Political Strategies." Paper presented at the Annual Meeting of the Academy of Management, Vancouver, B.C. Canada, August, 1995.

Selznick, P. *TVA and the Grassroots*. New York: Harper and Row, 1949.

Shabecoff, P. "Bill for Hazardous Waste Cleanup Stuck in Senate with Recess Near." *New York Times*, October 1, 1980, 20.

Shaffer, B. "Regulations, Competition, and Strategy: The Case of Automobile Fuel Economy Standards." In *Research in Corporate Social Performance and Policy*, Vol. 13, edited by J. E. Post, 191–218. Greenwich, Conn.: JAI Press, 1992.

Shapiro, I. "We Can Manage Hazardous Wastes." Speech before the National Conference of Lieutenant Governors, Atlantic City, N.J., August 19, 1980.

Simon, H. A. *Administrative Behavior*. 3rd ed. New York: Macmillan, 1976.

Smircich, L., and Stubbart, C. "Strategic Management in an Enacted World." *Academy of Management Review* 7 (1982): 25–34.

Stover, W. Interview by author. Washington, D.C., January 7, 1981.

"Superfund Compromise Wins 'Grudging' Nod." *Chemical Week*, June 18, 1980, 63.

"Superfund Finale Wrenches CMA." *Chemical Week*, December 3, 1980, 16.

"Superfund Stalls in Senate." *St. Louis Post Dispatch*, September 14, 1980, 1, 7K.

Syrre, S. "Scandals Raise Question: Who Is Minding the Store?" *Boston Globe*, September 28, 1995, 37, 39.

Taylor, G. D., and Sudnick, P. E. *Du Pont and The International Chemical Industry*. Boston: Twayne Publishers, 1984.

Tedlow, R. *Keeping the Corporate Image: Public Relations and Business, 1900–1950*. Greenwich, Conn.: JAI Press, 1976.

Tennant, R. *The American Cigarette Industry*. New Haven: Yale University Press, 1950.

Tipermas, M. Interview by author. Washington, D.C., January 6, 1981.

"The Tobacco Lobby." *Fortune*, August 17, 1987, 71.

Tobacco Tax Council. *The Tax Burden on Tobacco: Historical Compilation*, Vol. 29. Richmond, Va.: Tobacco Institute Publication, 1994.

"Toxic Clean up Suffers a Reversal." *New York Times*, November 15, 1980, A26.

Troy, M., and Markle, B. *Cooperative Lobbying: The Power of Pressure*. Tucson: University of Arizona Press, 1986.

Tye, J. *Newsletter of STAT* (Stop Teenage Abuse of Tobacco), 1986 to 1993.

U.S. Congress, House, Committee on Interstate and Foreign Commerce. *Hazardous Waste Disposal, Part 1, Hearings before a Subcommittee of the House Committee on Interstate and Foreign Commerce*. 96th Cong., 1st sess., March 21, 22; April 5, 10; May 16, 23, 30; June 1, 4, 5, 15, 18, 19, 1979.

————. *Hazardous Waste Disposal Report*. 96th Cong., 1st sess., September 26, 1979.

U.S. Congress, Senate, Committee on Environment and Public Works. *Hazardous and Toxic Waste Disposal Field Hearing. Hearings before Subcommittees of the Senate Committee on Environment and Public Works*. 96th Cong., 1st sess., May 18; June 22, 1979.

Utterback, J. M. "Environmental Analysis and Forecasting." In *Strategic Management: A New View of Business Policy and Planning*, edited by D. E. Schendel and C. W. Hofer, 134–143. Boston: Little, Brown, 1979.

Van Gelder, L. "New Troubles for the Tobacco Industry." *New York Times*, June 14, 1988, D1.

Waddock, S. A., and Mahon, J. F. "Corporate Social Performance Revisited: Dimensions of Efficacy, Effectiveness, and Efficiency." In *Research in Corporate Social Performance and Policy*, Vol. 12, edited by J. E. Post, 231–262. Greenwich, Conn.: JAI Press, 1991.

Walker, J. *Mobilizing Interest Groups in America*. Ann Arbor: University of Michigan Press, 1991.

Warner, K. E. "Cigarette Taxation: Doing Good by Doing Well." *Journal of Public Health* 5 (3; 1980): 312–319.

Wartick, S. L., and Cochran, P. L. "The Evolution of the Corporate Social Performance Model." *Academy of Management Review* 10 (4; 1985): 758–769.

Wartick, S. L., and Mahon, J. F. "Issues Management Theory Building: Defining the Corporate Issue Concept." In *Managing in a Global Economy V, Proceedings of the Fifth International Conference of the Eastern Academy of Management*, edited by E. Kaplan and R. Pieper, 1–4. Berlin: Eastern Academy of Management, 1993.

————. "Toward a Substantive Definition of the Corporate Issue Construct: A Review and Synthesis of the Literature." *Business and Society* 33 (3; 1994): 293–311.

Weick, K. *The Social Psychology of Organizing*. Reading, Mass.: Addison-Wesley, 1969.

White, L. *The Merchants of Death: The American Tobacco Industry*. Beech Tree, Tenn.: William Morrow, 1988.

"Who Pays for Poison?" *Washington Post*, April 12, 1979, 16.

"Why Poisons Fester . . ." *New York Times*, September 26, 1980, A34.

Wolfe, T. *Bonfire of the Vanities*. New York: Farrar, Straus, Giroux, 1987.

Wood, D. L. "Corporate Social Performance Revisited." *Academy of Management Review* 16 (4; 1991a): 691–718.

————. "Social Issues in Management: Theory and Research in Corporate Social Performance." *Journal of Management* 17 (2; 1991b): 383–406.

[] [] []

NAME INDEX

[] [] []

SUBJECT INDEX

ABOUT THE AUTHORS

JOHN F. MAHON is Professor of Management Policy in the School of Management at Boston University. Dr. Mahon has written many articles and three books on related subjects.

RICHARD A. McGOWAN is Assistant Provost and Associate Professor at the University of Scranton. Dr. McGowan is the author of two books, *Business, Politics, and Cigarettes: Multiple Levels, Multiple Agendas* (Quorum, 1995) and *State Lotteries and Legalized Gambling: Painless Revenue or Painful Mirage* (Quorum, 1994).

ISBN 0-89930-978-X